Summary of Contents

JQUERY: NOVICE TO NINJA

BY **EARLE CASTLEDINE**
& CRAIG SHARKIE

jQuery: Novice to Ninja

by Earle Castledine and Craig Sharkie

Program Director: Andrew Tetlaw

Technical Editor: Louis Simoneau

Chief Technical Officer: Kevin Yank

Printing History:

    First Edition: February 2010

Indexer: Fred Brown

Editor: Kelly Steele

Cover Design: Alex Walker

Published by SitePoint Pty. Ltd.

48 Cambridge Street Collingwood
VIC Australia 3066
Web: www.sitepoint.com
Email: business@sitepoint.com

ISBN 978-0-9805768-5-6
Printed and bound in the United States of America

About Earle Castledine

Sporting a Masters in Information Technology and a lifetime of experience on the Web of Hard Knocks, Earle Castledine (aka Mr Speaker) holds an interest in everything computery. Raised in the wild by various 8-bit home computers, he settled in the Internet during the mid-nineties and has been living and working there ever since.

A Senior Systems Analyst and JavaScript flâneur, he is equally happy in the muddy pits of .NET code, the dense foliage of mobile apps and games, and the fluffy clouds of client-side interaction development.

As co-creator of the client-side opus TurnTubelist,[1] as well as countless web-based experiments, Earle recognizes the Internet not as a lubricant for social change but as a vehicle for unleashing frivolous ECMAScript gadgets and interesting time-wasting technologies.

About Craig Sharkie

A degree in Fine Art is a strange entrance to a career with a passion for programming, but that's where Craig started. A right-brain approach to code and problem solving has seen him plying his craft for many of the big names of the Web—AOL, Microsoft, Yahoo!, Ziff-Davis, and now Atlassian.

That passion, and a fondness for serial commas and the like, have led him on a path from journalism, through development, on to conferences, and now into print. Taking up JavaScript in 1995, he was an evangelist for the "good parts" before Crockford coined the term, and now has brought that keenness to jQuery.

About the Technical Editor

Louis Simoneau joined SitePoint in 2009, after traveling from his native Montréal to Calgary, Taipei, and finally Melbourne. He now gets to spend his days learning about cool web technologies, an activity that had previously been relegated to nights and weekends. He enjoys hip-hop, spicy food, and all things geeky.

About the Chief Technical Officer

As Chief Technical Officer for SitePoint, Kevin Yank keeps abreast of all that is new and exciting in web technology. Best known for his book, *Build Your Own Database Driven Web Site Using PHP & MySQL*, he also co-authored *Simply JavaScript* with Cameron Adams and

---

[1] http://www.turntubelist.com/

Everything You Know About CSS Is Wrong! with Rachel Andrew. In addition, Kevin hosts the *SitePoint Podcast* and co-writes the *SitePoint Tech Times*, a free email newsletter that goes out to over 240,000 subscribers worldwide.

Kevin lives in Melbourne, Australia and enjoys speaking at conferences, as well as visiting friends and family in Canada. He's also passionate about performing improvised comedy theater with Impro Melbourne (http://www.impromelbourne.com.au/) and flying light aircraft. Kevin's personal blog is *Yes, I'm Canadian* (http://yesimcanadian.com/).

About SitePoint

SitePoint specializes in publishing fun, practical, and easy-to-understand content for Web professionals. Visit http://www.sitepoint.com/ to access our blogs, books, newsletters, articles, and community forums.

For Amelia.

*I wanted to have a picture here of
me holding a boombox above my
head, but they wouldn't let me.*

Will you marry me?

—Earle

For Jennifer:

*People who've met me
Only since I've known you
Never understand the
Good you've lead me to*

Always

—Craig

Table of Contents

Chapter 2   Selecting, Decorating, and Enhancing

Chapter 3   Animating, Scrolling, and Resizing

Chapter 6   Construction, Ajax, and Interactivity <span></span>

Chapter 9   Plugins, Themes, and Advanced Topics

Appendix A   Reference Material

Preface

No matter what kind of ninja you are—a cooking ninja, a corporate lawyer ninja, or an actual *ninja* ninja—virtuosity lies in first mastering the basic tools of the trade. Once conquered, it's then up to the full-fledged ninja to apply that knowledge in creative and inventive ways.

In recent times, jQuery has proven itself to be a simple but powerful tool for taming and transforming web pages, bending even the most stubborn and aging browsers to our will. jQuery is a library with two principal purposes: manipulating elements on a web page, and helping out with Ajax requests. Sure, there are quite a few commands available to do this—but they're all consistent and easy to learn. Once you've chained together your first few actions, you'll be addicted to the jQuery building blocks, and your friends and family will wish you'd never discovered it!

On top of the core jQuery library is jQuery UI: a set of fine-looking controls and widgets (such as accordions, tabs, and dialogs), combined with a collection of full-featured behaviors for implementing controls of your own. jQuery UI lets you quickly throw together awesome interfaces with little effort, and serves as a great example of what you can achieve with a little jQuery know-how.

At its core, jQuery is a tool to help us improve the usability of our sites and create a better user experience. **Usability** refers to the study of the principles behind an object's *perceived efficiency or elegance*. Far from being merely flashy, trendy design, jQuery lets us speedily and enjoyably sculpt our pages in ways both subtle and extreme: from finessing a simple sliding panel to implementing a brand-new user interaction you invented in your sleep.

Becoming a ninja isn't about learning an API inside out and back to front—that's just called having a good memory. The real skill and value comes when you can apply your knowledge to making something exceptional: something that builds on the combined insights of the past to be even slightly better than anything anyone has done before. This is certainly not easy—but thanks to jQuery, it's fun just trying.

Who Should Read This Book

If you're a front-end web designer looking to add a dash of cool interactivity to your sites, and you've heard all the buzz about jQuery and want to find out what the fuss is about, this book will put you on the right track. If you've dabbled with JavaScript, but been frustrated by the complexity of many seemingly simple tasks, we'll show you how jQuery can help you. Even if you're familiar with the basics of jQuery, but you want to take your skills to the next level, you'll find a wealth of good coding advice and in-depth knowledge.

You should already have intermediate to advanced HTML and CSS skills, as jQuery uses CSS-style selectors to zero in on page elements. Some rudimentary programming knowledge will be helpful to have, as jQuery—despite its clever abstractions—is still based on JavaScript. That said, we've tried to explain any JavaScript concepts as we use them, so with a little willingness to learn you'll do fine.

What's in This Book

By the end of this book, you'll be able to take your static HTML and CSS web pages and bring them to life with a bit of jQuery magic. You'll learn how to select elements on the page, move them around, remove them entirely, add new ones with Ajax, animate them … in short, you'll be able to bend HTML and CSS to your will! We also cover the powerful functionality of the jQuery UI library.

This book comprises the following nine chapters. Read them in order from beginning to end to gain a complete understanding of the subject, or skip around if you only need a refresher on a particular topic.

Chapter 1: *Falling in Love with jQuery*
Before we dive into learning all the ins and outs of jQuery, we'll have a quick look at why you'd want to use it in the first place: why it's better than writing your own JavaScript, and why it's better than the other JavaScript libraries out there. We'll brush up on some CSS concepts that are key to understanding jQuery, and briefly touch on the basic syntax required to call jQuery into action.

Chapter 2: *Selecting, Decorating, and Enhancing*
Ostensibly, jQuery's most significant advantage over plain JavaScript is the ease with which it lets you select elements on the page to play with. We'll start off

this chapter by teaching you how to use jQuery's selectors to zero in on your target elements, and then we'll look at how you can use jQuery to alter those elements' CSS properties.

Chapter 3: *Animating, Scrolling, and Resizing*

jQuery excels at animation: whether you'd like to gently slide open a menu, or send a dialog whizzing across the screen, jQuery can help you out. In this chapter, we'll explore jQuery's wide range of animation helpers, and put them into practice by enhancing a few simple user interface components. We'll also have a quick look at some animation-like helpers for scrolling the page and making elements resizable.

Chapter 4: *Images, Slideshows, and Cross-fading*

With the basics well and truly under our belts, we'll turn to building some of the most common jQuery widgets out there: image galleries and slideshows. We'll learn how to build lightbox displays, scrolling thumbnail galleries, cross-fading galleries, and even take a stab at an iPhoto-style flip-book.

Chapter 5: *Menus, Tabs, Tooltips, and Panels*

Now that we're comfortable with building cool UI widgets with jQuery, we'll dive into some slightly more sophisticated controls: drop-down and accordion-style menus, tabbed interfaces, tooltips, and various types of content panels. We're really on a roll now: our sites are looking less and less like the brochure-style pages of the nineties, and more and more like the Rich Internet Applications of the twenty-first century!

Chapter 6: *Construction, Ajax, and Interactivity*

This is the one you've all been waiting for: Ajax! In order to make truly desktop-style applications on the Web, you need to be able to pass data back and forth to and from the server, without any of those pesky refreshes clearing your interface from the screen—and that's what Ajax is all about. jQuery includes a raft of convenient methods for handling Ajax requests in a simple, cross-browser manner, letting you leave work with a smile on your face. But before we get too carried away—our code is growing more complex, so we'd better take a look at some best practices for organizing it. All this and more, in Chapter 6.

Chapter 7: *Forms, Controls, and Dialogs*

The bane of every designer, forms are nonetheless a pivotal cornerstone of any web application. In this chapter, we'll learn what jQuery has to offer us in terms of simplifying our form-related scripting. We'll learn how to validate forms on the fly, offer assistance to our users, and manipulate checkboxes, radio buttons, and select lists with ease. Then we'll have a look at some less conventional ways of allowing a site's users to interact with it: a variety of advanced controls like date pickers, sliders, and drag and drop. We'll round it off with a look at modal dialogs in the post-popup world, as well as a few original nonmodal notification styles. What a chapter!

Chapter 8: *Lists, Trees, and Tables*

No matter how "Web 2.0" your application may be, chances are you'll still need to fall back on the everyday list, the humdrum tree, or even the oft-derided table to present information to your users. This chapter shows how jQuery can make even the boring stuff fun, as we'll learn how to turn lists into dynamic, sortable data, and transform tables into data grids with sophisticated functionality.

Chapter 9: *Plugins, Themes, and Advanced Topics*

jQuery is more than just cool DOM manipulation, easy Ajax requests, and funky UI components. It has a wealth of functionality aimed at the more *ninja-level* developer: a fantastic plugin architecture, a highly extensible and flexible core, customizable events, and a whole lot more. In this chapter, we'll also cover the jQuery UI theme system, which lets you easily tailor the appearance of jQuery UI widgets to suit your site, and even make your own plugins skinnable with themes.

Where to Find Help

jQuery is under active development, so chances are good that, by the time you read this, some minor detail or other of these technologies will have changed from what's described in this book. Thankfully, SitePoint has a thriving community of JavaScript and jQuery developers ready and waiting to help you out if you run into trouble. We also maintain a list of known errata for this book, which you can consult for the latest updates; the details are below.

The SitePoint Forums

The SitePoint Forums[1] are discussion forums where you can ask questions about anything related to web development. You may, of course, answer questions too. That's how a discussion forum site works—some people ask, some people answer, and most people do a bit of both. Sharing your knowledge benefits others and strengthens the community. A lot of interesting and experienced web designers and developers hang out there. It's a good way to learn new stuff, have questions answered in a hurry, and have a blast.

The JavaScript Forum[2] is where you'll want to head to ask any questions about jQuery.

The Book's Web Site

Located at http://www.sitepoint.com/books/jquery1/, the web site that supports this book will give you access to the following facilities:

The Code Archive

As you progress through this book, you'll note a number of references to the code archive. This is a downloadable ZIP archive that contains each and every line of example source code that's printed in this book. If you want to cheat (or save yourself from carpal tunnel syndrome), go ahead and download the archive.[3]

Updates and Errata

No book is perfect, and we expect that watchful readers will be able to spot at least one or two mistakes before the end of this one. The Errata page[4] on the book's web site will always have the latest information about known typographical and code errors.

The SitePoint Newsletters

In addition to books like this one, SitePoint publishes free email newsletters, such as the *SitePoint Tech Times*, *SitePoint Tribune*, and *SitePoint Design View*, to name

---

[1] http://www.sitepoint.com/forums/
[2] http://www.sitepoint.com/forums/forumdisplay.php?f=15
[3] http://www.sitepoint.com/books/jquery1/code.php
[4] http://www.sitepoint.com/books/jquery1/errata.php

a few. In them, you'll read about the latest news, product releases, trends, tips, and techniques for all aspects of web development. Sign up to one or more SitePoint newsletters at http://www.sitepoint.com/newsletter/.

The SitePoint Podcast

Join the SitePoint Podcast team for news, interviews, opinion, and fresh thinking for web developers and designers. We discuss the latest web industry topics, present guest speakers, and interview some of the best minds in the industry. You can catch up on the latest and previous podcasts at http://www.sitepoint.com/podcast/, or subscribe via iTunes.

Your Feedback

If you're unable to find an answer through the forums, or if you wish to contact us for any other reason, the best place to write is books@sitepoint.com. We have a well-staffed email support system set up to track your inquiries, and if our support team members are unable to answer your question, they'll send it straight to us. Suggestions for improvements, as well as notices of any mistakes you may find, are especially welcome.

Acknowledgments

Earle Castledine

I'd like to thank the good folks at Agency Rainford for running Jelly (and getting me out of the house), Stuart Horton-Stephens for teaching me how to do Bézier Curves (and puppet shows), Andrew Tetlaw, Louis Simoneau, and Kelly Steele from Site-Point for turning pages of rambling nonsense into English, the Sydney web community (who do truly rock), the jQuery team (and related fellows) for being a JavaScript-fueled inspiration to us all, and finally, my awesome Mum and Dad for getting me a Spectravideo 318 instead of a Commodore 64—thus forcing me to read the manuals instead of playing games, all those years ago.

Craig Sharkie

Firstly, I'd like to thank Earle for bringing me onto the project and introducing me to the real SitePoint. I'd met some great SitePointers at Web Directions, but dealing with them professionally has been a real eye-opener. I'd also like to thank my wonderful wife Jennifer for understanding when I typed into the wee small hours, and my parents for letting me read into the wee small hours when I was only wee small. Lastly, I'd like to thank the web community that have inspired me—some have inspired me to reach their standard, some have inspired me to help them reach a higher standard.

Conventions Used in This Book

You'll notice that we've used certain typographic and layout styles throughout the book to signify different types of information. Look out for the following items.

Code Samples

Code in this book will be displayed using a fixed-width font, like so:

```
<h1>A Perfect Summer's Day</h1>
<p>It was a lovely day for a walk in the park. The birds
were singing and the kids were all back at school.</p>
```

If the code is to be found in the book's code archive, the name of the file will appear at the top of the program listing, like this:

```
                                                          example.css
.footer {
  background-color: #CCC;
  border-top: 1px solid #333;
}
```

If only part of the file is displayed, this is indicated by the word *excerpt*:

```
                                                     example.css (excerpt)
  border-top: 1px solid #333;
```

If additional code is to be inserted into an existing example, the new code will be displayed in bold:

```
function animate() {
  new_variable = "Hello";
}
```

Also, where existing code is required for context, rather than repeat all the code, a vertical ellipsis will be displayed:

```
function animate() {
  ⋮
  return new_variable;
}
```

Some lines of code are intended to be entered on one line, but we've had to wrap them because of page constraints. A ➥ indicates a line break that exists for formatting purposes only, and should be ignored:

```
URL.open("http://www.sitepoint.com/blogs/2007/05/28/user-style-she
➥ets-come-of-age/");
```

Tips, Notes, and Warnings

 Hey, You!

Tips will give you helpful little pointers.

 Ahem, Excuse Me ...

Notes are useful asides that are related—but not critical—to the topic at hand. Think of them as extra tidbits of information.

 Make Sure You Always ...

... pay attention to these important points.

 Watch Out!

Warnings will highlight any gotchas that are likely to trip you up along the way.

Chapter 1

Falling in Love with jQuery

So you have the coding chops to write lean, semantic HTML—and you can back it up with masterful CSS to transform your design ideas into gorgeous web sites that enthrall your visitors. But these days, you realize, inspiring designs and impeccable HTML alone fall short when you're trying to create the next Facebook or Twitter. So, what's the missing piece of the front-end puzzle?

It's JavaScript. That rascally scripting language, cast as the black sheep of the web development family for so many years. JavaScript is how you add complex behaviors, sophisticated interactions, and extra pizazz to your site. To conquer the sleeping giant that is JavaScript, you just need to buckle down and spend the next few years learning about programming languages: functions, classes, design patterns, prototypes, closures ...

Or there's a secret that some of the biggest names on the Web—like Google, Digg, WordPress, and Amazon—will probably be okay about us sharing with you: "Just use jQuery!" Designers and developers the world over are using the jQuery library to elegantly and rapidly implement their interaction ideas, completing the web development puzzle.

In the following chapter we'll have a look at what makes jQuery so good, and how it complements HTML and CSS in a more natural way than our old friend and bitter enemy: plain old JavaScript. We'll also look at what's required to get jQuery up and running, and working with our current sites.

What's so good about jQuery?

You've read that jQuery makes it easy to play with the DOM, add effects, and execute Ajax requests, but what makes it better than, say, writing your own library, or using one of the other (also excellent) JavaScript libraries out there?

First off, did we mention that jQuery makes it easy to play with the DOM, add effects, and execute Ajax requests? In fact, it makes it so easy that it's downright good, nerdy fun—and you'll often need to pull back from some craziness you just invented, put on your web designer hat, and exercise a little bit of restraint (ah, the cool things we could create if good taste were not a barrier!). But there are a multitude of notable factors you should consider if you're going to invest your valuable time in learning a JavaScript library.

Cross-browser Compatibility

Aside from being a joy to use, one of the biggest benefits of jQuery is that it handles a lot of infuriating cross-browser issues for you. Anyone who has written serious JavaScript in the past can attest that cross-browser inconsistencies will drive you mad. For example, a design that renders perfectly in Mozilla Firefox and Internet Explorer 8 just falls apart in Internet Explorer 7, or an interface component you've spent days handcrafting works beautifully in all major browsers except Opera on Linux. And the client just happens to use Opera on Linux. These types of issues are never easy to track down, and even harder to completely eradicate.

Even when cross-browser problems are relatively simple to handle, you always need to maintain a mental knowledge bank of them. When it's 11:00 p.m. the night before a major project launch, you can only hope you recall why there's a weird padding bug on a browser you forgot to test!

The jQuery team is keenly aware of cross-browser issues, and more importantly they understand *why* these issues occur. They have written this knowledge into the library—so jQuery works around the caveats for you. Most of the code you write will run exactly the same on all the major browsers, including everybody's favorite little troublemaker: Internet Explorer 6.

This feature alone will save the average developer a lifetime of headaches. Of course, you should always aim to keep up to date with the latest developments and best practices in our industry—but leaving the task of hunting down obscure browser bugs to the jQuery Team (and they fix more and more with each new version) allows you more time to implement your ideas.

CSS3 Selectors

Making today's technologies cross-browser compliant is all well and good, but jQuery also fully supports the upcoming CSS3 selector specification. Yes, even in Internet Explorer 6.0! You can gain a head start on the future by learning and using CSS3 selectors right now in your production code. Selecting elements you want to change lies at the heart of jQuery's power, and CSS3 selectors give you even more tools to work with.

Helpful Utilities

Also included is an assortment of utility functions that implement common functions useful for writing jQuery (or are missing from JavaScript!): string trimming, the ability to easily extend objects, and more. These functions by themselves are particularly handy, but they help promote a seamless integration between jQuery and JavaScript which results in code that's easier to write and maintain.

One noteworthy utility is the `supports` function, which tests to find certain features are available on the current user's browser. Traditionally, developers have resorted to browser sniffing—determining which web browser the end user is using, based on information provided by the browser itself—to work around known issues. This has always been an unsatisfying and error-prone practice. Using the jQuery `supports` utility function, you can test to see if a certain feature is available to the user, and easily build applications that degrade gracefully on older browsers, or those not standards-compliant.

jQuery UI

jQuery has already been used to make some impressive widgets and effects, some of which were useful enough to justify inclusion in the core jQuery library itself.

However, the jQuery team wisely decided that in order to keep the core library focused, they'd separate out higher-level constructs and package them into a neat library that sits on top of jQuery.

That library is called **jQuery User Interface** (generally abbreviated to just **jQuery UI**), and it comprises a menagerie of useful effects and advanced widgets that are accessible and highly customizable through the use of themes. Some of these features are illustrated in Figure 1.1.

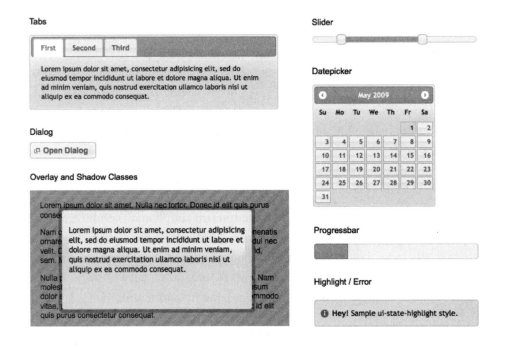

Figure 1.1. A few jQuery UI widgets

Accordions, sliders, dialog boxes, date pickers, and more—all ready to be used right now! You could spend a bunch of time creating them yourself in jQuery (as these have been) but the jQuery UI controls are configurable and sophisticated enough that your time would be better spent elsewhere—namely implementing your unique project requirements rather than ensuring your custom date picker appears correctly across different browsers!

We'll certainly be using a bunch of jQuery UI functionality as we progress through the book. We'll even integrate some of the funky themes available, and learn how to create our own themes using the jQuery UI ThemeRoller tool.

Plugins

The jQuery team has taken great care in making the jQuery library extensible. By including only a core set of features while providing a framework for extending the library, they've made it easy to create plugins that you can reuse in all your jQuery projects, as well as share with other developers. A lot of fairly common functionality has been omitted from the jQuery core library, and relegated to the realm of the plugin. Don't worry, this is a feature, not a flaw. Any additional required functionality can be included easily on a page-by-page basis to keep bandwidth and code bloat to a minimum.

Thankfully, a lot of people have taken advantage of jQuery's extensibility, so there are already hundreds of excellent, downloadable plugins available from the jQuery plugin repository, with new ones added all the time. A portion of this can be seen in Figure 1.2.

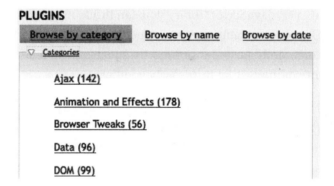

Figure 1.2. The jQuery plugin repository

Whenever you're presented with a task or problem, it's worth checking first to see if there's a plugin that might suit your needs. That's because almost any functionality you might require has likely already been turned into a plugin, and is available and ready for you to start using. Even if it turns out that you need to do some work yourself, the plugin repository is often the best place to steer you in the right direction.

Keeping Markup Clean

Separating script behavior from page presentation is best practice in the web development game—though it does present its share of challenges. jQuery makes it a cinch to completely rid your markup of inline scripting, thanks to its ability to easily hook elements on the page and attach code to them in a natural, CSS-like manner. jQuery lacks a mechanism for adding inline code, so this separation of concerns leads to leaner, cleaner, and more maintainable code. Hence, it's easy to do things the right way, and almost impossible to do them the wrong way!

And jQuery isn't limited to meddling with a page's existing HTML—it can also add new page elements and document fragments via a collection of handy functions. There are functions to insert, append, and prepend new chunks of HTML anywhere on the page. You can even replace, remove, or clone existing elements—all functions that help you to progressively enhance your sites, thus providing a fully featured experience to users whose browsers allow it, and an acceptable experience to everyone else.

Widespread Adoption

If you care to put every JavaScript library you can think of into Google Trends,[1] you'll witness jQuery's exponential rise to superstardom. It's good to be in the in crowd when it comes to libraries, as popularity equates to more active code development and plenty of interesting third-party goodies.

Countless big players on the Web are jumping on the jQuery bandwagon: IBM, Netflix, Google (which both uses and hosts the jQuery library), and even Microsoft, which now includes jQuery with its MVC framework. With such a vast range of large companies on side, it's a safe bet that jQuery will be around for some time to come—so the time and effort you invest in learning it will be well worth your while!

jQuery's popularity has also spawned a large and generous community that's surprisingly helpful. No matter what your level of skill, you'll find other developers patient enough to help you out and work through any issues you have. This caring and sharing spirit has also spread out to the wider Internet, blossoming into an encyclopedia of high quality tutorials, blog posts, and documentation.

---

[1] http://www.google.com/trends/

What's the downside?

There barely is a downside! The main arguments against using any JavaScript library have always been speed and size: some say that using a library adds too much download bloat to pages, while others claim that libraries perform poorly compared with leaner custom code. Though these arguments are worth considering, their relevance is quickly fading.

First, as far as size is concerned, jQuery is lightweight. The core jQuery library has always had a fairly small footprint—about 19KB for the basics, less than your average JPG image. Any extras your project needs (such as plugins or components from the jQuery UI library) can be added in a modular fashion—so you can easily count your bandwidth calories.

Speed (like size) is becoming a decreasing concern as computer hardware specifications rise and browsers' JavaScript engines grow faster and faster. Of course, this is far from implying that jQuery is slow—the jQuery team seem to be obsessed with speed! Every new release is faster than the last, so any benefit you might derive from rolling your own JavaScript is shrinking every day.

When it comes to competing JavaScript libraries (and there are more than a handful out there), jQuery is the best at doing what jQuery does: manipulating the DOM, adding effects, and making Ajax requests. Still, many of the libraries out there are of excellent quality and excel in other areas, such as complex class-based programming. It's always worth looking at the alternatives, but if the reasons we've outlined appeal to you, jQuery is probably the way to go.

But enough talk: time for jQuery to put its money where its mouth is!

Downloading and Including jQuery

Before you can fall in love with jQuery (or at least, judge it for yourself) you need to obtain the latest version of the code and add it to your web pages. There are a few ways to do this, each with a couple of options available. Whatever you choose, you'll need to include jQuery in your HTML page, just as you would any other JavaScript source file.

It's Just JavaScript!

Never forget that jQuery is just JavaScript! It may look and act superficially different—but underneath it's written in JavaScript, and consequently it's unable to do anything that plain old JavaScript can't. This means we'll include it in our pages the same way we would any other JavaScript file.

Downloading jQuery

This is the most common method of acquiring the jQuery library—just download it! The latest version is always available from the jQuery web site.[2] The big shiny download button will lead us to the Google code repository, where we can grab the latest "production compression level" version.

Click the download link and save the JavaScript file to a new working folder, ready for playing with. You'll need to put it where our HTML files can see it: commonly in a **scripts** or **javascript** directory beneath your site's document root. For the following example, we'll keep it very simple and put the library in the same directory as the HTML file.

To make it all work, we need to tell our HTML file to include the jQuery library. This is done by using a `script` tag inside the `head` section of the HTML document. The `head` element of a very basic HTML file including jQuery would look a little like this:

```
<head>
  <title>Hello jQuery world!</title>
  <script type='text/javascript' src='jquery-1.4-min.js'></script>
  <script type='text/javascript' src='script.js'></script>
</head>
```

The first script tag on the page loads the jQuery library, and the second script tag points to a **script.js** file, which is where we'll run our own jQuery code. And that's it: you're ready to start using jQuery.

We said earlier that downloading the jQuery file is the most common approach—but there are a few other options available to you, so let's have a quick look at them

---

[2] http://jquery.com/

before we move on. If you just want to start playing with jQuery, you can safely skip the rest of this section.

The Google CDN

An alternative method for including the jQuery library that's worth considering is via the Google **Content Delivery Network (CDN)**. A CDN is a network of computers that are specifically designed to serve content to users in a fast and scalable manner. These servers are often distributed geographically, with each request being served by the nearest server in the network.

Google hosts several popular, open-source libraries on their CDN, including jQuery (and jQuery UI—which we'll visit shortly). So, instead of hosting the jQuery files on your own web server as we did above, you have the option of letting Google pick up part of your bandwidth bill. You benefit from the speed and reliability of Google's vast infrastructure, with the added bonus of the option to always use the latest version of jQuery.

Another benefit of using the Google CDN is that many users will already have downloaded jQuery from Google when visiting another site. As a result, it will be loaded from cache when they visit your site (since the URL to the JavaScript file will be the same), leading to significantly faster load times. You can also include the more hefty jQuery UI library via the same method, which makes the Google CDN well worth thinking about for your projects: it's going to save you money and increase performance when your latest work goes viral!

There are a few different ways of including jQuery from the Google CDN. We're going to use the simpler (though slightly less flexible) path-based method:

```
<head>
  <title>Hello jQuery world!</title>
  <script type="text/javascript" src="http://ajax.googleapis.com/
➥ajax/libs/jquery/1.4.0/jquery.min.js"></script>
  <script type='text/javascript' src='script.js'></script>
</head>
```

It looks suspiciously like our original example—but instead of pointing the `script` tag to a local copy of jQuery, it points to one of Google's servers.

Obtaining the Latest Version with Google CDN

If you look closely at the URL pointing to Google's servers, you'll see that the version of jQuery is specified by one of the path elements (the `1.4.0` in our example). If you like using the latest and greatest, however, you can remove a number from the end of the version string (for example, 1.4) and it will return the latest release available in the 1.4 series (1.4.1, 1.4.2, and so on). You can even take it up to the whole number (1), in which case Google will give you the latest version even when jQuery 1.5 and beyond are released!

Be careful though: there'll be no need to update your HTML files when a new version of jQuery is released, but it will be necessary to look out for any library changes that might affect your existing functionality.

If you'd like to examine the slightly more complex "Google loader" method of including libraries, there's plenty to read about the Google CDN on its web site.[3]

Nightlies and Subversion

Still more advanced options for obtaining jQuery are listed on the official Downloading jQuery documentation page.[4] The first of these options is the nightly builds. **Nightlies** are automated builds of the jQuery library that include all new code added or modified during the course of the day. Every night the very latest development versions are made available for download, and can be included in the same manner as the regular, stable library.

And if every single night is *still* too infrequent for you, you can use the Subversion repository to retrieve the latest up-to-the-minute source code. **Subversion** is an open-source version control system that the jQuery team uses. Every time a developer submits a change to jQuery, you can download it instantly.

Beware, however: both the nightly and Subversion jQuery libraries are often untested. They can (and will) contain bugs, and are subject to frequent changes. Unless you're looking to work on the jQuery library itself, it's probably best to skip these options.

---

[3] http://code.google.com/apis/ajaxlibs/documentation/
[4] http://docs.jquery.com/Downloading_jQuery

Uncompressed or compressed?

If you had a poke around on the jQuery download page, you might have also spied a couple of different download format options: compressed (also called **minified**), and uncompressed (also called "development").

Typically, you'll want to use the minified version for your production code, where the jQuery source code is compressed: spaces and line breaks have been removed and variable names are shortened. The result is exactly the same jQuery library, but contained in a JavaScript file that's much smaller than the original. This is great for reducing bandwidth costs for you, and speeding up page requests for the end user.

The downside of the compressed file is readability. If you examine the minified jQuery file in your text editor (go on!), you'll see that it's practically illegible: a single line of garbled-looking JavaScript. The readability of the library is inconsequential most of the time, but if you're interested in how jQuery is actually working, the uncompressed development version is a commented, readable, and quite beautiful example of JavaScript.

Anatomy of a jQuery Script

Now that we've included jQuery in our web page, let's have a look at what this baby can do. The jQuery syntax may look a little bit odd the first time you see it, but it's really quite straightforward, and best of all, it's highly consistent. After writing your first few commands, the style and syntax will be stuck in your head and will leave you wanting to write more.

The jQuery Alias

Including jQuery in your page gives you access to a single magical function called (strangely enough) jQuery. Just one function? It's through this one function that jQuery exposes hundreds of powerful tools to help add another dimension to your web pages.

Because a single function acts as a gateway to the entire jQuery library, there's little chance of the library function names conflicting with other libraries, or with your own JavaScript code. Otherwise, a situation like this could occur: let's say jQuery defined a function called hide (which it has) and you also had a function called `hide` in your own code, one of the functions would be overwritten, leading to unanticipated events and errors.

We say that the jQuery library is contained in the jQuery *namespace*. Namespacing is an excellent approach for playing nicely with other code on a page, but if we're going to use a lot of jQuery (and we are), it will quickly become annoying to have to type the full jQuery function name for every command we use. To combat this issue, jQuery provides a shorter alias for accessing the library. Simply, it's $.

The dollar sign is a short, valid, and cool-looking JavaScript variable name. It might seem a bit lazy (after all, you're only saving five keystrokes by using the alias), but a full page of jQuery will contain scores of library calls, and using the alias will make the code much more readable and maintainable.

Using Multiple Libraries

The main reason you might want to use the full `jQuery` call rather than the alias is when you have multiple JavaScript libraries on the same page, all fighting for control of the dollar sign function name. The dollar sign is a common function name in several libraries, often used for selecting elements. If you're having issues with multiple libraries, check out Appendix A: Dealing with Conflicts.

Dissecting a jQuery Statement

We know that jQuery commands begin with a call to the `jQuery` function, or its alias. Let's now take out our scalpels and examine the remaining component parts of a jQuery statement. Figure 1.3 shows both variants of the same jQuery statement (using the full function name or the $ alias).

selector	action	parameters
jQuery('p')	.css	('color', 'blue');
$('p')	.css	('color', 'blue');

Figure 1.3. A typical jQuery statement

Each command is made up of four parts: the jQuery function (or its alias), selectors, actions, and parameters. We already know about the jQuery function, so let's look at each of the other elements in turn. First, we use a selector to select one or more elements on the web page. Next, we choose an action to be applied to each element we've selected. We'll see more and more actions as we implement effects throughout the book. And finally, we specify some parameters to tell jQuery how exactly we want to apply the chosen action. Whenever you see jQuery code, try to break it up into these component parts. It will make it a lot easier to comprehend when you're just starting out.

In our example above, we've asked the selector to select all the paragraph tags (the HTML <p> tags) on the page. Next, we've chosen jQuery's `css` action, which is used to modify a CSS property of the paragraph elements that were initially selected. Finally, we've passed in some parameters to set the CSS `color` property to the value `blue`. The end result? All our paragraphs are now blue! We'll delve deeper into selectors and the `css` action in Chapter 2.

Our example passed two parameters (`color` and `blue`) to the `css` action, but the number of parameters passed to an action can vary. Some require zero parameters, some accept multiple sets of parameters (for changing a whole bunch of properties at once), and some require that we specify another JavaScript function for running code when an event (like an element being clicked) happens. But all commands follow this basic anatomy.

Bits of HTML—aka "The DOM"

jQuery has been designed to integrate seamlessly with HTML and CSS. If you're well-versed in CSS selectors and know, for example, that `div#heading` would refer to a `div` element with an `id` of `heading`, you might want to skip this section. Otherwise, a short crash course in CSS selectors and the **Document Object Model (DOM)** is in order.

The DOM doesn't pertain specifically to jQuery; it's a standard way of representing objects in HTML that all browser makers agreed to follow. A good working knowledge of the DOM will ensure a smooth transition to jQuery ninja-hood.

The DOM is what you call bits of rendered HTML when you're talking to the cool kids around the water cooler. It's a hierarchal representation of your HTML markup—where each element (such as a `div` or a `p`) has a **parent** (its "container"), and can also have one or more nested **child** elements. Each element can have an `id` and/or it can have one or more `class` attributes—which generally you assign in your HTML source file. When the browser reads an HTML page and constructs the DOM, it displays it as a web page comprising objects that can either sit there looking pretty (as a static page) or, more interestingly, be manipulated by our code.

A sample DOM fragment is illustrated in Figure 1.4. As you can see, body has two child elements: an h1 and a p. These two elements, by virtue of being contained in the same parent element, are referred to as **siblings**.

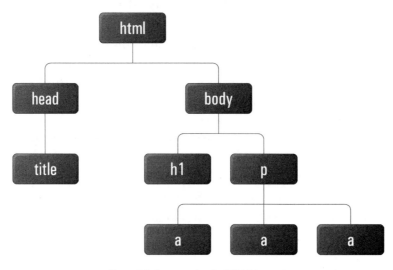

Figure 1.4. An example of a DOM fragment

An element's id uniquely identifies the element on the page:

```
<div id="footer">Come back and visit us soon!</div>
```

The div has been assigned an id of footer. It uses an id because it's unique: there should be one, and only one, on the page. The DOM also lets us assign the same name to multiple page elements via the class attribute. This is usually done on elements that share a characteristic:

```
<p class="warning">Sorry, this field must be filled in!</p>
<span class="warning">Please try again</span>
```

In this example, multiple elements on the same page are classified as a "warning." Any CSS applied to the warning class will apply to both elements. Multiple class attributes on the same element (when they're required) are separated by spaces.

When you write your CSS, you can hook elements by `id` with a hash symbol, or by `class` with a period:

```
#footer { border: 2px solid black }
.warning { color: red }
```

These CSS rules will give a black border to the element with an `id` of `footer`, and ensure that all elements with a `class` of `warning` will be displayed in red text.

When it comes time to write some jQuery, you will find that knowing about CSS selectors and the DOM is important: jQuery uses the same syntax as CSS for selecting elements on the page to manipulate. And once you've mastered selecting, the rest is easy—thanks to jQuery!

If You Choose to Accept It ...

jQuery is a stable and mature product that's ready for use on web sites of any size, demonstrated by its adoption by some of the veritable giants of the Internet. Despite this, it's still a dynamic project under constant development and improvement, with each new version offering up performance boosts and clever additional functionality. There's no better time than now to start learning and using jQuery!

As we work through the book you'll see that there's a lot of truth in the jQuery motto, "write less, do more." It's an easy and fun library with a gentle learning curve that lets you do a lot of cool stuff with very little code. And as you progress down the path to jQuery ninja-hood, we hope you'll also acquire a bit of respect for and understanding of JavaScript itself.

In the Chapter 2, we'll dive into jQuery and start using it to add some shine to our client's web site. Speaking of our client, it's time we met him ...

Chapter 2

Selecting, Decorating, and Enhancing

"In phase two, we are going to want to harness the social and enable Web 2.0 community-based, crowd-sourced, Ajax, um, interactions," says our new client. "But for now we just need some basic stuff changed on our site."

Our client is launching a startup called StarTrackr! It uses GPS and RFID technology to track popular celebrities' exact physical location—then sells that information to fans. It's been going great guns operating out of a friend's local store, but now they're taking the venture online.

"Can you do it? Here's a list that needs to be live by Friday, close of business."

You survey the list. By amazing coincidence you notice that all of the requests can be implemented using jQuery. You look at your calendar. It's Friday morning. Let's get started!

The first task on the list is to add a simple JavaScript alert when the existing site loads. This is to let visitors know that StarTrackr! is not currently being sued for invasion of privacy (which was recently implied in a local newspaper).

Sure, we could use plain old JavaScript to do it, but we know that using jQuery will make our lives a lot easier—plus we can learn a new technology as we go along! We already saw the anatomy of a jQuery statement in Chapter 1; now let's look at the steps required to put jQuery into action: we wait until the page is ready, select our target, and then change it.

You may have probably guessed that jQuery can be more complicated than this—but only a little! Even advanced effects will rely on this basic formula, with multiple iterations of the last two steps, and perhaps a bit of JavaScript know-how. For now, let's start nice and easy.

Making Sure the Page Is Ready

Before we can interact with HTML elements on a page, those elements need to have been loaded: we can only change them once they're already there. In the old days of JavaScript, the only reliable way to do this was to wait for the entire page (including images) to finish loading before we ran any scripts.

Fortunately for us, jQuery has a very cool built-in event that executes our magic as soon as possible. Because of this, our pages and applications appear to load much faster to the end user:

```
chapter_02/01_document_ready/script.js
$(document).ready(function() {
  alert('Welcome to StarTrackr! Now no longer under police …');
});
```

The important bits here (highlighted in bold) say, "When our document is ready, run our function." This is one of the most common snippets of jQuery you're likely to see. It's usually a good idea to do a simple alert test like this to ensure you've properly included the jQuery library—and that nothing funny is going on.

You'll Be Seeing $(document).ready() a Lot!

Almost everything you do in jQuery will need to be done *after* the document is ready—so we'll be using this action a lot. It will be referred to as the document-ready event from now on. Every example that follows in this book, unless otherwise stated, needs to be run from inside the document-ready event. You should only need to declare it once per page though.

The document-ready idiom is so common, in fact, that there's a shortcut version of it:

```
$(function() { alert('Ready to do your bidding!'); });
```

If you'd like to use the shortcut method, go ahead! The expanded version is arguably a better example of self-documenting code; it's much easier to see at a glance exactly what's going on—especially if it's buried in a page of another developer's JavaScript!

At a cursory glance, the document-ready event looks much removed from the structure we encountered back in our jQuery anatomy class, but on closer inspection we can see that the requisite parts are all accounted for: the selector is `document`; the action is `ready`; and the parameter is a function that runs some code (our `alert`).

Selecting: The Core of jQuery

Time is ticking, and deadlines wait for no one. The client has noted that people have been having quoting incorrect celebrity IDs from the web site. This is because the celebrities' names are all laid out in one big table and it's difficult for users to line up a celebrity with the correct reference ID. Our client tells us that he wants every other row to be a light gray color so the users can easily find their favorite celebrity.

We have jQuery ready to do our bidding—it just needs us to choose a target for it. Selecting the elements you want to modify on the page is really the art of jQuery. One of the biggest differences between being a novice and ninja is the amount of time it takes you to grab the elements you want to play with!

You might remember from our jQuery anatomy class that all of our selectors are wrapped in the `jQuery` function:

```
jQuery(<selectors go here>)
```

Or the alias:

```
$(<selectors go here>)
```

We'll be using the shortcut alias for the remainder of the book—it's much more convenient. As we mentioned earlier, there's no real reason to use the full jQuery name unless you're having conflict issues with other libraries (see the section called "Avoiding Conflicts" in Chapter 9).

Simple Selecting

Our task is to select alternate table rows on the celebrity table. How do we do this? When selecting with jQuery, your goal should be to be only as specific as required: you want to find out the most concise selector that returns exactly what you want to change. Let's start by taking a look at the markup of the Celebrities table, shown in Figure 2.1.

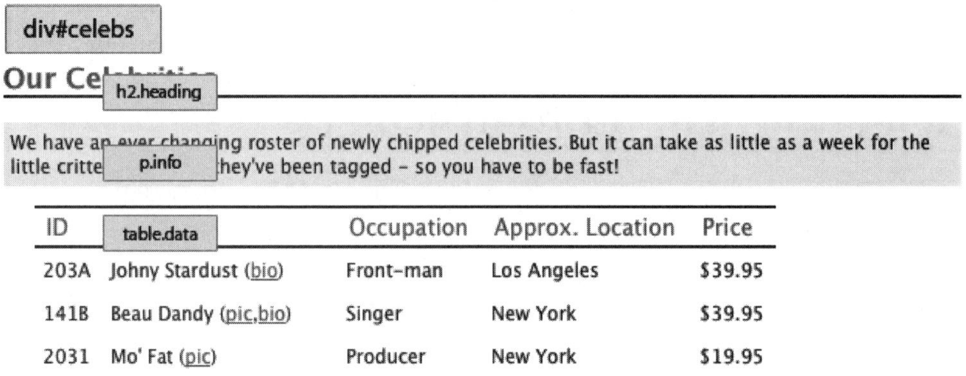

Figure 2.1. class and id attributes in the HTML page

We could start by selecting every table row element on the entire page. To select by element type, you simply pass the element's HTML name as a string parameter to the $ function. To select all table row elements (which are marked up with the <tr> tag), you would simply write:

```
$('tr')
```

Nothing Happens!

If you run this command, nothing will happen on the page. This is expected—after all, we're just selecting elements. But there's no need to worry; soon enough we'll be modifying our selections in all sorts of weird and wonderful ways.

Similarly, if we wanted to select every paragraph, `div` element, `h1` heading, or `input` box on the page, we would use these selectors accordingly:

```
$('p')
$('div')
$('h1')
$('input')
```

But we don't want to change *every* table row on the celebrity page: just the rows in the table that have the celebrity data. We need to be a bit more specific, and select first the containing element that holds the list of celebrities. If you have a look at the HTML and at Figure 2.1, you can see that the `div` that contains our celebrity `table` has an `id` of `celebs`, while the `table` itself has a `class` of `data`. We could use either of these to select the `table`.

jQuery borrows the conventions from CSS for referring to `id` and `class` names. To select by `id`, use the hash symbol (#) followed by the element's `id`, and pass this as a string to the jQuery function:

```
$('#celebs')
```

You should note that the string we pass to the jQuery function is exactly the same format as a CSS `id` selector. Because `id`s should be unique, we expect this to only return one element. jQuery now holds a reference to this element.

Similarly, we can use a CSS `class` selector to select by `class`. We pass a string consisting of a period (.) followed by the element's `class` name to the jQuery function:

```
$('.data')
```

Both of these statements will select the table but, as mentioned earlier when we talked about the DOM, a `class` can be shared by multiple elements—and jQuery will happily select as many elements as we point it to. If there were multiple tables (or any other elements for that matter) that also had the `class` `data`, they'd all be selected. For that reason, we'll stick to using the `id` for this one!

Can You Be More Specific?

Just like with CSS, we can select either `$('.data')` or the more specific `$('table.data')`. By specifying an element type in addition to the `class`, the selector will only return `table` elements with the `class` `data`—rather than *all* elements with the class `data`. Also, like CSS, you can add parent container selectors to narrow your selection even further.

Narrowing Down Our Selection

We've selected the table successfully, though the table itself is of no interest to us—we want *every other row* inside it. We've selected the containing element, and from that containing element we want to pick out all the descendants that are table rows: that is, we want to specify all table rows *inside* the containing `table`. To do this, we put a space between the ancestor and the descendant:

```
$('#celebs tr')
```

You can use this construct to drill down to the elements that you're looking for, but for clarity's sake try to keep your selectors as succinct as possible.

Let's take this idea a step further. Say we wanted to select all `span` elements inside of p elements, which are themselves inside `div` elements—but only if those `div`s happen to have a class of `fancy`. We would use the selector:

```
$('div.fancy p span')
```

If you can follow this, you're ready to select just about anything!

Testing Our Selection

Right, back to our task at hand. It feels like we're getting closer, but so far we've just been selecting blindly with no way of knowing if we're on the right path. We need a way of confirming that we're selecting the correct elements. A simple way to achieve this is to take advantage of the `length` property. `length` returns the number of elements currently matched by the selector. We can combine this with the good ol' trusty `alert` statement to ensure that our elements have been selected:

```
chapter_02/02_selecting/script.js
$(document).ready(function() {
  alert($('#celebs tr').length + ' elements!');
});
```

This will alert the length of the selection—7 elements—for the celebrity `table`. This result might be different from what you'd expect, as there are only six celebrities in the table! If you have a look at the HTML, you'll see where our problem lies: the `table` header is also a `tr`, so there are seven rows in total. A quick fix involves narrowing down our selector to find only table rows that lie inside the `tbody` element:

```
chapter_02/03_narrowing_selection/script.js
$(document).ready(function() {
  alert($('#celebs tbody tr').length + ' elements!');
});
```

This will alert the correct length of 6 elements—the jQuery object is now holding our six celebrity table row elements.

If the alert shows 0, you'll know there's a mistake in your selector. A good way to troubleshoot this sort of issue is to reduce your selector to the smallest, simplest one possible.

In our example, we could simply write `$('#celebs')`, which would select just the table element and alert a length of 1. From here you can make your selectors more specific, and check that you're selecting the correct number of elements as you go.

Filters

With the knowledge that we've successfully selected all of the table rows, narrowing our selection down to every other row is simple—because jQuery has a **filter** to do it. A filter removes certain items, and keeps only the ones we want. You'll acquire a feel for what can be filtered as we work through some more examples, but for now we'll just jump straight to the filter we need for our zebra stripes:

```
$(document).ready(function() {
  alert($('#celebs tbody tr:even').length + ' elements!');
});
```

Filters are attached to the item you want to filter (in this case, the table rows) and are defined by a colon, followed by the filter name. The `:even` filter used here keeps every even-indexed element in the selection and removes the rest, which is what we want. When we alert the selection length now, we see 3, as expected. All of our odd-numbered rows have been filtered out of the selection. There is a wide array of jQuery selector filters available to us: `:odd` (as you might expect), `:first`, `:last`, `:eq()` (for selecting, for example, the third element), and more. We'll look at each of these in more detail as we need them throughout the book.

Selecting Multiple Elements

One last trick for basic selecting is the ability to select multiple elements in a single statement. This is very useful, as we'll often want to apply the same action to several elements in unrelated parts of the page. Separating the selector strings with commas allows you to do this. For example, if we wanted to select every paragraph, `div` element, `h1` heading, and `input` box on the page, we'd use this selector:

```
$('p,div,h1,input')
```

Learning how to use all these different selectors together to access exactly the page elements you want is a big part of mastering jQuery. It's also one of the most satisfying parts of using jQuery, since you can pack some fairly complex selection logic into a single short line of code!

Becoming a Good Selector

Selecting may seem quite easy and, up to a point, it is. But what we've covered so far has only just scratched the surface of selecting. In most cases the basics are all you'll need: if you're simply trying to target an element or a bunch of related elements, the element name, `id`, and `class` are the most efficient and easiest ways to achieve this.

When moving around the DOM from a given element, the situation becomes a little trickier. jQuery provides a myriad of selectors and actions for traversing the DOM. **Traversing** means traveling up and down the page hierarchy, through parent and child elements. You can add and remove elements as you go, applying different actions at each step—which lets you perform some mind-bogglingly complex actions in a single jQuery statement!

If you're a wiz at CSS, you'll already be familiar with a lot of the statements; they're mostly borrowed directly from the CSS specification. But there are probably a few that you're unfamiliar with, especially if you've yet to spend much time learning CSS3 selectors. Of course, we'll be covering and learning advanced selection techniques as we implement them in our examples and demos. For this reason, any time you want to find out more about all the jQuery selectors available, you can just head over to the online documentation[1] and browse away!

Decorating: CSS with jQuery

Selecting elements in jQuery is the hard part. Everything else is both easy and fun. After we have selected our targets, we are able to manipulate them to build effects or interfaces. In this section we will cover a series of jQuery actions relating to CSS: adding and removing styles, classes, and more. The actions we execute will be applied individually to every element we've selected, letting us bend the page to our will!

Reading CSS Properties

Before we try changing CSS properties, let's look first into how we can simply access them. jQuery lets us do this with the `css` function. Try this:

chapter_02/05_reading_css_properties/script.js

```javascript
$(document).ready(function() {
  var fontSize = $('#celebs tbody tr:first').css('font-size');
  alert(fontSize);
});
```

---

[1] http://api.jquery.com/category/selectors/

This code will alert the font size of the first element matched by the selector (as you've likely guessed, the `:first` filter will return the first element among those matched by the selector).

 CSS Properties of Multiple Elements

You *can* ask for a CSS property after selecting multiple elements, but this is almost always a bad idea: a function can only return a single result, so you'll still only obtain the property for the first matched element.

The nifty aspect about retrieving CSS properties with this method is that jQuery gives you the element's *calculated* style. This means that you'll receive the value that's been rendered in the user's browser, rather than the value entered in the CSS definition. So, if you gave a `div` a height of, say, 200 pixels in the CSS file, but the content inside it pushed the height over 200 pixels, jQuery would provide you with the actual height of the element, rather than the 200 pixels you'd specified.

We'll see why that's really important when we come to implement some funky tricks a bit later.

Setting CSS Properties

So far we've yet to see jQuery actually *do* anything, and it's high time to remedy that. We know the page is ready (since we popped up an alert), and we're fairly sure we've selected the elements we're interested in. Let's check that we really have:

chapter_02/06_zebra_striping/script.js

```
$(document).ready(function() {
  $('#celebs tbody tr:even').css('background-color','#dddddd');
});
```

You probably saw that coming! This is the same `css` function we used to read a CSS property, but now it's being passed an extra parameter: the value we wish to set for that property. We've used the action to set the `background-color` to the value `#dddddd` (a light gray). Open the file from the code archive in your browser and test that it's working correctly. You can see the result in Figure 2.2.

ID	Name	Occupation	Approx. Location	Price
203A	Johny Stardust (bio)	Front–man	Los Angeles	$39.95
141B	Beau Dandy (pic,bio)	Singer	New York	$39.95
2031	Mo' Fat (pic)	Producer	New York	$19.95
007F	Kellie Kelly (bio,press)	Singer	Omaha	$11.95
8A05	Darth Fader (pic)	DJ	London	$19.95
6636	Glendatronix (bio,press)	Keytarist	London	$39.95

Figure 2.2. Zebra striping implemented with jQuery

 Were You Ready?

As mentioned previously, this command must be issued from within our document-ready function. If we run the command before the DOM is ready, the selector will go looking for the `#celebs` element, but will find nothing that matches. At this point it will give up; it won't even look for the `tr` elements, let alone change the background style.

This is true for all of the examples that follow, so remember to wrap your code in the document-ready function.

It's looking good! But perhaps we should add a little extra to it—after all, more is more! What about a shade lighter font color to really define our stripes? There are a few ways we could add a second CSS property. The simplest way is to repeat the entire jQuery statement with our new values:

```
chapter_02/07_multiple_properties_1/script.js (excerpt)

$('#celebs tbody tr:even').css('background-color','#dddddd');
$('#celebs tbody tr:even').css('color', '#666666');
```

These lines are executed one after the other. Though the end result is correct, it will become quite messy and inefficient if we have to change a whole slew of properties. Thankfully, jQuery provides us with a nice way to set multiple properties at the same time, using an **object literal**. Object literals are a JavaScript concept beyond the scope of this book, but for our purposes, all you need to know is that they provide an easy way of grouping together key/value pairs. For CSS, object literals allow us to match up our CSS properties (the keys) with the matching CSS values (the values) in a neat package:

```
                              chapter_02/08_multiple_properties_2/script.js (excerpt)

$('#celebs tbody tr:even').css(
  {'background-color': '#dddddd', 'color': '#666666'}
);
```

The object literal is wrapped in curly braces, with each key separated from its corresponding value by a colon, and each key/value pair separated by a comma. It's passed as a single parameter to the `css` function. Using this method you can specify as many key/value pairs as you like—just separate them with commas. It's a good idea to lay out your key/value pairs in a readable manner so you can easily see what's going on when you come back to your code later. This is especially helpful if you need to set a larger number of properties. As an example:

```
                              chapter_02/09_multiple_properties_3/script.js (excerpt)

$('#celebs tbody tr:even').css({
  'background-color': '#dddddd',
  'color': '#666666',
  'font-size': '11pt',
  'line-height': '2.5em'
});
```

 To Quote or Not to Quote

In general, when dealing with JavaScript objects, it's unnecessary for the keys to be in quotes. However, for jQuery to work properly, any key that contains a hyphen (as our `background-color` and `font-size` examples do) must be placed in quotes, or written in camel case (like `backgroundColor`).

Additionally, any key that's already a keyword in the JavaScript language (such as `float` and `class`) must also be written in quotes.

It can be confusing trying to remember which keys need to be quoted and which don't, so it's to be recommended that you just put all object keys in quotes each time.

Classes

Excellent! We've already struck two tasks off the client's list, and we have some funky jQuery happening. But if you stop and have a look at our last solution, you might notice something a little fishy. If you were to inspect the zebra-striped rows in a development tool such as Firebug, you'd notice that the CSS properties have been added to the paragraphs *inline*, as illustrated in Figure 2.3.

```
▼ <table id="celebs" class="data">
  ▼ <tbody>
    ▶ <tr>
    ▶ <tr style="background-color: rgb(221, 221, 221);
    ▶ <tr>
    ▶ <tr style="background-color: rgb(221, 221, 221);">
    ▶ <tr>
    ▶ <tr style="background-color: rgb(221, 221, 221);">
  </tbody>
</table>
```

Figure 2.3. Inline styles viewed with Firebug

Firebug

Firebug is a particularly useful tool for examining the DOM in your browser, as well as monitoring and editing CSS, HTML, and JavaScript (including jQuery). A debugger's Swiss Army knife for the Web, it will save you hours by helping you see exactly what your browser thinks is going on. It's available as a Mozilla Firefox extension, or as a stand-alone JavaScript file that you can include in your projects if you develop using another browser.

Inline styles are a big no-no in HTML/CSS best practice, right? That's quite true, and this also applies in jQuery: to keep your code clear and maintainable, it makes more sense for all the styling information to be in the same place, in your CSS files. Then, as we'll soon see, you can simply toggle those styles by attaching or removing `class` attributes to your HTML tags.

There are times when it *is* a good idea to use the `css` jQuery method in the way we've just seen. The most common application is when quickly debugging code: if you just want to outline an element in red to make sure you've selected it correctly, switching to your CSS file to add a new rule seems like a waste of time.

Adding and Removing Classes

If we need to remove the CSS from inline style rules, where should we put it? In a separate style sheet, of course! We can put the styles we want in a rule in our CSS that's targeted to a given `class`, and use jQuery to add or remove that class from targeted elements in the HTML. Perhaps unsurprisingly, jQuery provides some handy methods for manipulating the `class` attributes of DOM elements. We'll use the most common of these, `addClass`, to move our zebra stripe styles into the CSS file where they belong.

The `addClass` function accepts a string containing a `class` name as a parameter. You can also add multiple `classes` at the same time by separating the `class` names with a space, just as you do when writing HTML:

```
$('div').addClass('class_name');
$('div').addClass('class_name1 class_name2 class_name3');
```

We only want to add one `class` name, though, which we'll call zebra. First, we'll add the rule to a new CSS file (including it with a `link` tag in our HTML page):

chapter_02/10_adding_classes/zebra.css

```
.zebra {
  background-color: #dddddd;
  color: #666666;
}
```

Then, back in our JavaScript file, we'll modify the selector to use jQuery's `addClass` method rather than `css`:

chapter_02/10_adding_classes/script.js

```
$('#celebs tr:even').addClass('zebra');
```

The result is exactly the same, but now when we inspect the table in Firebug, we'll see that the inline styles are gone—replaced by our new class definition. This is shown in Figure 2.4.

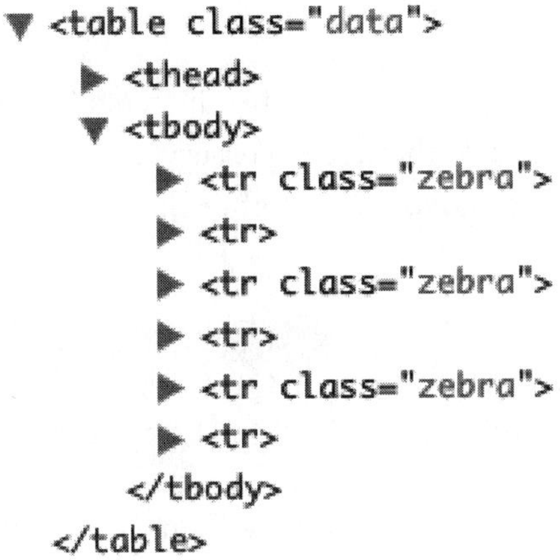

```
▼ <table class="data">
    ▶ <thead>
    ▼ <tbody>
        ▶ <tr class="zebra">
        ▶ <tr>
        ▶ <tr class="zebra">
        ▶ <tr>
        ▶ <tr class="zebra">
        ▶ <tr>
    </tbody>
</table>
```

Figure 2.4. Adding classes to table rows

That's much better. Now, if we want to change the appearance of the zebra stripes in the future, we can simply modify the CSS file; this will save us hunting through our jQuery code (potentially in multiple locations) to change the values.

There'll also be times when we want to remove class names from elements (we'll see an example of when this is necessary very soon). The action to remove a class is conveniently known as removeClass. This function is used in exactly the same way as addClass; we just pass the (un)desired class name as a parameter:

```
$('#celebs tr.zebra').removeClass('zebra');
```

It's also possible to manipulate the id attribute, or any other attribute for that matter, using jQuery's attr method. We'll cover this method in more detail later in the book.

Enhancing: Adding Effects with jQuery

Now you've reached an important milestone. You've learned the component parts of a jQuery statement: the selector, the action, and the parameters. And you've learned the steps to use the statement: make sure the document is ready, select elements, and change them.

In the following section, we'll apply these lessons to implement some cool and useful effects—and with any luck reinforce your understanding of the jQuery basics.

Hiding and Revealing Elements

The client dislikes the disclaimer on the site—he feels it reflects badly on the product—but his lawyer insists that it's necessary. So the client has requested that you add a button that will remove the text after the user has had a chance to read it:

```
chapter_02/11_hiding/index.html (excerpt)

<input type="button" id="hideButton" value="hide" />
```

We've added an HTML button on the page with an ID of hideButton. When a user clicks on this button we want the disclaimer element, which has an ID of disclaimer, to be hidden:

```
chapter_02/11_hiding/script.js (excerpt)

$('#hideButton').click(function() {
  $('#disclaimer').hide();
});
```

Run this code and make sure the disclaimer element disappears when you click the hide button.

The part in this example that makes the element actually disappear is the hide action. So, you might ask, what's all the other code that surrounds that line? It's what's called an event handler—an understanding of which is crucial to becoming a jQuery ninja. There are many event handlers we can use (we've used the click event handler here) and we'll be using a lot of them as we move on.

Event Handlers

Event handlers are named for their function of handling events. Events are actions and user interactions that occur on the web page. When an event happens, we say that it has *fired*. And when we write some code to handle the event, we say we *caught* the event.

There are thousands of events fired on a web page all the time: when a user moves the mouse, or clicks a button, or when a browser window is resized, or the scroll bar moved. We can catch, and act on, any of these events.

The first event that you were introduced to in this book was the document-ready event. Yes, that was an event handler: when the document said, "I'm ready" it fired an event, which our jQuery statement caught.

We used the `click` event handler to tell jQuery to hide the disclaimer when the button is clicked:

```
$('#hideButton').click(function() {
  $('#disclaimer').hide();
});
```

this

When an event fires, we will often want to refer to the element that fired it. For example, we might want to modify the button that the user has just clicked on in some way. Such a reference is available inside our event handler code via the JavaScript keyword `this`. To convert the JavaScript object to a jQuery object, we wrap it in the jQuery selector:

```
                                      chapter_02/12_this/script.js (excerpt)

$('#hideButton').click(function() {
  $(this).hide(); // a curious disappearing button.
});
```

`$(this)` provides a nicer way to talk about the element that fired the event, rather than having to re-select it.

Where's the Action?

This might be a bit confusing when you're starting out, as the "action" component of a jQuery statement seems to have several purposes: we've seen it used to run animations, retrieve values and now, handle events! It's true—it gets around! Usually the action's name gives you a good clue to its purpose, but if you become lost, it's best to consult the index. After a while, you'll sort out the handlers from the animations from the utilities.

Revealing Hidden Elements

On with our task! The client has also specified that the user needs to be able to re-trieve the disclaimer in case they close it by mistake. So let's add another button to the HTML, this time with an id of showButton:

```
chapter_02/13_revealing/index.html (excerpt)
<input type="button" id="showButton" value="show" />
```

We'll also add another jQuery statement to our script file, to handle showing the disclaimer when the **show** button is clicked:

```
chapter_02/13_revealing/script.js (excerpt)
$('#showButton').click(function() {
  $('#disclaimer').show();
});
```

Toggling Elements

Having separate buttons for hiding and showing the disclaimer seems like a waste of valuable screen real estate. It would be better to have one button that performed both tasks—hiding the disclaimer when it's visible, and showing it when it's hidden. One way we could do this is by checking if the element is visible or not, and then showing or hiding accordingly. We'll remove the old buttons and add this nice new one:

```
chapter_02/14_toggle_1/index.html (excerpt)
<input type="button" id="toggleButton" value="toggle" />
```

When it's clicked, we check to find out if we should show or hide the disclaimer:

```
chapter_02/14_toggle_1/script.js (excerpt)
$('#toggleButton').click(function() {
  if ($('#disclaimer').is(':visible')) {
    $('#disclaimer').hide();
  } else {
```

```
    $('#disclaimer').show();
  }
});
```

This introduces the `is` action. `is` takes any of the same selectors we normally pass to the jQuery function, and checks to see if they match the elements it was called on. In this case, we're checking to see if our selected `#disclaimer` is also selected by the pseudo-selector `:visible`. It can also be used to check for other attributes: if a selection is a `form` or `div`, or is enabled.

 The `if` Statement

If you're entirely new to programming (that is, if you've only ever worked with HTML and CSS), that whole block of code is probably quite confusing! Don't worry, it's actually quite straightforward:

```
if (condition) {
    // this part happens if the condition is true
} else {
    // this part happens if the condition is false
}
```

The condition can be anything that JavaScript will evaluate to `true` or `false`. This sort of structure is extremely common in any type of programming, and we'll be using it a lot for the rest of the book. If you're uncomfortable with it, the best way to learn is to play around: try writing different `if` / `else` blocks using jQuery's `is` action like the one we wrote above. You'll get the hang of it in no time!

`is` will return `true` or `false` depending on whether the elements match the selector. For our purposes we'll show the element if it's hidden, and hide it if it's visible. This type of logic—where we flip between two states—is called a **toggle** and is a very useful construct.

Toggling elements between two states is so common that many jQuery functions have a version that allows for toggling. The toggle version of `show`/`hide` is simply called `toggle`, and works like this:

```
chapter_02/15_toggle_2/script.js (excerpt)
$('#toggleButton').click(function() {
  $('#disclaimer').toggle();
});
```

Every time you click the button, the element toggles between visible and hidden.

It would be nice, however, if the button was labeled with a more useful word than "toggle," which might be confusing to our users. What if you want to toggle the text of the button as well? As is often the case when working with jQuery, there are a few ways we could approach this problem. Here's one:

```
chapter_02/16_toggle_text/script.js (excerpt)
$('#toggleButton').click(function() {
  $('#disclaimer').toggle();

  if ($('#disclaimer').is(':visible')) {
    $(this).val('Hide');
  } else {
    $(this).val('Show');
  }
});
```

There's a lot in this code that will be new to you. We'll save most of the details for later, but have a look at it and see if you can figure it out yourself. (Hint: remember that the selector $(this) refers to the element that caused the event to fire—in this case, the button.)

Progressive Enhancement

Our disclaimer functionality is working perfectly—and our client will doubtlessly be impressed with it. However, there's one subtle aspect of our solution that we should be aware of: if a user came to our site using a browser lacking support for JavaScript, they'd see a button on the page that would do nothing when they clicked it. This would lead to a very confused user, who might even abandon our site.

"No support for JavaScript?" you might snort. "What kind of browser is unable to run JavaScript?!"

There might be more people than you think browsing the Web without JavaScript: users on very old computers or limited devices (like mobile phones); people with visual impairments who require screen readers to use the Web; and those who worry that JavaScript is an unnecessary security risk and so choose to disable it.

Depending on your site's demographic, anywhere between 5% and 10% of your users might be browsing without JavaScript capabilities, and nobody wants to alienate 10% of their customers! The solution is to provide an acceptable experience to these users—and beef it up for everyone else. This practice is known as progressive enhancement.

For our disclaimer functionality, we might settle on this compromise: we want the disclaimer to be visible to all users, so we place it in our HTML. Then, we add the ability to hide it for users with JavaScript. That said, we'd prefer to avoid displaying the show/hide button to users who'll be unable to make use of it.

One way of accomplishing this might be to hide our button with CSS, and only show it via a jQuery `css` statement. The problem with this trick is that it will fail if the user's browser also lacks support for CSS. What we'd really like to do is add the button to the page via jQuery; that way, only users with JavaScript will see the button at all. Perfect!

Adding New Elements

So far we've seen the jQuery function used for selecting, but it does have another function of equal importance: creating new elements. In fact, any valid HTML string you put inside the jQuery function will be created and made ready for you to stick on the page. Here's how we might create a simple paragraph element:

```
$('<p>A new paragraph!</p>')
```

jQuery performs several useful actions when you write this code: it parses the HTML into a DOM fragment and selects it—just as an ordinary jQuery selector does. That means it's instantly ready for further jQuery processing. For example, to add a `class` to our newly created element, we can simply write:

```
$('<p>A new paragraph!</p>').addClass('new');
```

The new paragraph will now be given the class new. Using this method you can create any new elements you need via jQuery itself, rather than defining them in your HTML markup. This way, we can complete our goal of progressively enhancing our page.

 innerHTML

> Internally, the HTML string is parsed by creating a simple element (such as a div) and setting the innerHTML property of that div to the markup you provide. Some content you pass in is unable to convert quite as easily—so it's best to keep the HTML fragments as simple as possible.

Once we've created our new elements, we need a way to insert in the page where we'd like them to go. There are several jQuery functions available for this purpose. The first one we'll look at is the insertAfter function. insertAfter will take our current jQuery selection (in this case, our newly created elements) and insert it after another selected element, which we pass as a parameter to the function.

An example is the easiest way to show how this works. This is how we'd create the toggle button using jQuery:

chapter_02/17_insert_after/script.js (excerpt)

```
$('<input type="button" value="toggle" id="toggleButton">')
  .insertAfter('#disclaimer');
$('#toggleButton').click(function() {
  $('#disclaimer').toggle();
});
```

As shown in Figure 2.5, the button is inserted into our page after the disclaimer, just as if we'd put it there in our HTML file.

Disclaimer! This service is not intended for people so their privacy should be respected

(toggle)

Figure 2.5. A button created and inserted with jQuery

The insertAfter function adds the new element as a sibling directly after the disclaimer element. If you want the button to appear *before* the disclaimer element, you could either target the element before the disclaimer and use `insertAfter`, or, more logically, use the `insertBefore` method. `insertBefore` will also place the new element as a sibling to the existing element, but it will appear immediately before it:

chapter_02/18_insert_before/script.js *(excerpt)*

```
$('<input type="button" value="toggle" id="toggleButton">')
  .insertBefore('#disclaimer');
```

A quick refresher: when we talk about the DOM, *siblings* refer to elements on the same level in the DOM hierarchy. If you have a `div` that contains two `span` elements, the `span` elements are siblings.

If you want to add your new element as a *child* of an existing element (that is, if you want the new element to appear *inside* the existing element) then you can use the `prependTo` or `appendTo` functions:

chapter_02/19_prepend_append/script.js *(excerpt)*

```
$('<strong>START!</strong>').prependTo('#disclaimer');
$('<strong>END!</strong>').appendTo('#disclaimer');
```

As you can see in Figure 2.6, our new elements have been added to the start and the end of the actual disclaimer `div`, rather than before or after it. There are more actions for inserting and removing elements, but as they're unneeded in this round of changes, we'll address them later on.

START! Disclaimer! This service is not intended for the those with criminal intent. Celebrities are kind of like people so their privacy should be respected. **END!**

Figure 2.6. `prependTo` and `appendTo` in action

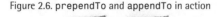

Inserting Multiple Elements

A new item is inserted *once for each element that's matched with the selector*. If your selector matches every paragraph tag, for example, the `insertAfter` action will add a new element after *every* paragraph tag. Which makes it a fairly powerful function!

Removing Existing Elements

We informed the client that up to 10% of his users might lack JavaScript capabilities and would therefore miss out on some of the advanced features we're building. He asked if we could add a message explaining that JavaScript was recommended for those people. Obviously the message should be hidden from those who *do* have JavaScript.

This seems like a perfect opportunity to learn how to remove HTML elements from a page using jQuery. We'll put the message in our HTML and remove it with jQuery; that way, only those visitors without JavaScript will see it.

Let's go ahead and add the new warning to our HTML page:

chapter_02/20_removing_elements/index.html (excerpt)

```
<p id="no-script">
  We recommend that you have JavaScript enabled!
</p>
```

Now we need to run our code to remove the element from the page. If a user has JavaScript disabled, our jQuery statements will fail to run and the message will remain on the screen. To remove elements in jQuery, you first select them (as usual) with a selector, and then call the `remove` method:

chapter_02/20_removing_elements/script.js (excerpt)

```
$('#no-script').remove();
```

The `remove` action will remove all of the selected elements from the DOM, and will also remove any event handlers or data attached to those elements. The `remove` action does not require any parameters, though you can also specify an expression to refine the selection further. Try this example:

```
chapter_02/21_removing_with_selector/script.js (excerpt)
$('#celebs tr').remove(':contains("Singer")');
```

Rather than removing every `tr` in the `#celebs div`, this code will remove only those rows which contain the text "Singer." This will come in handy when we look at some advanced effects in the next chapter.

Thanks to these changes, our page will work nicely for the 10% of our users without JavaScript, and even better for the remaining 90%! This is a very simple example of progressive enhancement, but it gives you a good understanding of the fundamental idea: rather than using jQuery as the underpinnings of your UI, use it to add some sugar to an already functioning experience. That way, you know no one's left behind.

In the interests of keeping our sample code small and focused, we'll stop short of delving much further into the topic. But go off and research it for yourself—it's the kind of best practice that makes you a better web developer.

Modifying Content

We can do just about anything we want to our elements now: show them, hide them, add new ones, remove old ones, style them however we like … but what if we want to change the actual content of an element? Again, jQuery provides a couple of methods for just this purpose: `text` and `html`.

The `text` and `html` actions are quite similar, as both set the content for the elements we've selected. We simply pass a string to either function:

```
chapter_02/22_modifying_content/script.js (excerpt)
$('p').html('good bye, cruel paragraphs!');
$('h2').text('All your titles are belong to us');
```

In both these examples the matched elements' contents will change to the string we've provided: every paragraph and `h2` tag on the page will be overwritten with our new content. The difference between `text` and `html` can be seen if we try adding some HTML to the content string:

```
chapter_02/23_text_vs_html/script.js (excerpt)
$('p').html('<strong>Warning!</strong> Text has been replaced … ');
$('h2').text('<strong>Warning!</strong> Title elements can be …');
```

In this case, our paragraphs will contain bold-faced text, but our h2 tags will contain the entire content string exactly as defined, including the <strong> tags. The action you use to modify content will depend on your requirements: text for plain text or html for HTML.

You might wonder, "Can these new actions only *set* content?" At this stage it should be no surprise to you that we can also fetch content from our jQuery selections using the same actions:

```
chapter_02/24_get_content/script.js (excerpt)
alert($('h2:first').text());
```

We use the text action supplying no parameters, which returns the text content of the first h2 tag on the page ("Welcome!"). Like other actions that retrieve values, this can be particularly useful for conditional statements, and it can also be great for adding essential information to our user interactions.

Basic Animation: Hiding and Revealing with Flair

All this showing and hiding and changing is useful, though visually it's somewhat unimpressive. It's time to move on to some jQuery techniques that are a bit more, shall we say, *animated*.

The core jQuery library includes a handful of basic effects that we can use to spice up our pages. And once you've had enough of these, mosey on over to the jQuery plugin repository, where you'll find hundreds more crazy effects.

 Keep It Sensible

When dealing with effects and animation on the Web, it's probably a wise idea to proceed with your good taste sensors engaged. Remember, at one time the <blink> tag was considered perfectly sensible!

Fading In and Out

One of the most common (and timeless) effects in jQuery is the built-in fade effect. To use fading in its simplest form, just replace `show` with `fadeIn` or `hide` with `fadeOut`:

chapter_02/25_fade_in_out/script.js *(excerpt)*

```
$('#hideButton').click(function() {
  $('#disclaimer').fadeOut();
});
```

There are also a few optional parameters we can use to modify the effect, the first of which is used to control the time it takes for the fade to complete. Many jQuery effects and animations accept the time parameter—which can be passed either as a string or an integer.

We can specify the time span as a string using one of the following predefined words: `slow`, `fast`, or `normal`. For example: `fadeIn('fast')`. If you'd rather have more fine-grained control over the duration of the animation, you can also specify the time in milliseconds, as in: `fadeIn(1000)`.

Toggling Effects and Animations

Although jQuery has no specific action for toggling using fades, here's a little secret: our original `toggle` action has a few more tricks up its sleeve than we first thought. If we pass it a time span parameter, we'll see that `toggle` has the ability to animate:

chapter_02/26_toggle_fade/script.js *(excerpt)*

```
$('#toggleButton').click(function() {
  $('#disclaimer').toggle('slow');
});
```

You can see that the width, height, and opacity of the entire element are animated. If this is a bit much for you, there's another core jQuery animation effect that *does* include built-in toggle actions: sliding.

Sliding eases an element into and out of view, as if it were sliding out from a hidden compartment. It's implemented in the same manner as our fade, but with the slideDown, slideUp, and slideToggle actions. As with the fade effect, we can also specify a time span:

chapter_02/27_slide_toggle/script.js *(excerpt)*

```
$('#toggleButton').click(function() {
  $('#disclaimer').slideToggle('slow');
});
```

Callback Functions

Many effects (including our slide and fade effects) accept a special parameter known as a **callback function**. Callbacks specify code that needs to run after the effect has finished doing whatever it needs to do. In our case, when the slide has finished sliding it will run our callback code:

chapter_02/28_callback_functions/script.js *(excerpt)*

```
$('#disclaimer').slideToggle('slow', function() {
  alert('The slide has finished sliding!')
});
```

The callback function is simply passed in as a second parameter to the effect action, as an anonymous function, much in the same way we provide functions as parameters to event handlers.

 Anonymous Functions

In JavaScript, functions that are defined inline (such as our callbacks and event handlers) are called **anonymous functions**. They are referred to as "anonymous" simply because they don't have a name! You use anonymous functions when you only require the function to be run from one particular location.

In any situation where we're using anonymous functions, it's also possible to pass a function name yet define the function elsewhere. This is best done when the same function needs to be called in several different places. In simple cases like our examples, this can make the code a bit harder to follow, so we'll stick with anonymous functions for the moment.

Let's put our callback functions to practical use. If we want to hide our button after the disclaimer has finished sliding out of view:

```
chapter_02/29_callback_functions_2/script.js (excerpt)
$('#disclaimer').slideUp('slow', function() {
  $('#hideButton').fadeOut();
});
```

The disclaimer will slide up, and only once that animation is complete will the button fade from view.

A Few Tricks

Now that we've struck a few high priority requests off the client's to-do list, let's be a bit more showy and add some extra sizzle to the site. We'll add a few effects and visual highlights by building on what we've learned so far. There'll be some new constructs and actions introduced, so it's worth working through them if this is your first venture into the world of jQuery.

Highlighting When Hovering

The client is really keen about the zebra-striping usability issue. He's requested that, as well as changing the row colors, there should be an additional highlight that occurs when the user runs the mouse over the `table`.

We could implement this effect by adding event handlers to the `table` that deal with both the `mouseover` and `mouseout` events. Then we could add or remove a CSS `class` containing a background color specific to elements over which the mouse is hovering. This is much the same way we'd do it in plain old JavaScript too:

```
chapter_02/30_hover_highlight/script.css (excerpt)
$('#celebs tr').mouseover(function() {
  $(this).addClass('zebraHover');
});
$('#celebs tr').mouseout(function() {
  $(this).removeClass('zebraHover');
});
```

Remember that `$(this)` refers to the selected object—so we're adding and removing the `zebraHover` class to each row as the user hovers the mouse over it. Now we simply need to add a style rule to our CSS file:

chapter_02/30_hover_highlight/zebra.css (excerpt)

```css
tr.zebraHover {
  background-color: #FFFACD;
}
```

Try this out in your browser and you'll see how great it works. However, it turns out there's an even simpler way of achieving the same result: jQuery includes a `hover` action, which combines `mouseover` and `mouseout` into a single handler:

chapter_02/31_hover_action/script.js (excerpt)

```js
$('#celebs tbody tr').hover(function() {
  $(this).addClass('zebraHover');
}, function() {
  $(this).removeClass('zebraHover');
});
```

Notice something odd about the `hover` event handler? Instead of one, it requires two functions as parameters: one to handle the `mouseover` event, and one to handle the `mouseout` event.

How Many Callbacks?

Some event handlers require a different number of functions. For example, the toggle event handler can accept any number of functions; it will simply cycle through each callback one by one each time it fires.

We're becoming handy at adding and removing `class` attributes, so it's probably a good time to point out another helpful `class`-related action: `toggleClass`. You can guess what it does. It's an incredibly useful action that adds a `class` if the element doesn't already have it, and removes it if it does.

For example, say we wanted users to be able to select multiple rows from our table. Clicking once on a table row should highlight it, and clicking again should remove the highlight. This is easy to implement with our new jQuery skills:

```
                              chapter_02/32_toggle_class/script.js (excerpt)
$('#celebs tbody tr').click(function() {
  $(this).toggleClass('zebraHover');
});
```

Try clicking on the table rows. Cool, huh?

Spoiler Revealer

The latest news section of the StarTrackr! site provides up-to-the-minute juicy gossip about a range of popular celebrities. The news is a real drawcard on the site—most users return every day to catch the latest update. The client would like to build on the hype it's generating and add to the excitement, so he's asked for our help. We've suggested a spoiler revealer: the user can try to guess which celebrity the news is about, before clicking to find the answer.

This kind of functionality would also make a great addition to a site containing movie reviews, for example. You could hide any parts of the review that give away details of the movie's story, but allow users to reveal them if they've already seen the film.

To set up our spoiler revealer, we need to add a new element to the news section of the site. Any "secrets" that should be hidden by default will be wrapped in a span element with the class spoiler attached to it:

```
                           chapter_02/33_spoiler_revealer/index.html (excerpt)
Who lost their recording contract today?
<span class='spoiler'>The Zaxntines!</span>
```

Let's break down what our script needs to do: first, we need to hide the answers and add a new element that enables them to be revealed if the user desires. When that element is clicked, we need to disclose the answer. Hiding? Adding? Handling clicks? We know how to do all of that:

chapter_02/33_spoiler_revealer/script.js *(excerpt)*

```
$('.spoiler').hide();
$('<span class="revealer">Tell me!</span>')
  .insertBefore('.spoiler');
$('.revealer').click(function() {
  $(this).hide();
  $(this).next().fadeIn();
});
```

There's a lot going on here, some of it new, but if you read through the lines one at a time, you'll make sense of it. First, we instantly hide all the spoiler elements, and use the `insertBefore` action to add a new button before each of them. At this point the page will display the new "Tell Me!" buttons, and the original spoiler spans will be hidden.

Next, we select the new buttons we just added and attach `click` event handlers to them. When one of the buttons is clicked, we remove the new revealer element (which we find with `$(this)`), and fade in the spoiler element that's next to it. `next` is an action we've yet to cover. It's used for traversing the DOM, and unsurprisingly gives us access to an element's next sibling (that is, the next element inside the same container).

If we look at our modified DOM shown in Figure 2.7, we can see that the spoiler span is the next element after the revealer button. The `next` action simply moves our selection to that element. jQuery also gives us access to a `previous` action that moves the selection to the element before the one that's currently selected.

```
▼ <p>
    Who lost their recording contract today?
    <input class="revealer" type="button" value="Tell Me!"/>
    <span class="spoiler" style="display: none;"> The Zaxntines! </span>
  </p>
```

Figure 2.7. The modified DOM

In fact, jQuery has about a dozen different actions you can use to move around the DOM; `previous` and `next` are just two particularly useful ones. We'll discover more of them as we proceed through the book, or you can consult the jQuery API documentation[2] to see them all.

With the hidden spoiler element now under jQuery's control, we can simply call `fadeIn` to reveal the spoiler with a smooth transition.

Before We Move On

We've covered so much in the initial chapters that you should now be gaining a sense of jQuery's structure and power. With any luck, you've already hatched plans for using it in your current projects. Please do! Whether you're using it to solve a pernicious problem or just to add a bell here and a whistle there, dirtying your hands is by far the best way to cement your knowledge.

One small word of warning—remember the old saying: "When the only tool you have is a hammer, everything looks like a nail." jQuery is a great tool, but may be inappropriate in some instances. If a problem is better solved with simple changes to your CSS or HTML, that's what should be done. Of course, while you're learning, feel free to do *everything* with jQuery; just remember that when the time comes to put your skills into practice, you should always use the best tool for the job.

In the pages that follow, we'll take the simple jQuery building blocks we've learned here and use them to construct some very cool widgets, effects, and user interaction that you can start using immediately.

---

[2] http://docs.jquery.com/Traversing

Animating, Scrolling, and Resizing

The client is extremely happy with our rapid and inspired first-round changes and wants to take it further. His company deals with the entertainment industry, and he believes that the web site should reflect what he perceives as the exciting and dynamic nature intrinsic to the business. Also, he believes flashy animations will help boost sales.

"I think it needs some of that Web 2.0 that I've been hearing about," he says confidently. "Can you make it look more like a Web 2.0?"

"Errrm, indeed we can," you assure him, as he passes you his next wish list chock-full of exciting changes—a list that will allow us to move beyond simply hiding and showing, and closer to our goal of being a jQuery ninja.

Animating

jQuery was built to animate. Whether it's fading out a warning message after a failed login, sliding down a menu control, or even powering a complete side-scrolling, "shoot 'em up" game—it's all a snap with some powerful built-in methods, augmented with an extensive array of plugins.

Animating CSS Properties

We have mastered some valuable examples of animation so far—sliding, fading, and some fancy hiding and showing—but we haven't had a lot of control over what exactly is animated and exactly how it happens. It's time to introduce a very exciting jQuery function, helpfully called `animate`, which lets you animate a whole host of CSS properties to fashion some striking effects of your own. Let's have a look at an example of `animate` in action:

chapter_03/01_animating_css/script.js *(excerpt)*

```
$('p').animate({
    padding: '20px',
    borderBottom: '3px solid #8f8f8f',
    borderRight: '3px solid #bfbfbf'
}, 2000);
```

This code will animate all paragraphs on the page, changing the padding from its initial state to 20px and adding a beveled border over a period of 2 seconds (2,000 milliseconds).

To use `animate`, we pass an object literal containing the properties we would like to animate specified as key/value pairs—much the same as when you assign multiple properties with the `css` function. There's one caveat that you'll need to remember: property names must be camel-cased in order to be used by the animate function; that is to say, you'll need to write `marginLeft`, instead of `margin-left` and `backgroundColor` instead of `background-color`. Any property name made up of multiple words needs to be modified in this way.

The time span parameter works exactly the same way as the simple animations we saw in Chapter 2: you can pass a number of milliseconds, or one of the strings `slow`, `fast`, or `normal`. Values for CSS properties can be set in pixels, ems, percentages, or points. For example, you could write `100px`, `10em`, `50%`, or `16pt`.

Even more excitingly, the values you define can be *relative* to the element's current values: all you need to do is specify `+=` or `-=` in front of the value, and that value will be added to or subtracted from the element's current property. Let's use this ability to make our navigation menu swing as we pass our mouse over the menu items using the `hover` function:

chapter_03/02_relative_css_animation/script.js (excerpt)

```
$('#navigation li').hover(function() {
  $(this).animate({paddingLeft: '+=15px'}, 200);
}, function() {
  $(this).animate({paddingLeft: '-=15px'}, 200);
});
```

Mouse over the navigation menu, and you'll see the links wobble around nicely.

You can also use `animate` to achieve fine-grained control over the showing, hiding, and toggling functions we saw in Chapter 2. We simply specify a property's animation value as `show`, `hide`, or `toggle` rather than a numeric amount:

chapter_03/03_animate_show_hide (excerpt)

```
$('#disclaimer').animate({
  opacity: 'hide',
  height: 'hide'
}, 'slow');
```

It's terribly satisfying seeing elements animate. As an exercise, try animating every element property you can think of—you'll stumble on some interesting effects! The `animate` function also has some powerful advanced options, which we'll examine in detail over the course of this chapter.

Color Animation

Once you realize how cool the `animate` function is, you'll probably want to animate an element's color. However, animating color is a little bit tricky, because the color values "in between" the start and end colors need to be calculated in a special way. Unlike a height or width value that moves from one value to another in a simple, linear manner, jQuery needs to do some extra math to figure out what color is, say, three-quarters of the way between light blue and orange.

This color-calculating functionality is omitted from the core library. This makes sense when you think about it: most projects have no need for this functionality, so jQuery can keep the size of the core library to a minimum. If you want to animate color, you're going to need to download the Color Animations plugin.[1]

---

[1] http://plugins.jquery.com/project/color

Using Plugins

The official jQuery plugin repository[2] contains an ever-increasing number of plugins—some more useful than others. You can search for plugins by name, category (such as effects or utilities), or by the rating it's received from the jQuery community.

Once you've found a plugin you're interested in, download it to a suitable location for your project (most likely the same place as your jQuery source file). It's a good idea to peruse the **readme** file or related documentation before you use a plugin, but generally all you need to do is include it in your HTML files, in much the same way as we've been including our custom JavaScript file.

How you make use of your newfound functionality varies from plugin to plugin, so you'll have to consult each plugin's documentation to put it to the best use.

After downloading and including the Color Animations plugin, you can now animate color properties in your jQuery animation code, just as you would other CSS properties. Let's gradually highlight our disclaimer message over a period of two seconds as the page loads, to make sure no one misses it:

chapter_03/04_color_animation (excerpt)

```
$('#disclaimer').animate({'backgroundColor':'#ff9f5f'}, 2000);
```

See how animating the disclaimer makes it so much more noticeable?

Easing

Easing refers to the acceleration and deceleration that occurs during an animation to give it a more natural feel. Easing applies a mathematical algorithm to alter the speed of an animation as it progresses. Thankfully, we're using jQuery, so you can leave your high school math skills safely locked away.

There are two types of easing available to use in jQuery: `linear` and `swing`. Any time you use an animation function in jQuery, you can specify either of these parameters to control the animation's easing. The difference between them can be

---

[2] http://plugins.jquery.com/

seen in Figure 3.1, which shows how a property is adjusted over the period of an animation depending on which easing option you select.

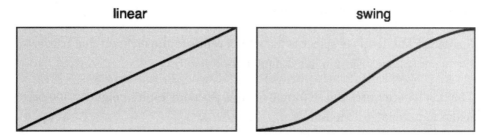

Figure 3.1. jQuery's easing options

swing easing starts off slowly before gaining speed, then towards the end of the animation it slows down again, nice and gently. Visually, swing easing looks far more natural than linear easing, and jQuery uses it by default if no easing parameter is specified.

The linear easing method has no acceleration or deceleration: animations occur at a constant rate. It looks fairly boring and a bit rigid in most circumstances, but it's worth giving it a try—it might just be appropriate for your purposes.

As an example, we'll animate the first paragraph tag so that when clicked, it grows and shrinks; we'll use linear easing as it grows, and swing easing as it shrinks. The difference is quite subtle, but if you repeat the animations a few times you should be able to distinguish between them; the shrinking animation feels a little bit more natural:

chapter_03/05_easing/script.js (excerpt)

```
$('p:first').toggle(function() {
  $(this).animate({'height':'+=150px'}, 1000, 'linear');
}, function() {
  $(this).animate({'height':'-=150px'}, 1000, 'swing');
});
```

There's quite a lot of jQuery in this statement, so now might be a good time to pause and make sure you understand everything that's going on here:

■ We use a filter with a selector to grab only the first paragraph tag.

■ A toggle event handler (which executes each passed function on successive clicks) is attached to the paragraph.

■ Inside the handlers we select `this`, which refers to the element that triggered the event (in our example, it's the paragraph itself).

■ The first handler uses the `+=` format to grow the paragraph's height by 300 pixels, using the `linear` easing function.

■ The second handler uses the `-=` format to shrink the paragraph's height by 300 pixels, using the `swing` easing function.

If you managed to follow along and understand each of these steps, pat yourself on the back! You're really getting the hang of jQuery!

Advanced Easing

As stated, swing easing provides a much more visually pleasing transition, and is probably adequate for most tasks. But swing and linear easing are just the tip of the iceberg. There is a vast array of easing options beyond these two basic types included in the core jQuery library. Most of these are available in the easing plugin,[3] available from the jQuery plugin repository.

 jQuery UI Includes Several Plugins

The easing library is also included in the effects section of the jQuery UI library, which we'll be visiting shortly. If you're starting to suffer from plugin fatigue, then you might like to skip forward to the section called "The jQuery User Interface Library"—this library includes several common plugins, including color animation, class transitions, and easing. By including the jQuery UI library, you'll avoid needing to include each plugin separately in your pages.

Just download and include the plugin's JavaScript file in your HTML page, anywhere after the jQuery library. Rather than providing you with new functions, the easing plugin simply gives you access to over 30 new easing options. Explaining what all of these easing functions do would test even the most imaginative writer, so we'll

---

[3] http://plugins.jquery.com/project/Easing

simply direct your attention to Figure 3.2, where you can see a few of the algorithms represented graphically.

You'll notice that some of the algorithms move out of the graph area; when animated elements reach this part of the transition, they'll move *past* their destination and finally turn back to settle there. The effect is that of an element attached to a piece of elastic, which gently pulls everything back into place.

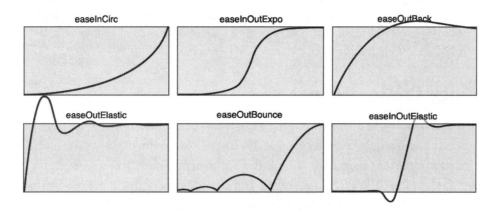

Figure 3.2. Advanced easing options

To use one of the new algorithms, we just need to pass its name to our `animate` function. There are lots to choose from, so we might as well jump straight into it and try a few different ones:

```
chapter_03/06_other_easing_options/script.js (excerpt)

$('p:first').animate({height: '+=300px'}, 2000, 'easeOutBounce');
$('p:first').animate({height: '-=300px'}, 2000, 'easeInOutExpo');
$('p:first').animate({height: 'hide'}, 2000, 'easeOutCirc');
$('p:first').animate({height: 'show'}, 2000, 'easeOutElastic');
```

Look at that paragraph go! You might want to know where these easing option names are coming from—or where you can see the full list. The algorithms originated from Robert Penner's easing equations, which are described in detail on his web site.[4]

---

[4] http://www.robertpenner.com/easing/

The best way to see all the available equations is to view the plugin's source code. If you use your text editor to open up the file you downloaded, you'll see a list of the functions you can use in jQuery animations.

 Time to Play Around

Take a break and test out all of the easing functions that the plugin makes available. It's unlikely you'll ever need to use all of them, but becoming familiar with them will let you choose the right one to give your interface the precise feel you want. Moreover, playing around with the `animate` function will cement your knowledge of it: it's an important part of a jQuery ninja's arsenal!

Bouncy Content Panes

Now that we've learned a bit about how the `animate` function works, let's have a look at our client's latest round of requests. Today's to-do list includes the addition of a vitally important page component: the *StarTrackr! Daily "Who's Hot Right Now?" List* (or the SDWHRNL for short). The list consists of the latest celebrities to fall in or out of favor, along with an accompanying photo and brief bio. We'll apply some of the animation and easing techniques we've just learned to implement the list as panes that can be opened and closed independently.

The appearance of the widget in the page is shown in Figure 3.3.

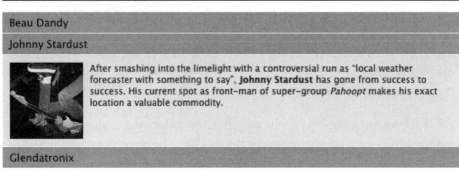

Figure 3.3. Biography panes

In our HTML, we'll implement the section as a `div` element containing all of our celebrities. Each celebrity's pane will be marked up as an `h3`, followed by another `div` containing an image and a short paragraph:

chapter_03/07_bouncy_content_panes/index.html *(excerpt)*

```html
<div id="bio">
  <h2>Who's Hot Right Now?</h2>

  <h3>Beau Dandy</h3>
  <div>
    <img src="../images/beau_100.jpg" width="100"
      height="100" alt="Beau Dandy"/>
    <p>Content about Beau Dandy</p>
  </div>

  <h3>Johnny Stardust</h3>
  <div>
    <img src="../images/johnny_100.jpg" width="100"
      height="100" alt="Johny Stardust"/>
    <p>Content about Johny Stardust</p>
  </div>

  <h3>Glendatronix</h3>
  <div>
    <img src="../images/glenda_100.jpg" width="100"
      height="100" alt="Glendatronix"/>
    <p>Content about Glendatronix</p>
  </div>
</div>
```

When a user clicks on one of the headings, we want the associated content pane to toggle open and closed. You can style your panes however you see fit, but having a block-level element for a heading with a different-colored background is a common technique: it provides a clear call to action for the user to click on it.

 "Jumpy" Animation?

One quirk to be aware of is that animating an element directly next to a heading tag can sometimes look "jumpy"—especially when the element hides. This is due to the heading's margin, which collapses as the following element hides. A simple workaround, which we've used here, is to remove margins from the heading tag entirely.

We want to avoid showing any content when the page loads, so the first thing to do is to hide all of the content containers:

chapter_03/07_bouncy_content_panes/script.js (excerpt)

```
$('#bio > div').hide();
```

If, instead, you'd prefer to have one pane open by default, you could specify it here. This can help to make it more evident to users that there's content "hidden" in the panes, and that they're meant to click on the headings to reveal it. Making this work in jQuery is simple: we merely apply the `:first` filter and call the `show` action to reveal only the first pane:

```
$('#bio > div:first').show();
```

 ### The Child Selector

There's a new selector feature in these examples that we've yet to cover. It's the **child** selector, and it's indicated by the greater-than angle bracket (>). A child selector selects all the immediate children that match the selector. If we'd omitted the child selector, our code would select all `div` elements underneath the bio `div` element, even if they were nested inside other elements. For more details and code examples using this selector, feel free to look it up in the jQuery API documentation.[5]

Now that our content is marked up the way we want it, we simply need to add some jQuery interaction magic to it. To reveal our secret content we'll take the familiar approach of capturing the `click` event, finding the next element (which contains our content), and showing it—as we did in Chapter 2. But this time, we'll employ a touch of "bounce," easing to the content's height so that the panes bounce in and out of view:

---

[5] http://docs.jquery.com/Selectors/child

```
chapter_03/example_07/script.js (excerpt)
$('#bio h3').click(function() {
  $(this).next().animate(
    {'height':'toggle'}, 'slow', 'easeOutBounce'
  );
});
```

The easing function `easeOutBounce` produces a great bouncing ball effect, which works wonderfully for content panes like this. Give it a spin in your browser and see for yourself!

The Animation Queue

The last topic we're going to look at with regards to animation is another advanced use of the `animate` function. It turns out `animate` can be called with a set of extra options, like this:

```
animate(parameters, options);
```

The options parameter is a bundle of options packaged together as an object literal made up of key/value pairs. We're already familiar with several of the available options: `duration`, `easing`, and `complete` (the callback method). There are, however, a couple of new ones: `step` and `queue`. Before we explain them, let's take a look at the syntax for calling the `animate` function with an options parameter:

```
chapter_03/08_animation_queue/script.js (excerpt)
$('p:first').animate(
  {
    height: '+=100px',
    backgroundColor: 'green'
  },
  {
    duration: 'slow',
    easing: 'swing',
    complete: function() {alert('done!');},
    queue: false
  }
);
```

Notice that you can accomplish almost all of this with the simpler format that we've already seen. You only need the advanced version if you want to specify additional settings, like the `queue` parameter.

The queue is the list of animations waiting to occur on a particular element. Every time we ask jQuery to perform an animation on an element, that animation is added to the queue. The element executes the queue one at a time until everything is complete. You've probably already seen this if you've gone click-happy on one of our demos.

There are many situations where this will be undesirable though. Sometimes you'll want multiple animations to occur at the same time. If you disable the queue when you specify an animation, further animations can run in parallel.

The animation queue can be controlled by using the `queue` option, as well as with the jQuery actions `stop`, `queue`, and `dequeue`. This combination of actions and options gives us super-fine control over how our animations run. But before we can really sink our teeth into these juicy options, it's time to unveil one of the most important jQuery techniques around.

Chaining Actions

So far we've been writing statements one at a time—either one after the other, or nested inside callback functions. We've needed to either rewrite our selectors, or make use of the `this` keyword to find our targets again. However, there's a technique that allows us to run multiple jQuery commands, one after the other, on the same element(s). We call this chaining—and to release the ninja inside of you, you'd better pay attention to this bit.

Chaining links two or more jQuery actions into a single statement. To chain an action you simply append it to the previous action. For example, let's chain together the `hide`, `slideDown`, and `fadeOut` actions. Our element quickly hides and then slides into view, before fading away:

```
$('p:first').hide().slideDown('slow').fadeOut();
```

You can chain together as many actions as you like. Be careful though: chaining can quickly become addictive! As well as being able to chain actions based on your initial selector, you can also move around the DOM, adding and removing elements as you go—which can lead to some quite hairy statements.

It's often good to lay out your actions on separate lines for clarity. This takes up a lot more space, but is much easier to read and maintain. Our previous example could be rewritten like this:

```
$('p:first')
  .hide()
  .slideDown('slow')
  .fadeOut();
```

It's important to realize that the jQuery selector contains the modified results of each action that runs before running the next action. This means that we can add and remove elements as we go along, only applying actions to the current selection.

If you revisit a few of our earlier examples, you might spot a few chained actions hidden in the code—for example, when we wrote: `$(this).next().toggle()`. The `next` action moved our selection to the next DOM element, and then the `toggle` action toggled it without affecting the original element.

You'll have plenty of chances from now on to play with chaining; the rest of this book is going to be filled with it. It's the most fun part of jQuery!

Pausing the Chain

If you'd like to pause briefly in the middle of a jQuery chain, you can use the `delay` action. Simply give it a number, and it will hold the chain for that many milliseconds before continuing. So, referring to the same example, we could write:

```
$('p:first')
  .hide()
  .slideDown('slow')
  .delay(2000)
  .fadeOut();
```

This code will slide down the paragraph, and then wait two seconds before fading it out. This can be a great way to control your animations more precisely.

Animated Navigation

The client is sticking to his guns on this issue: he wants the top-level navigation to be a Flash control that wobbles and zooms around as the user interacts with it. Flash, he explains, looks better. You assure him your Flash skills are second to none, and that you'll whip up a proof of concept for him right away.

Okay. Now, with the client out of the room, let's apply our newly discovered jQuery power to create a Flash-like navigation bar. It will have a background "blob" that wobbles around to highlight the menu choice the user is hovering over. And we'll do it all with free, standard technologies: HTML, CSS, and JavaScript. Flash? We don't need no stinkin' Flash!

We're sticking with a fairly basic animation so that the steps are easier to follow. First off, we've modified the CSS pertaining to our navigation menu so that it's laid out horizontally rather than vertically. As a refresher, here's what the HTML for the navigation looks like:

chapter_03/09_animated_navigation/index.html *(excerpt)*

```html
<ul id="navigation">
  <li><a href="#">Home</a></li>
  <li><a href="#">About Us</a></li>
  <li><a href="#">Buy!</a></li>
  <li><a href="#">Gift Ideas</a></li>
</ul>
```

Our background color blob will be an empty div element, positioned behind whichever navigation link the user is mousing over. Our first task, therefore, will be to create the element and append it to the document:

chapter_03/09_animated_navigation/script.js *(excerpt)*

```javascript
$('<div id="navigation_blob"></div>').css({
  width: $('#navigation li:first a').width() + 10,
  height: $('#navigation li:first a').height() + 10
}).appendTo('#navigation');
```

Notice that we're selecting the navigation link *inside* the object literal to provide values for the width and height. This may seem strange if you're new to programming, but you shouldn't let it frighten you—in general, you can use the returned (or calculated) value of a function anywhere you can put a static value. We're also adding 10 to each of those values, so that the blob is slightly larger than the anchor tag it will sit behind.

With the blob in place, we need to set up a trigger that will set it in motion. This should occur when the user hovers over one of the navigation links, so we'll use the hover function. Remember that hover accepts two parameters: the function that runs when the mouse moves *over* the element, and the one that runs when the mouse moves *off* the element. This is the general outline of our event handler:

chapter_03/09_animated_navigation/script.js *(excerpt)*

```
$('#navigation a').hover(function() {
  // Mouse over function
    ⋮
}, function() {
  // Mouse out function
    ⋮
});
```

Now for some fun stuff. Let's look at the first function, which occurs when the mouse moves over the element:

chapter_03/09_animated_navigation/script.js *(excerpt)*

```
// Mouse over function
$('#navigation_blob').animate(
  {width: $(this).width() + 10, left: $(this).position().left},
  {duration: 'slow', easing: 'easeOutElastic', queue: false}
);
```

When the user mouses over the menu item, we animate two properties of the blob: its width and its position.

The link's position on the page can be determined using a jQuery method called position. This is an action that does nothing on its own, but when called exposes two properties: left and top; these are the left and top offsets of the selected element relative to its parent. In this case we want the left property, so we know where to move the blob to in our navigation menu.

We set the `queue` option to `false` to ensure that our animations won't pile up in a line waiting to execute if our user is hover-happy. When you move to a different link, a new animation will start regardless of whether the current one is finished or not.

We still need to tell jQuery what to do when our user moves the mouse *off* the link. This block of code is fairly similar to the one we just saw, although it includes a few more chained actions:

chapter_03/09_animated_navigation/script.js *(excerpt)*

```
// Mouse out function
$('#navigation_blob')
  .stop(true)
  .animate(
    {width: 'hide'},
    {duration: 'slow', easing: 'easeOutCirc', queue: false}
  )
  .animate(
    {left: $('#navigation li:first a').position().left;},
    'fast'
  );
}
```

This time we've chained two `animate` actions together: the first one hides the blob with a bit of nice easing applied, and the second whisks it off to the side (to the position of the first link in the navigation).

You might notice that there's an extra action chained into our animation, the `stop` action. `stop` does exactly what you'd expect—it stops the animation! It accepts two optional parameters: `clearQueue` and `gotoEnd`. We're setting the `clearQueue` parameter to `true`, so that any queued animations are cleared.

The `gotoEnd` parameter is used if you want jQuery to determine what an element's state will be at the end of the current animation queue, and then jump immediately to that state. We don't want to use that here, as we want our animations to start from the blob's current position—even if it's only halfway through moving.

Give the menu a spin in your browser, and see how the appropriate use of easing has given our control a natural feel.

Now's a great time to try some different easing functions. Just replace the ones used here with any of the others from the easing plugin—you'll be amazed at how much difference they make to the feel of the component. You can also try animating other values: changing the blob's color, for instance.

Animated Navigation, Take 2

One of the great advantages to using a library such as jQuery is that you can try out a bunch of different alternatives fairly quickly, and pick the one you like best.

We still have a few hours left before our client will want to see the progress of our animated navigation. Let's try to approach the same problem from a different angle and see what we can come up with.

For this animation, our menu items will each have a hidden icon that will bounce into view when the link is moused over (as shown in Figure 3.4).

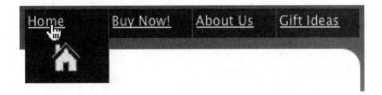

Figure 3.4. Bouncy animated menu

The setup for this effect is nice and simple. It's a regular unordered list, configured as a horizontal menu—but we've stashed a secret icon underneath the normally visible area. This is just a matter of setting the list item's height so that you can only see the link text by default, but as we animate the height the icon bounces into view.

We'll start with the CSS: we've moved our menu to be absolutely positioned at the top-right of the container `div`, where there's space for the icons to expand. We've set a background color for the icons to be set against, and employed a clever trick to keep the background images out of view; notice that the list items are 20px in height, but that the background is offset 30px from the top. As a result, they'll be invisible until we expand the height of the list items.

We'll also set the background image of each link to a different icon:

```css
#container {
  position: relative;
}

#navigation {
  position:absolute;
  width: inherit;
  top: 0;
  right: 0;
  margin: 0;
}

#navigation li {
  height:20px;
  float:left;
  list-style-type: none;
  width:70px;
  padding:3px;
  border-right:1px solid #3687AF;
  background-color: #015287;
  background-repeat: no-repeat;
  background-position: center 30px;
}

#navigation li a {
  color: #FFFFFF;
}

#navigation #home{
  background-image:url('icon_home.png');
}
```

The only new aspect for this effect's code is that we use the `stop` action to clear the queue for both the mouseover event and the mouseout event. Then we just animate the height to display the hidden icons and shrink it back to normal when the hover finishes. Some carefully chosen duration and easing settings give us the groovy bouncing effect that we're after. Make sure you experiment with the settings in order to match the feel of your site:

chapter_03/10_animated_navigation_2/script.js *(excerpt)*

```
$('#nav_stretch li').hover(
  function() {
    $(this)
      .stop(true)
      .animate(
        {height: '60px'},
        {duration: 500, easing: 'easeOutBounce'}
      )
  },
  function() {
    $(this)
      .stop(true)
      .animate(
        {height:'20px'},
        {duration: 500, easing: 'easeOutCirc'}
      )
  }
);
```

Now we have not one, but two funky examples of animated navigation to show our client!

The jQuery User Interface Library

As mentioned in Chapter 1, the jQuery UI library is a collection of advanced jQuery widgets, effects, and interactions—such as date pickers, accordions, and drag-and-drop functionality—that are widely applicable to web development. But before we start the fun stuff, it's time to have a look at downloading and including the jQuery UI library—a procedure that's marginally more complicated to set up than the core library and plugins we've been using so far. This is because the full jQuery UI library is nearly 500KB in size (300KB when minified)! That's a lot of code! Fortunately, any given project will normally only require a small subset of the functionality contained in jQuery UI, and the jQuery web site provides us with a handy tool to create our own custom version of jQuery UI that contains only what we need and nothing more.

The options can appear a bit daunting the first time you visit the download builder page, which you can reach by clicking the **Build custom download** link from the jQuery UI homepage.[6]

The download builder is broken into several sections: Core, Interaction, Widgets, Effects, and Themes. Core is the main jQuery UI library—the Widgets and Interaction components all rely on it. A good way to approach the builder is to deselect everything and then add only what you require. If a component relies on another component to function,it will be automatically selected for you.

While we're developing, it's safe to grab the full library. That way everything will be there for us to use if we need it. Once you're happy with the functionality on your web site, you can always return to the download builder and create a custom library, omitting anything unused. The difference in file size between the full library and a customized version can be quite significant, as illustrated in Figure 3.5.

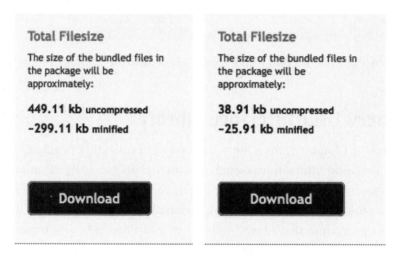

Figure 3.5. Full jQuery UI library versus customized download

One option that will greatly affect the visual output of the widgets and interactions is the *theme*. There are a number of themes you can choose from using the drop-down box. In Chapter 9 we'll have an in-depth look at themes, including making your own. But in the interests of progressing with the more exciting stuff, we'll use the default theme and return to work.

---

[6] http://jqueryui.com/

The custom download archive contains a lot of files. There are heaps of demos and documentation for you to try out and explore in the **development-bundle** directory, but to use jQuery UI you'll simply need the **jQuery-ui-1.7.2-min.js** file (or whichever version is current at the time you're reading this), and the directory that contains the theme you've chosen.

You'll have to put the theme's directory in a location where your HTML page can reach it. For this book's examples, jQuery UI has been placed in the **lib** directory (alongside jQuery itself), and the theme files in the **css** directory.

The jQuery UI library contains an Effects package that enables us to implement some interesting effects. It also includes useful methods and functionality for doing advanced animation. We've seen some of this functionality already, thanks to the Color Animation plugin and the Easing plugin. These are included in the Effects package, so you no longer need to include them if you're going to use the jQuery UI effects library.

Before we move on, let's just have a quick look at a few of the available effects. We'll take our much-maligned first paragraph element and shake it about, highlight it in yellow, then explode it to pieces:

chapter_03/11_jquery_ui_effects/script.js *(excerpt)*

```
$('p:first')
  .effect('shake', {times:3}, 300)
  .effect('highlight', {}, 3000)
  .hide('explode', {}, 1000);
```

Look at it go! Of course, this is just a tiny sample of the available effects. Some of them can only be used in this way, via the `effect` action, while others can be used either in this way or in place of `hide`, `show`, or `toggle` parameters. Some examples of the latter are `blind`, `clip`, `puff`, `fold`, and `slide`.

We'll refrain from going through all of them in detail here—you're best off spending your Sunday afternoon exploring them. Not all of the effects are pure flair, however, but many are useful in common user interaction scenarios, such as `highlight`, which is a standard way to indicate a new message to the user.

It's a good idea to test out each function, so you'll remember them when they're appropriate. And if the jQuery UI assortment of effects just isn't enough for you, never mind—there are hundreds more available from the plugin repository!

Get Animated!

You now understand all the fundamentals of animating with jQuery: selectors, event handlers, callbacks, chaining, and the all-important `animate` function. You've also become briefly acquainted with the extensive jQuery UI library. The best way to really master these skills, however, is to put them into practice. Go out and animate everything you can get your hands on! Try playing with every property of every element on every page, until you feel like you can really bend them to your will.

Before we move on from animation to the next jQuery skill set for you to master, we'll turn our attention to scrolling and resizing: these topics might be less flashy than animation, but they're essential to a good many user interface components. They'll also help cement your understanding of jQuery selectors, actions, and chaining. So what are we waiting for?

Scrolling

Scrolling is, in a way, similar to animation, in that elements are moving around the page. Unlike animation though, the user is the one in control! Still, there's a plethora of ways to customize these interactions. In this section, we'll have a look at menus that stay put when the user scrolls, custom-themed scrollbars, and even how we can use the animation techniques we've just learned and apply them to scrolling the document.

The `scroll` Event

Before we can improve our users' scrolling experience, we need to know when and what they are scrolling. It turns out there is an event, called `scroll`, which fires when the user updates the scroll position of an element—such as the window or a scrollable `div`. So, every time one of your users interacts with a scroll bar on your site, an event will be fired that you can catch and respond to.

To capture the `scroll` event, we attach an event handler to an element that has scroll bars—most often the window element. The window itself is a JavaScript object, so all we need to do is wrap it in our jQuery function to select it.

Of course, to see the `scroll` event in action, we have to set up an area with scroll bars! We have a few ideas for scrolling effects that we'd like to pitch to the client, but in the interests of learning how the `scroll` event works, let's just fake a scrolling environment by setting `overflow: scroll;` on one of the `div`s in our page:

chapter_03/12_scroll_event/scroll.css (excerpt)

```css
#news {
  height: 100px;
  width: 300px;
  overflow: scroll;
}
```

This will turn our news section into a smaller scrolling pane inside the page. Now let's capture the `scroll` event and add some arbitrary text to the page every time the `scroll` event fires:

chapter_03/12_scroll_event/script.js (excerpt)

```js
$('#news').scroll(function() {
  $('#header')
    .append('<span class="scrolled">You scrolled!</span>');
});
```

Now whenever you scroll the news section, the text "You Scrolled!" will appear on a red background at the top of the page. Very annoying, but you get the picture. Try scrolling in different ways: dragging the scroll bar, using the mouse wheel, and clicking inside the scrollable zone to use the arrow keys. In all the above cases, the `scroll` event will fire.

Floating Navigation

We now know when a user scrolls, so how can we make use of this information to improve our site? Well, one fairly common example of a page reacting to users' scrolling is a floating navigation pane. This is when the main navigation element is always present at the top of the visible part of the screen, regardless of the scroll position; it's as if the navigation menu follows users as they scroll down the page. This is easy to implement using the `scroll` event: we simply need to find out where we are on the page, and then move the navigation to that point.

Our first task is to set up our CSS to prepare for the animated navigation. We'll add a `position: relative;` declaration to our navigation element so that we can easily move it up and down the page by adjusting its `top` property. For the purpose of this exercise, we've applied a very large `height` property to the content in order to force it to have a scroll bar (unless, of course, you have a huge monitor!):

chapter_03/13_floating_nav_1/scroll.css *(excerpt)*

```css
#navigation {
  position: relative;
}

#content {
  height: 2000px;
}
```

Now we can take a stab at our floating pane. At first glance it seems that nothing could be simpler—just respond to the `scroll` event of the main window by updating the `top` position of the navigation block:

chapter_03/13_floating_nav_1/script.js *(excerpt)*

```js
$(window).scroll(function() {
  $('#navigation').css('top', $(document).scrollTop());
});
```

Test this out in your browser and you'll see that we've achieved our goal: as you scroll down the page, the navigation box plods along with you. How does it know where the top is? We asked for the top of the screen by using the `scrollTop` action. `scrollTop` returns the top offset of the matched element—in our example we asked for the entire document's top position: `$(document).scrollTop()`. This will always be the very top of the screen.

It works, sure, but it's very jumpy, which makes it a little unattractive. The reason for this should be evident if you were paying attention when we first introduced the `scroll` event: every time the user moves the scroll bar, it fires *many* `scroll` events. Each one of those events triggers our code to update the navigation position—so it's no wonder the motion is jittery.

We saw how to stop animations from queuing up like this in the section called "Animated Navigation" with the `stop` command. This takes care of the jumpiness, but our effect could still use some refinement. How about we smarten it up with some animation and a little bit of bouncy easing? Here's how we do that:

```
                                chapter_03/14_floating_nav_2/script.js (excerpt)
$(window).scroll(function() {
  $('#navigation')
    .stop()
    .animate({top: $(document).scrollTop()},'slow','easeOutBack');
});
```

For such a significant effect, it requires a satisfyingly minimal amount of code!

Scrolling the Document

When a long list of information about related (yet varied) subjects needs to be displayed on a single HTML page, it's common to include a hyperlinked list of the subjects at the top of the page.

These internal links will immediately jump to the correct position for the menu item you selected. After the content, there's often a link to take you back to the top of the screen—so you can select another menu item. Let's try adding this functionality to our page.

The first task is add the link to our page's footer. To jump to the top of the page, all we need to do is set our link's href attribute to #.

If we think about it, all we want to do is animate the page's scrolling position, which is represented by scrollTop in jQuery. We'll also need to cancel the default link action—otherwise the page will jump before our animation has time to occur. If you're new to JavaScript, there's an easy way to accomplish this: any function handling a link's click event need simply include the statement return false to cancel the link's default behavior:

```
$('a[href=#]').click(function() {
  $('html').animate({scrollTop: 0},'slow');
  return false; // Return false to cancel the default link action
}
```

This code introduces a new kind of selector: the **attribute selector**. By enclosing an attribute and the value we want to look for in square brackets ([ ]), we can narrow a selection to include only elements with a specific attribute value. In this case, we're looking for only those links with an `href` value of `#`.

This code works, and is certainly clear and simple, but it does encounter a slight issue. If the user's browser is operating in quirks mode, the `$('html')` selector will fail. (Unsure what quirks mode means? Take the time to read the SitePoint CSS reference page on the topic[7] for a detailed explanation.) While you *should* be marking up your pages in a way that triggers standards mode, sometimes you'll be working with legacy code and thus be without that luxury. To make the above code work in quirks mode, you'd need to use the selector `$('body')`. We could also target both, just to be sure: `$('html, body')`. This in turn causes issues in certain versions of the Opera browser, which (probably correctly) tries to scroll both elements at the same time.

"But you said jQuery sorts out all our cross-browser issues!" you might exclaim. To be fair, it sorts out *most* cross-browser issues. This is a slightly trickier one, and is not addressed in the core jQuery library. Fortunately for us, it's fairly simple to work around. Even more fortunately for us, someone has taken the time to package that workaround (as well as a plethora of other scrolling functionality) into a plugin called ScrollTo.

The ScrollTo plugin, available from the plugin repository,[8] is a stable plugin for scrolling the screen and overflowed elements. It's more than capable of handling any of the scrolling tasks we've seen so far.

After you've downloaded and included the plugin, you can rewrite the top link functionality and forget all your worries about obscure browser bugs:

chapter_03/15_page_scroll/script.js *(excerpt)*

```
$('a[href=#]').click(function() {
   $.scrollTo(0,'slow');
   return false;
});
```

This syntax probably looks a little strange to you, in that we're calling `scrollTo` directly from the jQuery alias. The plugin is clever, and knows that if we call it

---

[7] http://reference.sitepoint.com/css/doctypesniffing
[8] http://plugins.jquery.com/project/ScrollTo

directly in this way, we want to scroll the entire window. If we wanted to scroll a specific overflowed element, we'd use the traditional selector syntax, for example: `$('div#scrolly').scrollTo(0, 'slow')`.

The ScrollTo plugin is feature-packed and not limited to scrolling by an integer value. You can pass in a relative value (like `+=50px`), a DOM element (it will scroll the page to find that element), a selector string, a hash-value containing `x` and `y` co-ordinates, or the keyword `max`, which will scroll to the end of the document. You can scroll horizontally as well as vertically, and it also has some great options for fine-tuning your destination. You can learn about all these options on the plugin's home page.[9]

Custom Scroll Bars

The client strolls over to your desk with a furrowed brow, holding a copy of the "absolutely final" signed-off designs in his hand. "Now," he starts, "these scroll bars here won't look like this, will they? I mean, they're all gray, and stand out badly."

Usually you only have to be working as a web developer for a very short time before a client asks you to replace the standard operating system scroll bars with custom ones—especially for internal elements, like scrolling divs. It does seem like a reasonable request, but it has some usability implications of which you should be aware.

People have certain expectations about how core interface components of their operating system will function, and custom implementations can sometimes have different features from the core elements that they are replacing. Breaking users' expectations in this way can be extremely frustrating, so this type of UI customization should be undertaken with extreme care.

That said, there are times when a well-placed custom UI element can make a world of difference to the overall feel of an interface. Ultimately, you will have to weigh the benefits and drawbacks for your intended audience. In our case, the client is paying—so we'll do it!

There's no need, however, to try and build it from scratch: a scroll bar is a complex user interface element, and the client would be unhappy if he found out we'd wasted

---

[9] http://flesler.blogspot.com/2007/10/jqueryscrollto.html

precious development hours building it ourselves, especially when there's a perfectly suitable plugin ready to go: it's called jScrollPane.

jScrollPane is a jQuery plugin that allows you to replace the browser's default vertical scroll bars with custom ones in any element with overflowed content. You can find the plugin in the official repository, but a more up-to-date version is available on Google Code.[10]

There are two files we need to include: the JavaScript code file, **jScrollPane-1.2.3.min.js**; and the accompanying CSS file, **jScrollPane.css**. The CSS file sets out some default styles for the scroll bars, and gives you a starting point for implementing your own customizations. Simply extend or overwrite the styles contained in this file with your own colors and images to create your customized scroll bars. We'll stick with the default style for our example: a sleek-looking gray bar that will fit in on just about any site (as illustrated in Figure 3.6).

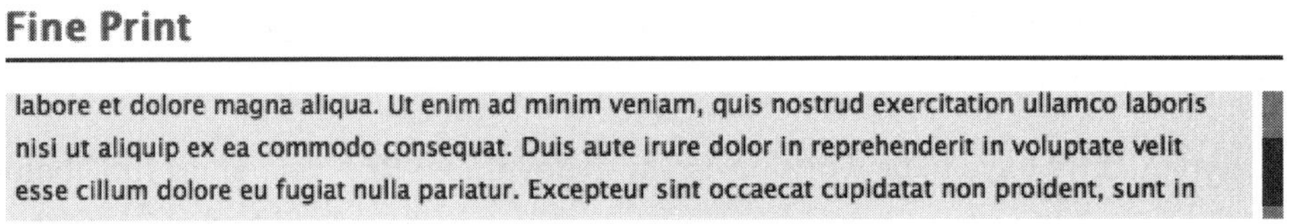

Fine Print

labore et dolore magna aliqua. Ut enim ad minim veniam, quis nostrud exercitation ullamco laboris nisi ut aliquip ex ea commodo consequat. Duis aute irure dolor in reprehenderit in voluptate velit esse cillum dolore eu fugiat nulla pariatur. Excepteur sint occaecat cupidatat non proident, sunt in

Figure 3.6. A custom scroll bar

You can activate custom scroll bars on any element by simply calling the jScrollPane function on it. Although parameters are optional, there are more than a dozen for you to tweak, such as showing scroll bar arrows, or moving the scroll bars to the left-hand side of the panel. You can see the full list on the plugin's home page.[11] For our example, we'll set a margin between our content and the scroll bar, set the width of the scroll bar, and choose to hide the top and bottom arrows:

chapter_03/16_custom_scrollbar/script.js (excerpt)

```
$('#fine_print').jScrollPane({
  scrollbarWidth: 10,
  scrollbarMargin: 10,
  showArrows: false
});
```

[10] http://code.google.com/p/jscrollpane/
[11] http://www.kelvinluck.com/assets/jquery/jScrollPane/jScrollPane.html

Our new scroll bar looks and works great, but you might notice that it fails to respond when you scroll the mouse wheel over the element. jQuery's core library has deliberately left out mouse wheel functionality to keep the library's size to a minimum, but there's a plugin to add it back in,[12] and jScrollPane has been written with this plugin in mind. As a result, all you need to do is include the mouse wheel plugin in your page and jScrollPane will automatically add mouse wheel event handling to all your scrolling content panes, letting you scroll them however you please!

Resizing

Resizing has a few different meanings in relation to a user interface: the first that comes to mind is the ability to resize the browser window (an event that has often caused headaches for web developers). But also common are resizing windows inside applications, and resizing images or other elements.

jQuery includes a way of gathering information about user-initiated window resizing, and also (via jQuery UI) a way to give users ultimate resizing power over any element on the page. Let's dive in!

The `resize` Event

The `resize` event is a core jQuery event that fires when a document view is resized. There are a number of reasons why you'd want to react to this event. But before we examine a practical example, let's make sure we understand how the event works:

chapter_03/17_resize_event/script.js *(excerpt)*

```
$(window).resize(function() {
  alert("You resized the window!");
});
```

Load the **index.html** page in your browser and try resizing the window: every time you do, an alert will pop up. Annoying users every time they change their browser window size will probably keep us from winning any user-experience points—so let's put this event to use in a more practical example.

---

[12] http://plugins.jquery.com/project/mousewheel

Layout Switcher

If you've worked with CSS for any length of time, you'll know that there's a constant debate about which is best: fluid or fixed-width layouts. On one hand, fluid layouts make maximal use of a user's screen real estate; on the other hand, fixed-width layouts allow you to design a pixel-perfect layout that you know won't break when a user is viewing it with a different viewport size.

For StarTrackr! we can offer the best of both worlds: design two separate, fixed-width layouts, and switch between them by catching the `resize` event.

Let's start! The default StarTrackr! web site we've been working with so far is a modest 650px wide. Our first task is to write some styles to make it wider—we'll go for 850px for the wider version:

```
                                   chapter_03/18_layout_switcher/wide.css

body #container {
  width: 850px;
}

body #container p {
  width: 650px;
}

body #header {
  background-image: url('../../css/images/header-corners-wide.png');
}

body #celebs table {
  width: 650px;
  margin-left: 5px;
}
```

Notice that we've added a seemingly superfluous body to the beginning of each rule. This is so that these rules will take precedence over any rules in our base style sheet targeting the same elements, because they're more specific.

The next step is to write the jQuery code to add or remove our new style sheet. All we need to do is test to see if the body element's width is greater than 900px, append the style sheet to our head element if it is, or remove it if it's not:

chapter_03/18_layout_switcher/script.js *(excerpt)*

```
if ($('body').width() > 900) {
  $('<link rel="stylesheet" href="wide.css" type="text/css" />')
    .appendTo('head');
} else {
  $('link[href=wide.css]').remove();
}
```

This puts us in a tight spot. We need to run this code in two different situations: once when we first load the page and then again whenever the page is resized. You might be tempted to just copy and paste that chunk of code, and be done with it.

Resist that temptation! Repeating yourself in code is almost always a bad idea: imagine a situation where, a few months down the line, you decide that 900px was the wrong cutoff point. You're now thinking that you should switch style sheets only around the 1000px mark. You go into your code, change the value, and reload the page. But it's broken, because you forgot to change the same value in the other, identical block of code. This kind of scenario can happen all too easily in any type of software development, and the more complicated your code becomes, the more likely it will happen—and the harder it will be to track down.

Fortunately, almost every programming language has constructs to help us out in these kinds of situations, and JavaScript (and hence jQuery) is no exception. So far we've been passing anonymous functions to all our event handlers, but now it's time to give our function a name:

```
                                     chapter_03/18_layout_switcher/script.js (excerpt)

$(document).ready(function() {
  stylesheetToggle();
  $(window).resize(stylesheetToggle);
});

function stylesheetToggle() {
  if ($('body').width() > 900) {
    $('<link rel="stylesheet" href="wide.css" type="text/css" />')
      .appendTo('head');
  } else {
    $('link[href=wide.css]').remove();
  }
}
```

We've named our function stylesheetToggle, and called it twice: once when the document first loads, and again whenever we resize. You'll notice that we only need to pass the function's *name* to the resize event handler; since we are not declaring a function here, we have no need for the the function keyword, or any curly braces or parentheses.

Resizable Elements

The jQuery UI library contains a Resizable plugin as part of its interaction functionality. The Resizable plugin makes elements that you select able to be resized by adding a small handle to the bottom corner of the element. This can be stretched around with the mouse (much like your operating system's windows). Like all jQuery UI components, it's highly configurable and easy to use. If you downloaded the full jQuery UI library earlier, you'll already have the class ready to go. Otherwise, you'll need to head back to the download builder and include the Resizable component—which will also require the core library and a theme.

Using the Resizable component in its most basic form is very easy. We simply select the element or elements we want to modify, and call the resizable function:

```
                                    chapter_03/19_resizable_elements/script.js (excerpt)

$('p').resizable();
```

If we run this on our StarTrackr! site, we're in for some unusual results: every paragraph element instantly becomes resizable!

It's a lot of fun to see this in action: suddenly our whole web page becomes malleable. By default, the Resizable interaction adds small handles in the bottom-right corners of the elements. These are styled in the jQuery UI style sheet, so have a look in there if you're interested in changing the way they look. The default handles are illustrated in Figure 3.7.

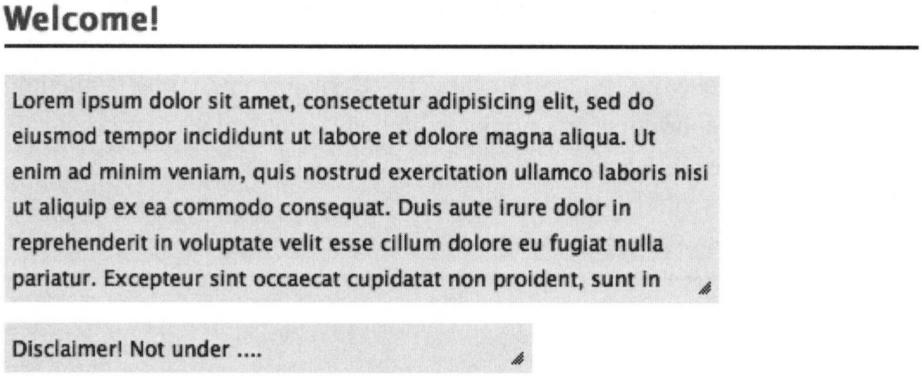

Welcome!

Lorem ipsum dolor sit amet, consectetur adipisicing elit, sed do eiusmod tempor incididunt ut labore et dolore magna aliqua. Ut enim ad minim veniam, quis nostrud exercitation ullamco laboris nisi ut aliquip ex ea commodo consequat. Duis aute irure dolor in reprehenderit in voluptate velit esse cillum dolore eu fugiat nulla pariatur. Excepteur sint occaecat cupidatat non proident, sunt in

Disclaimer! Not under ....

Figure 3.7. Resizable paragraphs

Now let's look at a simple situation where this functionality is very handy: resizing `textarea` elements.

Resizable `textarea`

Sometimes providing a usable interface can conflict with the desire to keep a design balanced and beautiful. But thanks to jQuery, we can have our cake and eat it too—and justify our way through those tricky client walk-throughs.

One area where form and function often clash is in HTML form design. This is partly because users to your site will often have wildly different requirements. For example, if you're providing an area for feedback, users will either want to write nothing, a little, or a lot. To strike a balance you could start a small `textarea`, but make it resizable. Therefore, the users with a lot to say will feel as if you're letting them say it. Here's how we can go about doing this using jQuery UI's Resizable functionality:

```
                              chapter_03/20_resizable_textarea/script.js (excerpt)
$('textarea').resizable({
  grid : [20, 20],
  minWidth : 153,
  minHeight : 30,
  maxHeight : 220,
  containment: 'parent'
});
```

This makes all our textarea elements resizeable, just like we did with the paragraph elements. The effect is shown in Figure 3.8. However, we've specified a few new parameters to improve the feel, and to show the Resizable component's flexibility. It has a plethora of configuration options, which you can explore in more detail on the jQuery UI documentation site.[13]

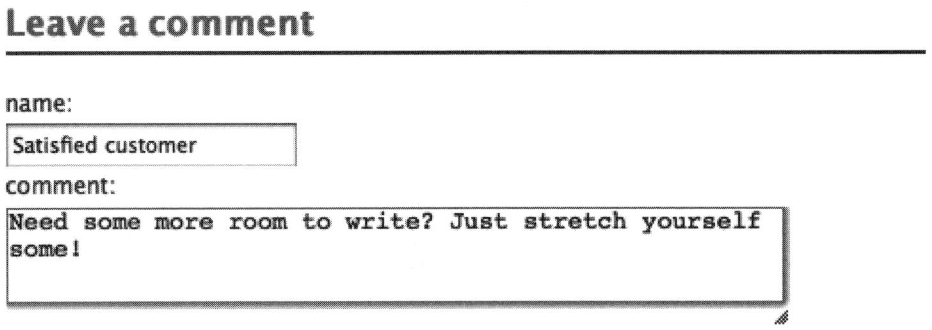

Leave a comment

name:

Satisfied customer

comment:

Need some more room to write? Just stretch yourself some!

Figure 3.8. Resizable textarea

We've also constrained how far the element can be stretched by specifying the minHeight, minWidth, and maxHeight properties. You'll notice that we've omitted the maxWidth property in favor of the containment parameter: this lets you specify a container restricting the resizable element. You can use either a jQuery selector as the parameter or the special keyword parent to refer to the resizable element's parent element.

We've also used the grid option to confine the resizable object to steps of a certain size. For some reason, this seems to add a nice feel to the resizing interaction. The

---

[13] http://docs.jquery.com/UI/API/1.7/Resizable

grid is specified as an array containing two elements: the horizontal grid size and the vertical grid size.

One other parameter you'll want to look into is the `handles` parameter. This specifies which sides of the element the handles will be attached to and, consequently, in which directions the element can be stretched. The parameter accepts the following options: `n`, `e`, `s`, `w`, `ne`, `se`, `sw`, `nw`, and `all`. You can specify any number of these by separating them with a comma. For example, `{ handles : 'n', 'se'}` adds handles to the top and bottom-right of the element.

It's common to see this kind of functionality built into input pages where content length will vary significantly.

Pane Splitter

Despite the disclaimer message functionality we've provided, our client's legal team is still worried about the possible repercussions that might extend from failing to properly outline the company's terms and conditions. The problem, from a design and usability perspective, is that there are pages and pages of terms and conditions divided into many subsections—yet they need to be prominently displayed on the home page. Perhaps a splitter could help us out.

A splitter is a UI component that divides multiple areas on a page in a way that allows users to resize elements; this way, users are able to decide how much space they want to allot each area. Splitters are commonplace in desktop applications, and with the explosion of Rich Internet Applications, they're making their way onto the Web. We can build on our experience with the Resizable component to simulate a simple splitter that contains a "Table of Contents" in one pane and StarTrackr!'s "Terms and Conditions" content in the other. The widget's appearance is shown in Figure 3.9.

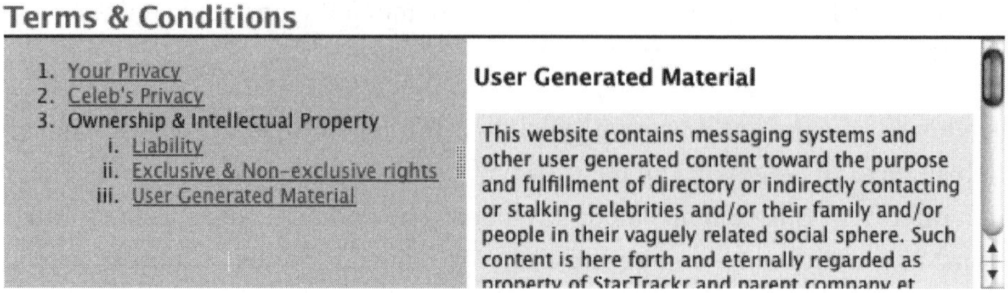

Figure 3.9. A horizontal pane splitter

For now we'll focus solely on the resizing functionality. Dynamically loading each section's content into the panes will be covered in plenty of detail in Chapter 5.

Our splitter will consist of two `div` elements, representing each pane, nested inside of a containing element that has fixed dimensions. We'll encase the table of contents in a block-level element, so that when the user resizes the panes the text won't wrap and mess up our nested list:

chapter_03/21_horizontal_pane_splitter/index.html *(excerpt)*

```
<div id="splitter">
  <div class="pane" id="tocPane">
    <div class="inner">
      ⋮
    </div>
  </div>
  <div class="pane" id="contentPane">
    <div class="inner">
      ⋮
    </div>
  </div>
</div>
```

We'll now add some simple styles in a new **splitter.css** style sheet. You can see that we've fixed the height of the containing `div`, and made the child elements each consume 50% of the width by default. You could change this to specify different values if it was necessary to start with an alternative to a 50:50 split. If you need to use a CSS border, you'll have to specify your widths in pixels and make sure they all add up:

chapter_03/21_horizontal_pane_splitter/splitter.css

```css
#splitter {
  height: 150px;
  margin-top: 30px;
  margin-bottom: 50px;
}

#splitter .pane {
  width: 50%;
  height: 100%;
  float: left;
}

#splitter h2 {
  margin-bottom: 0;
  padding-bottom: 0;
}

#tocPane {
  overflow: hidden;
  background: #d6dde5 url(../images/handle.png) no-repeat
➥right center;
}

#tocPane .inner {
  width: 300px;
}

#contentPane {
  overflow: auto;
}

#contentPane .inner {
  padding: 0 5px;
}
```

Next, our jQuery code. To create a horizontal splitter, we make the first element resizable and specify an east-facing handle—so only the right edge of the `div` will be resizable.

If you were to run the example with only a simple `resizable` statement, you'd notice that we're almost there: the two elements act *somewhat* like a split pane—except that the right element's width remains constant rather than expanding to fill the remaining space when you drag the handle. To take care of that, we're going to have to do some calculations inside the resizable widget's `resize` function. This is an event handler that fires as the component is being resized:

chapter_03/21_horizontal_pane_splitter/script.js *(excerpt)*

```
$('#splitter > div:first').resizable({
  handles: 'e',
  minWidth: '100',
  maxWidth: '400',
  resize: function() {
    var remainingSpace = $(this).parent().width() -
➡$(this).outerWidth();
    var divTwo = $(this).next();
    var divTwoWidth = remainingSpace - (divTwo.outerWidth() -
➡divTwo.width());
    divTwo.css('width', divTwoWidth + 'px');
  }
});
```

Every resizing will now also trigger a change in the second element's width. A bit of basic math helps us work out what the widths should be: we take the parent container's width (that is, the total width), then subtract the first div's `outerWidth`. The `outerWidth` function is a useful way to grab the total width of an element, including any padding and borders (it can also include margins if you pass it the optional parameter `true`). Perhaps unsurprisingly, there's a corresponding `outerHeight` function as well.

Having calculated how much space is left to use up, we're almost ready to set the first element's width. There's just one remaining catch: if the second `div` has borders or padding, we need to take these into consideration. Unfortunately the `outerWidth` function is read-only, so we're unable to use it to set the total height.

To calculate how much of the element's width consists of borders and padding, we need to subtract the element's `outerWidth` from its `width`. Subtracting that from the `remainingSpace` variable gives us exactly how many pixels wide the second div needs to be—and we can complete our horizontal splitter.

JavaScript Variables

The line `var remainingSpace = $(this).parent().width() - $(this).outerWidth();` assigns the result of the calculation to a variable called `remainingSpace`. From now on in our code, we can simply write `remainingSpace` whenever we need to access this value.

The following line (`var divTwo = $(this).next();`) is performing a very similar function, except that this time we're assigning a *jQuery selection* to a variable (`divTwo`). This can subsequently be used like any other jQuery selection.

Using variables like this helps to make your code more readable, as you can keep each line as concise as possible. It also makes your code more efficient; retrieving a value from a variable is much quicker for JavaScript than figuring out the value in the first place.

If we then wanted to have a go at implementing a vertical splitter, there's little to change: our pane elements stack on top of each other (rather than side by side), and our resizable call uses a south-facing handle instead of an east-facing one. The code is also almost identical—but now we're interested in the element's heights, not widths:

chapter_03/22_vertical_pane_splitter/script.js (excerpt)

```
$('#splitter > div:first').resizable({
  handles: 's',
  minHeight: '50',
  maxHeight: '200',
  resize: function() {
    var remainingSpace = $(this).parent().height() -
➡$(this).outerHeight();
    var divTwo = $(this).next();
    var divTwoHeight = remainingSpace -
➡(divTwo.outerHeight() - divTwo.height());
    divTwo.css('height', divTwoHeight + 'px');
  }
});
```

These simple splitters are quite useful, require very little code, and will be suitable for many purposes. But if you require complex splitter behavior, such as multiple split panes or nested panes, head over to the plugin repository and check out the jQuery Splitter plugin.

That's How We Scroll. And Animate.

What a chapter! We've mastered animation, scrolling, and resizing, and seen how chaining can help us easily write succinct, powerful functionality in a readable and natural manner. We're starting to apply our jQuery knowledge to create some great effects. However, what's important to concentrate on as you move through the book is not the effects themselves, but the underlying concepts that we use to implement them.

Even the most complex-looking effects tend to come out of a few simple actions chained together cleverly. It's up to you to sit down, think up some ideas, and try to implement them for yourself.

Chapter 4

Images and Slideshows

There's no more fooling around now. With the basics well and truly under our belts, we already have unlimited potential to create some world-class effects. Our client is over the moon; we've given him his "Web 2.0," and now his questionable startup has found favor with several of the big social networking sites. He's asked us to add in some "stuff" that really cooks: "image galleries, slideshows, fading effects—the works!" And why not? We have the tools, and we have the talent!

It would be a fairly boring Internet (at least visually) without images; much of the content we receive on our web-based travels is in the form of pictures and design elements such as borders, icons, and gradients that help to define our interaction with a web page. When we combine all of these elements with a healthy dose of jQuery, we start to see some vibrant and startling effects emerge. As well as the bog-standard components we've come to know and love, jQuery provides the means for implementing some less common, relatively new effects and features that would be difficult to do in JavaScript alone.

Lightboxes

Our client wants Web 2.0, so let's give him the quintessential Web 2.0 effect: the lightbox. A **lightbox**—a term borrowed from photography—is used is to display full-sized versions of an image thumbnail in a modal dialog. Typically, the entire background becomes darker to indicate that it's been disabled. The user must interact with the image (by hitting a close button, for example) to continue working on the page.

Custom Lightbox

Lightboxes are very common these days, and many feature some very complex functionality: animations, transitions, as well as the ability to display video, or to load content via Ajax. As always, there are some excellent plugins available that do all this, and we'll be visiting one of them in the next section—but for the moment, we'll build our own lightbox.

Why build our own? For our example, we just want a basic image view without any fanciness, and the kilobytes that fanciness costs us. We'll also have the chance to look under the hood and see how this type of functionality is implemented.

Our lightbox will be extremely simple: any HTML link that has a `class` name of `lightbox` will, when clicked, pop up the image file that the link points to. The picture will be centered on the screen, and the surrounding areas will be disabled and darkened as a visual cue. The effect is demonstrated in Figure 4.1.

Let's start with the HTML links. They're just tags pointing at image files with a `lightbox` class, so we can target them in our jQuery:

chapter_04/01_lightbox/index.html (excerpt)

```
<a href="/images/celeb01.jpg" class="lightbox">Pic</a>
```

When the image is displayed, we want the entire screen to go dark. How do we do this? The easiest way is to add a large `div` to the page that's as tall and wide as the screen itself. Inside that `div`, we'll add another `div` into which we'll load the image.

Figure 4.1. Our lightbox effect

The styling for the overlay is quite straightforward: 100% `height` and `width`, and a black background. Later, we'll fade the `opacity` of the element to give it its shadowy appearance. One other trick is to add a spinning loader image to the center of this element. When we start loading the image the spinner will display as part of the background. It will appear to vanish when the image loads, but in reality it will simply be hidden behind the image:

chapter_04/01_lightbox/lightbox.css

```css
#lightbox_overlay {
  position:absolute;
  top:0;
  left:0;
  height:100%;
  width:100%;
  background:black url(loader.gif) no-repeat scroll center center;
}
```

```
#lightbox_container {
  position:absolute;
}
```

Next, we add a `click` handler to our lightbox links. When they're clicked, we'll add the dark overlay element, the image container, and the image itself. The container isn't strictly necessary for our bare-bones example, but is helpful when you want to extend the lightbox's functionality, such as adding borders, descriptions, or **Next** and **Previous** buttons:

chapter_04/01_lightbox/script.js (excerpt)

```
$('a.lightbox').click(function(e) {
  // hide scrollbars!
  $('body').css('overflow-y', 'hidden');

  $('<div id="overlay"></div>')
    .css('top', $(document).scrollTop())
    .css('opacity', '0')
    .animate({'opacity': '0.5'}, 'slow')
    .appendTo('body');

  $('<div id="lightbox"></div>')
    .hide()
    .appendTo('body');

  $('<img />')
    .attr('src', $(this).attr('href'))
    .load(function() {
      positionLightboxImage();
    })
    .click(function() {
      removeLightbox();
    })
    .appendTo('#lightbox');

  return false;
});
```

The overlay is positioned at the top of the screen, and quickly faded from invisible to 50% opacity to provide the background effect. The lightbox container is added to the page and immediately hidden, awaiting the loading of our image. The image is added to the container, and its `src` attribute is set to the location of the image (extracted from the link's `href`). To do this we use jQuery's powerful `attr` method, which can be used to retrieve or set any attribute of a DOM element. When called with only one parameter (such as `$(this).attr('href')`), it returns the value of that attribute. With a second parameter (for instance, `$('<img />').attr('src', …)`), it sets the attribute to the value provided.

Then we attach a few event handlers to the image. One of these events is new to us: `load`. It's a close cousin to the `ready` event, but fires when an element (in this case our image) is 100% loaded.

Quick Element Construction

Creating new elements is very satisfying, and a task you'll have to do frequently. There's an alternative way to set up a new jQuery object, which involves passing an object as the second parameter. The object contains all of the attributes and settings you want the new item to have. For example:

```
$('<img />', {
  src: $(this).attr('href'),
  load: function() {
    positionLightboxImage();
  },
  .click: function() {
    removeLightbox();
  }
}).appendTo('#lightbox');
```

jQuery has a bit of smarts in how it reacts to the properties you set. If you give it an event, it will bind the provided handler to the event (as we've done with `load` and `click`). If you use a jQuery method name like `text`, `html`, or `val`, it will use the jQuery methods to set the property. Everything else will be treated as an attribute, as done with the `src` property. The end result is the same jQuery object as the one we constructed before, but if you're comfortable with JavaScript object notation, you might prefer this method of element construction.

Finally, we add a `return false;` to prevent the default behavior of the HTML link from occurring. Otherwise, the user would navigate away from our page and to the image itself.

Now let's have a look at the `positionLightbox` function:

chapter_04/01_lightbox/script.js *(excerpt)*

```
function positionLightboxImage() {
  var top = ($(window).height() - $('#lightbox').height()) / 2;
  var left = ($(window).width() - $('#lightbox').width()) / 2;
  $('#lightbox')
    .css({
      'top': top + $(document).scrollTop(),
      'left': left
    })
    .fadeIn();
}
```

When the image is done loading, the positionLightboxImage function is called. This takes care of displaying the image in the center of the screen. It calculates the central point by taking the window's height or width and subtracting the image's height or width, then dividing the result by 2. It then performs a nice fade to display the image.

The last task left to do is remove the lightbox when the user clicks on the image. We simply fade out our new elements and then remove them, so that the lightbox is ready to be triggered again for the next image:

chapter_04/01_lightbox/script.js *(excerpt)*

```
function removeLightbox() {
  $('#overlay, #lightbox')
    .fadeOut('slow', function() {
      $(this).remove();
      $('body').css('overflow-y', 'auto'); // show scrollbars!
    });
}
```

This is probably the most bare-bones lightbox you can imagine, but it's still satisfying to see in action. Now that you have an idea of how a lightbox is built, you can come up with improvements and customizations. Even though plugins may be plentiful, sometimes building them yourself is more satisfying!

Troubleshooting with `console.log`

If you've had a go at extending or customizing this simple lightbox (or, for that matter, any of the code we've seen so far), you'll no doubt have encountered a situation where your code fails to do what you expect it to. Figuring out exactly what's going on at any given moment in your code can be frustrating. Sometimes you need to know if a certain function is being called, or what the value of a variable is at a specific point in time.

Traditionally, this sort of debugging is often achieved with the trusty old `alert` method. For example, if you need to to know what value the code has stored in the `top` variable, you type `alert(top);`. But this interrupts the flow of the program—and forces you to close the alert before continuing. And if the code you're interested in is in the middle of a loop, you might wind up having to close a lot of alerts.

Thankfully, web development tools are constantly advancing, and if you use the excellent Firebug plugin for Firefox (introduced back in Chapter 2), you can take advantage of the built-in debugging options. One of Firebug's most handy features is the console, where instead of alerting the value of variables, you can use the command `console.log`:

chapter_04/01_lightbox/script.js *(excerpt)*

```
console.log(top,left);
```

Just open the **Console** tab of Firebug (you may need to enable it first), and you'll see the values displayed. No more annoying alert windows! You can specify as many variables or expressions as you would like in a single statement by separating them with commas. The outputs generated by different types of log statements are depicted in Figure 4.2: two simple string outputs, a multivariable output consisting of two numbers, and a jQuery selection.

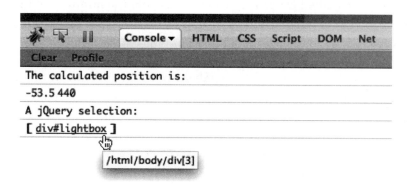

Figure 4.2. The Firebug console

If the variable is a JavaScript object, you can even click on it in the console to examine its contents. If it is a DOM node or jQuery object, clicking on it will highlight it on the page and jump to it in the Firebug DOM tree. This will save your sanity when you're stuck on those obnoxious bugs! Just remember to remove any `console.log` lines from your code when you release it.

ColorBox: A Lightbox Plugin

Our custom lightbox is a fine solution for our modest needs, but you'll have to admit that it's fairly limited as far as features go. Sometimes you'll need more. The principal contender for "more" for quite some time has been Cody Lindley's ThickBox. ThickBox has certainly fought the big fights, but like all true champions, you have to know when it's time to step out of the ring and hang up the gloves.

ThickBox is still a powerful plugin and suits many developers despite the fact that it's no longer maintained. It did what it did, and did it well. It's precisely that level of quality that has set the bar high for a new generation of lightbox plugins. Let's take a look at one of the big challengers: ColorBox.

ColorBox[1] is the brainchild of Jack Moore, and with an array of public methods and event hooks—and a staggering 37 options to choose from—it's likely that even seasoned users won't touch on everything it has to offer. Given ColorBox's focus on standards-based XHTML, reliance on CSS for styling, and wide support of content options, it's easy to see that the "lightweight" tag line on its web page refers only to its tiny 9KB footprint—and not to its huge feature set!

Grab ColorBox from the download area of the web site and examine its contents. There's a directory called ColorBox that contains both the minified and uncompressed version of the plugin code. As usual, you should use the minified version unless you're keen to understand the inner workings of ColorBox.

Also included in the download are a number of example directories; the examples all use the same markup and JavaScript code, but show how the lightbox can be styled to look completely different. The best way to start out is to have a look at the examples and choose the CSS file (and corresponding images) that you like best, and then build on that for your implementation.

---

[1] http://colorpowered.com/colorbox/

We've copied over the CSS and image files from one of the example directories, and included both that CSS file and the minified plugin file in our HTML:

chapter_04/02_colorbox_plugin/index.html *(excerpt)*

```
<link rel="stylesheet" href="colorbox.css" type="text/css">
<script src="jquery.colorbox-min.js" type="text/javascript">
➥</script>
```

ColorBox can work on a single image as we did in the previous section, but it excels at displaying slideshow-style galleries—letting the user move between the images, as illustrated in Figure 4.3. To take advantage of this we need to group the images we want to show, and ColorBox expects us to do this with the `rel` attribute of our links.

Figure 4.3. A styled gallery using the ColorBox plugin

In the markup, we've included `rel="celeb"` on all of the images we want to group together. Now we can use the jQuery attribute selector to find those images: `a[rel="celeb"]`. Calling the `colorbox` method on the selection gives us a fantastic-looking lightbox:

chapter_04/02_colorbox_plugin/script.js (excerpt)

```
$(document).ready(function() {
  $('a[rel="celeb"]').colorbox();
});
```

It looks and works briliiantly by default, but there are stacks and stacks of options to play around with. In the following example we give it a fading transition, rather than the default elastic resize (the **speed** option, as you might have guessed, specifies the duration of the fade). To suit the StarTrackr! style, we'll also customize the wording of the lightbox text. This is just the tip of the iceberg, though—poke around on the ColorBox site to explore all the other options and events available for customizing the lightbox:

chapter_04/02_colorbox_plugin/script.js (excerpt)

```
$('a[rel=celeb]').colorbox({
  transition: 'fade',
  speed: 500,
  current: "{current} of {total} celebrity photos"
});
```

What's great about ColorBox is that it's highly unobtrusive and customizable: you can alter behavior settings, add callbacks, and use event hooks without modifying your markup or the plugin's source files. ColorBox preloads any required images—and can even start preloading your gallery images—so it always appears snappy on your pages. And last, but by no means least, ColorBox is released under the permissive MIT License[2]—so you can use it in your commercial projects as you see fit.

---

[2] http://creativecommons.org/licenses/MIT/

Cropping Images with Jcrop

While we're looking at mature and excellent plugins and lightbox effects, we'd be remiss if we skipped over the Jcrop plugin[3] for defining regions of an image. The plugin adds a lightbox-style overlay on an image and lets the user drag a rectangle to select a required area of an image. This functionality is common on many large web sites, where it allows users to crop an uploaded image for their profile picture.

If you know a little about image manipulation on the Web, you're likely to know that image manipulation of this sort usually takes place on the server side. Right? Yes, that's correct—the Jcrop plugin doesn't actually crop images, it provides an intuitive interface for defining the bounding edges where the user would like to crop an image. The results returned from the plugin can then be fed to the server to perform the actual image manipulation. You can see an image being cropped with Jcrop in Figure 4.4.

Figure 4.4. The Jcrop plugin in action

---

[3] http://deepliquid.com/content/Jcrop.html

The typical workflow for using the Jcrop plugin would be to display an image to the user that needs to be cropped (either a stored image or a freshly uploaded one), and overlay the Jcrop interface. When the user has made their selection the coordinates are posted to the server, where the resulting image is created and saved for display or download.

To apply the Jcrop interaction, you first need to download it and extract the files. Contained in the download bundle is the Jcrop JavaScript file, a small CSS file, a clever animated GIF (that's responsible for the "moving lines" effect when you select a region), and some demo pages that highlight all of Jcrop's features.

You'll need to include the CSS (at the top of the page) and JavaScript (at the bottom of the page) files. The Jcrop.gif image should be in the same directory as your CSS file:

chapter_04/03_jcrop/index.html (excerpt)

```html
<link rel="stylesheet" href="css/jquery.Jcrop.css" type="text/css">
<script src="jquery.Jcrop.min.js" type="text/javascript"></script>
```

Once everything is in place, you just need to add an image that you'd like to make selectable to the page. We've given the image an ID so that it's nice and easy to select with jQuery. If you want the user to signal that they're happy with their selection, you can add a clickable button too:

chapter_04/03_jcrop/index.html (excerpt)

```html
<div id="crop">
  <img id="mofat" src="../../images/mofat_400.jpg" alt="Mo'Fat"/>
  <input type="button" value="crop"/>
</div>
```

In its simplest form, you just have to apply the jQuery plugin to the image. When you reload the page, the image will be augmented with draggable handles and an overlay:

```javascript
$('#mofat').Jcrop();
```

The plugin exposes a couple of useful events that you can use to keep an eye on what the user is selecting. It also has a handful of default options for customizing how the selector works. You can restrict the aspect ratio of the crop area and the minimum and maximum selection sizes, as well as the color and opacity of the background overlay:

```
var jcrop = $('#mofat).Jcrop({
  setSelect: [10,10,300,350],
  minSize:[50,50],
  onChange: function(coords) {
    // use the coordinates
  },
  onSelect: function(coords) {
    // use the coordinates
  }
});
```

Here we've included some default properties. `setSelect` allows us to define a default cropping area; we need to pass it an array of coordinates, in the format [x1, y1, x2, y2]. The `minSize` option is an array containing the selection's minimum width and height. We've also illustrated how you'd capture the `onChange` and `onSelect` events. The `onChange` event will fire many times as the user is dragging the handles or the selection around the image. The `onSelect` event, on the other hand, will only fire when a selection has been defined; that is, when the user has stopped dragging.

The handlers for the events receive a coordinates object that contains the x, y, x2, y2, w, and h properties. So, in your handler code, you'd write `coords.w` to obtain the current selection's width.

By far the most common use for the Jcrop plugin is to define points to send to the server after the user is done selecting. The events that the plugin fires are of no use to us for this purpose, as we have no way of knowing if the user is *really* finished selecting—that's why we added a button! We want to know where the selection is when the user clicks the button.

In order to do this, we'll need to modify our original code a little. When you call `Jcrop` on a jQuery object as we did above, the jQuery object is returned, ready to be chained into more jQuery methods. However, this gives us no access to the selection coordinates. In order to grab these, we'll need to call `Jcrop` differently, directly from `$`. When called in this way, it will return a special Jcrop object, which has properties and methods for accessing the selected coordinates (as well as modifying the selection programmatically). We need to pass it both a selector for the image to crop, and the set of options:

```
                                    chapter_04/03_jcrop/script.js (excerpt)

var jcrop = $.Jcrop('#mofat',{
  setSelect: [10,10,300,350],
  minSize:[50,50]
});

$('#crop :button').click(function() {
  var selection = jcrop.tellSelect();
  alert('selected size: ' + selection.w + 'x' + selection.h);
})
```

We're using the `tellSelect` method to obtain the current selection; this has the same properties as the event coordinates, so we can use them to send to the server and chop up our picture! In the absence of a server, we've chosen to simply alert them, to let you know what's going on.

Jcrop has a vast array of available options and methods, so it's strongly recommended that you inspect the demos included in the plugin download to see what's available.

Slideshows

Every night, customers of the StarTrackr! site use the location information they purchase to hunt down and photograph the world's social elite. Many of the photos are posted back to the web site, and the client wants to feature some of them on the home page. We're increasingly comfortable with jQuery, so we've told our client we'd mock up a few different slideshow ideas for him. First we'll look at some ways of cross-fading images; that is, fading an image out while another is fading in. Then we'll look at a few scrolling galleries, and finally a more sophisticated flip-book style gallery. Along the way we'll pick up a bunch of new jQuery tricks!

Cross–fading Slideshows

If you work in television, you'll know that unless you're George Lucas, the only transition effect they'll let you use is the cross-fade (aka the dissolve). The reason for this is that slides, starbursts, and swirl transitions nearly always look tacky. This also applies outside the realm of television; just think back to the last PowerPoint presentation you saw.

There are different techniques for cross-fading images on the Web—all with pros and cons mostly boiling down to simplicity versus functionality. We'll cover some of the main methods used to cross-fade items, so that you have a selection to choose from when necessary.

Rollover Fader

The first cross-fader we'll have a look at is a rudimentary rollover fader; it's much like the hover effects we've already looked at, except this time we'll perform a gradual fade between the two states. First, we need to tackle the problem of where and how to store the hover image.

This solution works by putting both of our images into a span (or whatever container you like). The hover image is positioned on top of the first image and hidden until the user mouses over it; then the hidden image fades in. To start, we set up our rollover container:

chapter_04/04_rollover_fade/index.html *(excerpt)*

```
<span id="fader">
  <img src="../../images/glenda_200.jpg" alt="Glendatronix"/>
  <img class="to" src="../../images/fader_200.jpg"
    alt="Darth Fader"/>
</span>
```

To hide the hover image, we employ the usual position and display properties:

chapter_04/04_rollover_fade/style.css *(excerpt)*

```
#fader {
  position: relative;
}

#fader .to {
  display: none;
  position: absolute;
  left: 0;
}
```

We now have something juicy to attach our `hover` event handler to. Knowing that we have two images trapped inside the container, we can access them with the `:eq` filter: image 0 is our visible image, and image 1 is our hover image.

There's More than One Way to Select a Cat

We've used this method primarily to highlight the `:eq` selector attribute. There are several other ways we could've accessed the two images inside the container: by using the `:first` and `:last` filters, the corresponding `.eq`, `.last`, or `.first` actions, the child (`>`) selector, or simply a `class` name. There are usually multiple ways to accomplish tasks with jQuery, and the choice often boils down to personal preference.

Here's the code we'll use to perform the rollover:

```
chapter_04/04_rollover_fade/script.js (excerpt)

$('#fader').hover(function() {
  $(this).find('img:eq(1)').stop(true,true).fadeIn();
}, function() {
  $(this).find('img:eq(1)').fadeOut();
})
```

There's nothing new to use here—except that we're using the advanced version of the `stop` command (which we first saw in the section called "Animated Navigation" in Chapter 3). We're specifying `true` for both `clearQueue` and `gotoEnd`, so our fade animation will immediately stop any other queued animations and jump straight to where it was headed (in this case, it will jump straight to the fully faded-out state, so we can fade it back in). This prevents animations from backing up if you mouse over and out quickly.

You'd probably be thinking of using this effect for navigation buttons—which is a good idea! Another consideration, though, is adding the hover image as the link's `:hover` state background image in CSS too. That way, your rollover will function as a traditional hover button for those without JavaScript.

JavaScript Timers

The Web is an event-driven environment. Elements mostly just sit on the page waiting patiently for a user to come along and click or scroll, select or submit. When they do, our code can spring to life and carry out our wishes. But there are times when we want to avoid waiting for the user to act, and want to perform a task with a regular frequency. This will be the case with the next few slideshows we're going to build: we want to rotate automatically through a series of images, displaying a new one every few seconds.

Unlike many other areas of the library, there's been no need for jQuery to expand on JavaScript's timer functionality; the basic JavaScript methods are simple, flexible, and work across browsers. There are two of them: `setTimeout` and `setInterval`.

The timer functions both work the same way: they wait a certain amount of time before executing the code we give them. The syntax used to call them is also much the same:

```
setTimeout(<code to run>, <number of milliseconds to wait>);
setInterval(<code to run>, <number of milliseconds to wait>);
```

The key difference is that `setTimeout` will wait the specified period of time, run the code we give it, and then stop. `setInterval`, on the other hand, will wait, run the code—then wait again and run the code again—repeating forever (or until we tell it to stop). If the code we pass it updates a visible property of an element, and the delay we assign it is relatively small, we can achieve the illusion of animation. In fact, behind the scenes, this is what jQuery is doing when we use any of its animation functions!

Timers can be tricky to use correctly, largely because they cause problems of *scope*, which we'll discuss in more detail in the section called "Scope" in Chapter 6. However, we want to master them, as timers are the key to freeing our pages from the tyranny of user-initiated events!

Setting up a Timer

Here's a small example to demonstrate timers at work: we'll simply move a green box smoothly across the screen. Of course, we could rely on jQuery's `animate` method to do this for us, but we want to learn what is really going on in the JavaScript. This will involve positioning a square `div` and continuously updating its `left` CSS property. Let's set up our boxes:

chapter_04/05_timers/index.html *(excerpt)*

```
<div>
  <div id="green" class="box">Go!</div>
  <div id="red" class="box">Go!</div>
</div>
```

The boxes are sitting still; to animate them we're going to need a timer. We'll use the setInterval timer, because we want our code to be executed repeatedly:

chapter_04/05_timers/script.js *(excerpt)*

```
var greenLeft = parseInt($('#green').css('left'));
setInterval(function() {
  $('#green').css('left', ++greenLeft);
}, 200);
```

Our div moves slowly across the screen: every 200 milliseconds, we're pushing it a pixel to the right. Changing the size of the delay affects the speed of the animation. Be careful, though: if you set the delay very low (say, less than 50 milliseconds) and you're doing a lot of DOM manipulation with each loop, the average user's browser will quickly grind to a halt. This is because their computer is not given enough time to do everything you asked it to before you come around asking it again. If you think your code might be at risk, it's best to test it on a variety of machines to ensure the performance is acceptable.

It's also possible to replicate setInterval's functionality using the setTimeout function, by structuring our code a bit differently:

chapter_04/05_timers/index.html *(excerpt)*

```
var redLeft = parseInt($('#red').css('left'));
function moveRed() {
  setTimeout(moveRed, 200);
  $('#red').css('left', ++redLeft);
}
moveRed();
```

Here we have a function called moveRed, inside of which we have a setTimeout timer that calls … moveRed! As setTimeout only runs once, it will only call moveRed once. But because `moveRed` *contains* the timer call, it will call itself again and again—achieving the same result as `setInterval`.

Stopping Timers

Usually it's undesirable (or unnecessary) for our timers to run forever. Thankfully, timers that you start running can be forced to stop by calling the appropriate JavaScript command, `clearInterval` or `clearTimeout`:

```
clearInterval(<timer id>);
clearTimeout(<timer id>);
```

To call either of these functions you need to pass in the timer's ID. How do we know what the ID is? The ID is an integer number that's assigned to the timer when you create it. If you know you might want to stop a timer in the future, you must store that number in a variable:

```
var animationTimer = setInterval(animate, 100);
```

The timer can now be stopped at any time with the following code:

```
clearInterval(animationTimer);
```

And that's all there is to know about `setTimeout` and `setInterval`! Don't worry if they still seem a little fuzzy: we'll be using them as required through the rest of the book, and seeing them in context will help you become more accustomed to them.

Fading Slideshow

Cross-fading between two images is fairly straightforward: it's always fading one image in as the other fades out. If we extend the idea to a whole bunch of images for, say, a rotating image gallery the task becomes a little more difficult. Now we'll need to calculate which picture to show next, and make sure we wrap around after we've shown the last image.

A common trick you'll see with jQuery image galleries is to fake the cross-fade by hiding all of the images except for the current image. When it comes time to swap, you simply hide the current image, and fade in the next one. Because there's no true overlap occurring with the images, this doesn't really qualify as a cross-fade;

however, it's a simple solution that might be all you need, so we'll look at it first. The next example we'll look at will be a true cross-fader.

Our basic slideshow will consist of a bunch of images inside a `div`. We'll designate one of the images as the visible image by assigning it the `class` show:

chapter_04/06_slideshow_fade/index.html *(excerpt)*

```
<div id="photos">
  <img alt="Glendatronix" class="show"
    src="../../images/glenda_200.jpg" />
  <img alt="Darth Fader" src="../../images/fader_200.jpg" />
  <img alt="Beau Dandy" src="../../images/beau_200.jpg" />
  <img alt="Johnny Stardust" src="../../images/johnny_200.jpg" />
  <img alt="Mo' Fat" src="../../images/mofat_200.jpg" />
</div>
```

We'll hide all the images by default. The `show` class has a double purpose for this slideshow: it enables us to target it in CSS to display it, and—equally importantly—it gives us a handle to the current image. There's no need to keep track of a variable, such as `var currentImage = 1`, because the `class` name itself is functioning as that variable.

Now we need to start running a JavaScript timer so we can loop around our images. We'll write a function that calls itself every three seconds:

chapter_04/06_slideshow_fade/script.js *(excerpt)*

```
$(document).ready(function() {
  slideShow();
});

function slideShow() {
  var current = $('#photos .show');
  var next = current.next().length ? current.next() :
➥current.parent().children(':first');

  current.hide().removeClass('show');
  next.fadeIn().addClass('show');

  setTimeout(slideShow, 3000);
}
```

We know the current image has the `class show`, so we use that to select it. To find the next image we want to show, we use a bit of conditional logic. If the next sibling exists, we select it. If it doesn't exist, we select the first image, so the slideshow wraps around.

Ternary Operator

You might be a little confused by the syntax we've used to assign a value to the `next` variable. In JavaScript (and in many other programming languages), this is called the **ternary operator**. It's a shortcut for setting a variable *conditionally*.

The syntax `a ? b : c` means that if `a` is `true`, return b; otherwise, return c. You can use this in variable assignment, as we did above, to assign different values to the same variable depending on some condition. Of course, a longer `if / else` statement can always do the same job, but the ternary operator is much more succinct, so it's well worth learning.

So, to resume, the line:

```
var next = current.next().length ? current.next() :
➥current.parent().children(':first');
```

can be translated into English as follows: if the current element has a sibling after it in the same container (if the `next` method returns a non-empty array), we'll use that. On the other hand, if `next` returns an empty array (so `length` is `0`, which is `false` in computer terms), we'll navigate up to the current element's parent (the `#photos div`) and select its first child (which will be the first photo in the slideshow).

Finally, we hide the current image and fade in the next one. We also swap the `show` class from the old photo onto the new one, and set a timeout for the `slideShow` method to call itself again after three seconds have passed.

True Cross-fading

Our last solution looks nice—but it's just a fade, rather than a true cross-fade. We want to be able to truly cross-fade: as the current picture is fading out, the next picture is fading in. There is more than one way to skin a jQuery effect, and the approach we'll take for our implementation is as follows:

1. Stack the images on top of each other, so that the picture with the highest z-index will be showing.

2. Fade out the top image so that the next image appears to fade in.

3. Once the fade has completed, reorder the z-index of the images so that the current image is on top.

4. Repeat steps 2 and 3.

A disadvantage of this technique is that we'll be stacking the images on top of each other, so they must all be the same size. This usually is a small issue, as it's fairly common on the Web to be constrained to a certain area. It should also be noted that it's very easy to switch out the images for divs and be able to cross-fade any HTML in their place.

z-index

z-index is a CSS property used to specify the visual stacking order of an element. Elements with higher z-index values will appear in front of those with lower values. This can be used in conjunction with absolute or relative positioning to stack elements on top of each other.

Looking back at our outline, you should be able to tell that steps 1 and 2 are straightforward. Let's start by stacking up our images:

chapter_04/07_slideshow_cross_fade/index.html *(excerpt)*

```
<p id="photos">
  <img src="images/BarronVonJovi.png" />
  <img src="images/TheComputadors.png" />
  <img src="images/Bosom.png" />
  ⋮
</p>
```

We need to position the images absolutely and contain them within a bounding box:

```
chapter_04/07_slideshow_cross_fade/style.css (excerpt)
```

```css
#photos img {
  position: absolute;
}

#photos {
  width: 180px;
  height: 180px;
  overflow: hidden;
}
```

Now that our images are stacked, let's step back and do some planning. In order to be able to execute step 4 (repeating the fade for the next image), we'll need to put our fading code in some sort of loop. As the loop needs to keep track of the current photo, we're going to move our code out into a named function, which we'll call from our $(document).ready block:

```
chapter_04/07_slideshow_cross_fade/script.js (excerpt)
```

```javascript
$(document).ready(function() {
  rotatePics(1);
}
```

Now we'll create the rotatePics function, which will do all the hard work. This method accepts a number, which should be the index of the current photo. We'll see how this is used shortly, but first, we store the total number of photos in a variable. We do this because we're going to be reusing it a few times in the code—and storing it in a variable means jQuery is spared from wasting time doing the same calculations over and over:

```
chapter_04/07_slideshow_cross_fade/script.js (excerpt)
```

```javascript
function rotatePics(currentPhoto) {
  var numberOfPhotos = $('#photos img').length;
  currentPhoto = currentPhoto % numberOfPhotos;
  ⋮
}
```

The second line of code is a common JavaScript trick for ensuring that values are confined to a given range. We never want the currentPhoto to be greater than the total number of photos, so we perform a calculation to ensure that the index of the photo we passed in is valid—by taking the **modulus** of the length. Modulus, represented in JavaScript by the % symbol, returns only the *remainder* of a division. So if we have five photos in total, and we pass in an index of six, the operation gives 6 % 5 = 1. The number is effectively wrapped around back to the start, and we can be sure we're never trying to display a photo that's nonexistent!

Now we can finally proceed with doing the actual cross-fade. As we described in our outline, the effect works by fading out the current image. This will give the appearance of the next image fading in.

We use jQuery's eq traversing command to grab the current photo. eq—short for "equals"—selects the element from a group whose index is equal to the number we pass in. We pass it our currentPhoto variable to select the current image. With the image selected, we simply fade it out and run a callback function to take care of the setup for the next fade:

```
                           chapter_04/07_slideshow_cross_fade/script.js (excerpt)
$('#photos img').eq(currentPhoto).fadeOut(function() {
  // re-order the z-index
  $('#photos img').each(function(i) {
    $(this).css(
      'zIndex', ((numberOfPhotos - i) + currentPhoto) %
➥numberOfPhotos
    );
  });

  $(this).show();
  setTimeout(function() {rotatePics(++currentPhoto);}, 4000);
});
```

There are a few things happening here. First, we do a bit of math to reorder the images. We offset each photo's index by the currently displayed photo index. Then our new modulus trick is put to use again, and the end result is each image's z-index shuffled along by 1. To see this in action, open up Firebug and inspect the images as the effect is running: you'll see the z-index properties shuffling each time a new image displays.

Once we've completed the reordering, the picture we just faded out will be on the bottom of the pile. This means that it's safe to show it again, ready for the next time it rises to the top: an easy $(this).show().

Then there's a call to the timer function `setTimeout` to set up the function to be run again after a delay of 4,000 milliseconds. We pass it the next photo's index by writing `++currentPhoto`.

Increment and Decrement

In JavaScript, if you follow or precede a numeric variable with `--` or `++`, the variable will be decremented or incremented by 1, respectively. This is a handy shortcut for the `-=` and `+=` operators we've already seen.

The difference between `++a` and `a++` is subtle, but important. If you are using it in your code, the first form (with the `++` or `--` *preceding* the variable name) will increment the variable *before* returning it. The second form will return the unmodified value, *then* increment it.

In our code above, we want to call our function with the new incremented value, so we use `++currentPhoto`.

Feel free to experiment with the type of effect; as well as fades, you can try using the `slideUp` effect, or one of the jQuery UI effect plugins.

Advanced Fading with Plugins

As you'd imagine, there are countless jQuery plugins already built for transitioning between images. If you have some advanced requirements (sometimes you just need to have a starburst wipe), heading straight for the plugin repository could be a good idea.

Before Using a Plugin

Many jQuery plugins you find on the Web were developed quite some time ago, and have been more or less abandoned since then. Without continued development and improvement, they'll often be comparatively slow and buggy. It's always a good idea to try to understand what you're adding to your site, instead of blindly including a half-dozen plugin files. If the code is heavy (in terms of file size) and has a lot of functionality unnecessary for your requirements, perhaps a more lightweight, tailor-made solution is in order.

That said, many plugins provide excellent, well-documented code that will save you enormous amounts of time and effort. Just be sure to adequately consider your options!

Now we'll look at two plugins you can use to achieve a slideshow effect; one is extremely lightweight, while the other has more features.

News Ticker with InnerFade

InnerFade[4] is a tiny plugin that lets you transition between a series of elements, much like the fading image gallery we just built. It does have a few benefits over our code that makes it worth considering. For one, it's a plugin—which means it's easy to drop in wherever we need it. Of course, we can easily turn our code into a plugin too (just jump to the section called "Plugins" in Chapter 9 to see how easy it is). It also has some extra options that give us more flexibility: the ability to show the items in a random order, give a `class` name to the active element, and choose different animation types.

You might be thinking that all these features would be fairly easy to add to our custom code—after all, we're well on our way to becoming jQuery ninjas! If you're feeling adventurous, open up the InnerFade plugin file to see how these features have been developed in there, which should give some idea about how you would implement them yourself.

As a departure from our image rotations, let's have a look at rotating list items to create a simple news ticker, where a list of text links will be displayed randomly. To kick it off, we need to include the plugin in our page.

The ZIP file is linked at the very bottom of the plugin's web page. It's over 100KB—but don't worry, most of that size consists of images used in the demos. The actual script weighs in at 8KB, and that's without being compressed!

chapter_04/08_innerfade/index.html *(excerpt)*

```
<script type="text/javascript" src="jquery.innerfade.js"></script>
```

Next, we'll set up our containing element and the items we'd like to scroll. The plugin will treat all first-level children of the container we pass to it as fair game to cycle through. We'll use an unordered list as the container, and the list items as the elements:

---

[4] http://medienfreunde.com/lab/innerfade/

chapter_04/08_innerfade/index.html *(excerpt)*

```
<div id="news">
  <h2>News</h2>
  <ul>
    <li><a href="#">Barron Von Jovi spotted … </a></li>
    <li><a href="#">Mo'Fat signs up-and-coming rapper … </a></li>
    <li><a href="#">Glendatronix rumored to be … </a></li>
    <li><a href="#">Man claims to be Darth Fader's son … </a></li>
  </ul>
</div>
```

When our document is ready, we use the plugin's provided `innerfade` method on the list. There are a number of options available to customize the way this method works; we're using a few here, and you should consult the plugin's documentation to discover all of them. We'll specify a slide effect, rather than a fade effect, to round out our news ticker style, and we'll have the elements rotate at random:

chapter_04/08_innerfade/script.js *(excerpt)*

```
$('#news ul').innerfade({
  animationtype: 'slide',
  speed: 750,
  timeout: 2000,
  type: 'random'
});
```

And there we have it: a simple and cool effect for displaying news items. The Inner-Fade plugin is also perfectly suitable for image galleries like the ones we've already built, though you should be aware of one important difference. InnerFade handles all of the item hiding, showing, and positioning in its code—so without JavaScript *all* of the elements will be displayed (whereas in our custom code, we hid all but one in CSS). You'll need to take this into consideration, and decide what you want the baseline experience of your site to be and how you'd like to enhance it with jQuery.

The Cycle Plugin

The Cycle plugin[5] is a very mature, full-featured plugin that—like all the fading we have been doing—enables you to transition between elements in a container. Its

---

[5] http://malsup.com/jquery/cycle/

completeness results in a comparatively hefty download (25KB for the complete minified version), but offers some impressive transition effects, well suited for displaying image galleries in a more interesting manner.

The setup should be very familiar to you now: download the plugin and add the JavaScript file to the head of your page. There are actually three different versions of the plugin contained in the download: a base version with only a slide transition (**jquery.cycle.min.js**, 16KB), a full-featured version with a wide range of available transitions (**jquery.cycle.all.min.js**, 25KB), and a stripped-down version with only the most basic options (**jquery.cycle.lite.min.js**, 4KB). For our example, we'll use the full-fledged version for the sake of illustrating the available options.

We'll start off with exactly the same markup we used for our previous slideshows. You can easily cross-fade images with the Cycle plugin, but given that it's provided us with a number of fancier options, let's try one and "shuffle" the images:

chapter_04/09_cycle_plugin/script.js *(excerpt)*

```
$('#photos').cycle({
  fx: 'shuffle'
});
```

This effect is illustrated in Figure 4.5.

Figure 4.5. The shuffle effect included in the Cycle plugin

The plugin gives us more than 20 ways to move around our gallery: shuffle, fade, zoom, wipe, toss, curtainX, growY ... for starters. Additionally, the plugin can be customized to include your own transition effects, if you're unable to find one that suits your needs.

The number of options offered in Cycle is quite astounding, probably far more than you'll ever need. Let's try out a more complicated example:

chapter_04/10_cycle_plugin_2/script.js *(excerpt)*

```
$('#photos').cycle({
  fx: 'scrollDown',
  speedIn: 2500,
  speedOut: 500,
  timeout: 0,
  next: '#photos'
});
```

The timeout setting controls the time between transitions—but what would a value of 0 mean? In this case it means "don't animate." Instead, we've used the next option to select an element that, when clicked, will advance to the next slide. That selector is the slideshow itself—so to move to the next picture, you just need to click on the picture.

Additionally, we've used the speedIn and speedOut options to specify the duration of the "in" and "out" animations: we've chosen to *sloooowly* bring the next picture into view, while quickly dismissing the last. There are so many options available that you'll need some serious playing with it to exhaust the possibilities for usable effects.

Scrolling Slideshows

As we saw when using the Cycle plugin, cross-fading is far from being the only way to transition between a set of images. In the next few examples, we'll explore another technique for creating interactive slideshows. We're going to throw all our images in a giant container, and use a wrapper element to hide all but one or a few from view. Then, when we want to display a different image, we'll just scroll the element to the desired position.

Thumbnail Scroller

Our first stab at a scrolling gallery will be a horizontal list of thumbnails. If you click on the control, the list scrolls along to reveal more images.

To build this control we'll need to have two nested elements. The child element will be large and contain all of the images. The parent element is only as big as the viewing area; that is, the area we want the user to see. As the child element moves around, it appears to the user that the content is scrolling in. Here's the markup:

chapter_04/11_thumbnail_scroller/index.html *(excerpt)*

```html
<div id="pic_scroller">
  <div id="pic_container">
    <img class="pic" src="Image_01.png" />
    <img class="pic" src="Image_02.png" />
    ...
    <img class="pic" src="Image_15.png" />
  </div>
<div>
```

The outer element needs to hide the excess content, and so needs to have overflow: hidden. For our scroller, we define the inner element to have a width wide enough to fit our 15 thumbnails:

chapter_04/11_thumbnail_scroller/style.css *(excerpt)*

```css
#photos {
  overflow: hidden;
}

#photos_inner {
  height: 100px;
  width: 600px;
  overflow: hidden;
  position: relative;
}

#photos_inner img {
  float: left;
  width: 100px;
  height: 100px;
}
```

With our container all set up, and an armful of images to show, let's take a first stab at scrolling the images:

```
chapter_04/11_thumbnail_scroller/script.js (excerpt)

$('#photos_inner').toggle(function() {
  var scrollAmount = $(this).width() - $(this).parent().width();
  $(this).animate({'left':'-=' + scrollAmount}, 'slow');
}, function() {
  $(this).animate({'left':'0'}, 'slow');
});
```

First we need to calculate how much to scroll. We take the width of the overflowed element that contains images and subtract that from the width of the parent container. The parent action selects an element's immediate parent (see the section called "Bits of HTML—aka "The DOM"" in Chapter 1). We use this to tell us how far we need to scroll to reach the very end of the images. When we click on the images, our scroll effect toggles between the start and end of the images.

This is great if we have less than two screen width's worth of images. But if we have more, we'll be unable to see all the images that lie in between the six on either end, so we need a different approach. A better way is to scroll, say, a half-screen's worth of images at a time. When we reach the end of the list, we'll scroll back to the start. Let's expand on our code to make it more bulletproof:

```
chapter_04/12_thumbnail_scroller_improved/script.js (excerpt)

$('#photos_inner').click(function() {
  var scrollAmount = $(this).width() - $(this).parent().width(); ❶
  var currentPos = Math.abs(parseInt($(this).css('left'))); ❷
  var remainingScroll = scrollAmount - currentPos; ❸

  // Scroll half-a-screen by default
  var nextScroll = Math.floor($(this).parent().width() / 2); ❹

  // But if there isn't a FULL scroll left,
  // only scroll the remaining amount.
  if (remainingScroll < nextScroll) { ❺
    nextScroll = remainingScroll;
  }

  if (currentScrollPos < scrollAmount) { ❻
    // Scroll left
    $(this).animate({'left':'-=' + nextScroll}, 'slow');
  }
  else{
    // Scroll right
    $(this).animate({'left':'0'}, 'fast');
  }
});
```

Woah, that's certainly more code—but if you walk through line by line, you'll see that it's all fairly uncomplicated. We're using quite a lot of variables, and because we've given them clear names, it helps to make the code a little easier to understand:

❶ As in the previous example, we first calculate the total amount of scrolling space we have: our `scrollAmount` variable.

❷ Because our new scroller needs to be able to handle more than two screens' worth of images, we also need to figure out how far along we currently are. We use the JavaScript function `Math.abs()` to convert the current scroll position to a positive number, because scrolling to the left means we're moving the elements into negative territory. If your high school math is deep down in your memory, here's a refresher: the absolute value of a number will always be its positive value, whether the number itself is positive or negative. So `Math.abs(3)` is 3, and `Math.abs(-3)` is also 3.

❸ We know how much space there is in total, and we also know how far along we are—so it's simple to find out how far we have to go! Just subtract the latter number from the former.

❹ Now for the real business: we need to calculate how far to scroll. By default, this will be half of the total width of our image container. (`Math.floor()` is a way of rounding an image down, so we're sure we end up with a round number.) We store the distance we want to scroll in the `nextScroll` variable.

❺ If there's less space left than what we want to scroll, we'll change our `nextScroll` variable to only bring us to the end of the images.

❻ Finally, we scroll. If we've yet to reach the end of the images (if our current position is less than the total scrollable width), we scroll to the left by the amount we calculated. Otherwise (if we're at the end of the images), we scroll all the way back to the beginning.

If you think that's a lot of code for a fairly basic effect, you're right! If only there was a way of scrolling content without doing all that math …

A Scrolling Gallery with scrollTo

You might remember that back when we looked at scrolling in Chapter 3, we mentioned a particularly useful plugin for scrolling the page: scrollTo. As well as scrolling the entire page, the scrollTo plugin excels in scrolling overflowed elements (like those in a picture gallery) too! In our first stab at a scrolling thumbnail gallery, we had to do quite a few of our own calculations to determine how big the scrollable area was, and whether we were at the end or the start of the container.

The scrollTo plugin automatically figures a lot of this out for us, so we can concentrate on adding more complex features. In this demo we're going to remove our list of thumbnails, and replace them with larger images. The large images will be contained in a grid—but we're only going to display one at a time. When the user clicks on the image, we'll scroll around the grid, and stop on a new random picture.

To start off, we'll need a list of pictures. For simplicity, we'll just set it up as a swag of image tags, inside a div container—itself contained inside another div. You might like to set it up as an unordered list of images inside a div, to be semantically nicer, but what we need to end up with is a block level element that's as big and wide as

our grid. This needs to be inside an element with `overflow: hidden` (or `auto`).
Here's what we mean:

```
chapter_04/13_scrolling_gallery/index.html (excerpt)
```

```html
<div id="photos">
  <div id="photos_inner">
    <img class="pic" src="Image_01.jpg" />
    <img class="pic" src="Image_02.jpg" />
    …
    <img class="pic" src="Image_12.jpg" />
  </div>
</div>
```

We'll make the pic_container `div` the width of, say, three images and the height of
four images; the pictures, therefore, will be confined to a 3x4 grid. For this demo,
we'll be using images that are 200x200px, so our container needs to be 800px wide
and 600px high. We'll then make the visible region the size of a single image, and
hide all the rest:

```
chapter_04/13_scrolling_gallery/style.css (excerpt)
```

```css
#pic_container {
  width:1200px;
  height:1000px;
}

#pic_scroller {
  overflow:hidden;
  height:250px;
  width:400px;
}
```

Now that our grid is ready, we can add some random scrolling pixie dust. We first
grab all the images, then choose a random one and scroll to it using `scrollTo`:

```
                      chapter_04/13_scrolling_gallery/script.js (excerpt)
$('#pic_scroller').click(function() {
  var numberOfPics = $(this).find('div > img').length;
  var next = Math.floor(Math.random() * numberOfPics);
  $(this)
    .scrollTo(
      '#photos_inner>img:eq(' + next + ')',
      {duration: 1000}
    );
});
```

That's certainly a lot simpler than our last example! The plugin takes care of almost all the complicated parts. That said, there are two new bits of jQuery in there: the `find` action, and the `:eq` filter. `find` functions in much the same way as the main jQuery `$` selector itself, except that it searches only within the currently selected element, rather than the whole document.

The `:eq` filter works exactly like the `eq` action we saw earlier, except that it's a filter, so you use it inside a selector string. We pass it a random number between 0 and the total number of images to select a random image.

 Random Numbers

> `Math.random` will give you a random number between 0 and 1. More often, though, you're looking for random whole numbers in a given range. The easiest way to achieve this is by writing `Math.floor(Math.random() * maximum)`. You multiply the fraction by the maximum number you'd like, then round it down to the nearest whole number.

Notice how easy it is to ask scrollTo to scroll to a specific element: we simply pass it a selector that will match that element!

Smarter Scrolling with the `data` Action

There's a fairly big problem with the component we've built, however, especially if you have a small number of images: the next random image to display might be the same one we're currently on! In this case no scrolling takes place, making it feel like a bug. To remedy this, we need to keep track of what the last image was:

```
                    chapter_04/14_scrolling_gallery_improved/script.js (excerpt)
$('#pic_scroller').click(function() {
  var numberOfPics = $(this).find('div > img').length;
  var last = $(this).data('last');
  var next = Math.floor(Math.random() * numberOfPics);
  if (next == last) {
    next = (next + 1) % numberOfPics;
  }
  $(this)
    .data('last', next)
    .scrollTo(
      '#photos_inner>img:eq(' + next + ')',
      {duration: 1000});
});
```

We're using a new and extremely powerful jQuery action: `data`. `data` is unlike any action we've seen so far, because it allows us to store information in any jQuery object. We call it with two parameters to store data. The first parameter becomes the name of the data item, and the second is the value to store. Then, to retrieve data, we pass in only one parameter: the name of the data item.

In our improved example, once we find the image we're going to scroll to, we store the number element with the command `$(this).data('last', next)`. The next time the scroller element is clicked, we read it back again with the command `$(this).data('last')`. If our new element is the same as our last, we simply add 1 to it to scroll to the next image. (We use the modulus again to ensure we stay within the total number of images).

You should carefully study the two lines of code where we retrieve and set data on the element (highlighted above). We'll be using this amazing jQuery feature a lot in the coming chapters, so do yourself a favor—commit it to memory, and play with it as much as you can!

iPhoto-like Slideshow widget

We'll look at a more advanced slideshow by building an iPhoto-like widget (iPhoto is the included image gallery application in Mac OS X). Mousing over the left or right side of the current image will scroll to the next or previous image, so the user can flip casually through the gallery. This is the most advanced jQuery we've seen so far, and it might be difficult for you to make complete sense of it the first time around. We'll be exploring many of the concepts employed here in more detail in the coming chapters, so don't worry if you need to skip this one for now and come back to it later.

Let's base our slideshow on a familiar list of images. We'll wrap the list in a `div`, which will allow us to constrain the thumbnails and add an anchor that will serve as our trigger:

chapter_04/15_iphoto_style_slideshow/index.html *(excerpt)*

```
<h2>Around town last night</h2>
<div id="photos">
  <a href="#" class="trigger">Image Gallery</a>
  <ul id="photos_inner">
    <li>
      <img alt="Glendatronix" src="../../images/glenda_400.jpg" />
    </li>
    <li>
      <img alt="Darth Fader" src="../../images/fader_400.jpg" />
    </li>
    ⋮
  </ul>
</div>
```

If a user views our page with both CSS and JavaScript turned off, they'll simply see a huge stack of images. While it's far from being the great experience we hoped to provide, we have given them full access to our content. If only JavaScript is disabled, all but one of the images will be hidden—but we'll overlay a link to the full gallery page on top of the gallery, so clicking it will bring users through to a traditional HTML gallery page. Let's start our slideshow enhancements with the CSS:

chapter_04/15_iphoto_style_slideshow/style.css *(excerpt)*

```css
#photos {
  border: 1px solid #BEBEBE;
  height: 400px;
  overflow: hidden;
  position: relative;
  width: 400px;
}

#photos ul {
  left: 0;
  list-style-type: none;
  margin: 0;
  padding: 0;
  position: absolute;
  top: 0;
  width: 2400px;
}

#photos li {
  float: left;
}

#photos .trigger {
  left: 0;
  position: absolute;
  top: 0;
  z-index: 10;
  text-indent: -9999px;
  height: 400px;
  width: 400px;
  display: block;
}
```

Starting with the container div, we set up the display constraints. Our images are 400 pixels square, so that's the dimensions for our container. Should the images have been of varying sizes, you could simply set the container's proportions to the size of the largest image it would need to contain. The overflow: hidden; means that none of our thumbnails will peek through unexpectedly. For our unordered list of images, we control the positioning ahead of creating the slide, and as we know we'll be using ten images, we set the list width to 2400px. In a dynamic web application, this would need to be set on the server side—depending on how many images were in the gallery, of course.

The last touch with the CSS positions the trigger anchor to cover the gallery image completely, and hide its text with `text-indent: -9999px`. That sorted, let's dive into the jQuery!

Creating a Widget

The definition of a widget is quite varied, but we're using it here to mean a stand-alone piece of functionality that we can reuse in our future projects. The real purpose of a widget is to cordon off our code into a handy package. We'll be doing this more and more throughout the book (and there's an in-depth look at it coming up in the section called "Namespacing Your Code" in Chapter 6), so the structure and ideas will become quite familiar to you by the end!

The basis for our widget is a JavaScript object literal (the same kind we've been using to pass sets of multiple options to jQuery actions) to define the name of our widget: `var gallery = {};`. As we've seen so far, object literals are enclosed in curly braces (`{}`). The object is empty to start with, but we'll be filling it up soon enough. Putting all our code in an object like this will give our code a named boundary, which limits the chance of any of our scripts conflicting with others that may be in the page. Setting up an empty object is how we'll begin implementing most of our widgets.

Next, we can add properties and methods to make our widget actually perform functions. By adding properties to our object, we remove the risk that any variables in the page might be overwritten by other scripts:

chapter_04/15_iphoto_style_slideshow/script.js *(excerpt)*

```
gallery.trigger = $("#photoshow .photoshow-trigger");
gallery.content = $("#photoshow .photoshow-content");
gallery.scroll = false;
gallery.width = 240;
gallery.innerWidth = gallery.content.width();
gallery.timer = false;
```

When we write `gallery.timer = false`, it's the same as if we'd written:

```
var gallery = {
  var timer = false;
}
```

The . (dot) notation is a shortcut for reading and writing properties of objects from outside of the object's declaration. If it's a little unclear, be assured it will make more and more sense as you see it used in our examples.

Let's take a look at what we've made for ourselves: `gallery.trigger` is a reference to a jQuery selection of our trigger link, and `gallery.content` is our list of images. We can now utilize these much shorter names, which saves us typing out the full selector string every time we want to use them. It also means we can easily point out a script at a different gallery on a different page, just by changing these values.

The next properties we assign to our `gallery` object are functions. We have `gallery.offset`, which sets how far we move the sliding list; `gallery.slide`, which moves the list and causes it to keep moving; the cunningly named `gallery.direction` that sets the direction of the slideshow's scroll; and a trusty initializing method, `gallery.init`. Let's take a look at each in turn:

chapter_04/15_iphoto_style_slideshow/script.js *(excerpt)*

```
gallery.offset = function() {
  var left = gallery.content.position().left;
  if (gallery.scroll == '>') {
    if (left < 0) {
      left += gallery.width;
    }
  } else {
    if (left <= 0 && left >= ((gallery.innerWidth * -1) +
➥(gallery.width * 2))) {
      left -= gallery.width;
    }
  }
  return left + "px";
}
```

The first task we do in `gallery.offset` is set a variable holding the `left` property of our list relative to the holding `div`. By using `position` rather than `offset`, jQuery saves us the trouble of working where the gallery is relative to the viewport.

We then check the direction we want to scroll the thumbnails, and that we still have room to scroll, and if all's well we generate the new value for `left` (by adding our 400px `width` property to the current `left` value) and return it. Note that we need to add `"px"` to the value before returning it, since we'll be using it as a CSS property.

So `gallery.offset` does nothing but calculate how far to slide the gallery along. You might be thinking, "Why not just calculate that inside the `gallery.slide` function?" By moving this functionality into its own method we make it more usable, should we ever need to access it from a different context than sliding the gallery. It also helps us to avoid nesting our code too deeply, which would make it more difficult to read. Here's the function:

```
                                    chapter_04/15_iphoto_style_slideshow/script.js (excerpt)
gallery.slide = function() {
  if (gallery.timer) {
    clearTimeout(gallery.timer);
  }
  if (gallery.scroll) {
    $(gallery.content)
      .stop(true,true)
      .animate({left: gallery.offset()}, 500);
    gallery.timer = setTimeout(gallery.slide, 1000);
  }
}
```

Our `slide` method's first job is to check if `gallery.timer` is set. If it is, `setTimeout` has already been called, so we call `clearTimeout` just to be on the safe side. We don't let the scroll happen unless we're sure we want it! We then check `gallery.scroll` to see if the scroll should happen. If the user moves the cursor off the widget between scrolls, we want to stop any more scrolling from occurring. If they're still hovering over the widget, though, we call jQuery's `animate` method on the `left` property of `gallery.content`. This will scroll our gallery smoothly to the side. We're again making use of `stop(true,true)` to prevent animations from piling up in the queue.

The `animate` duration is set to 500, so it's nice and zippy, and happens in plenty of time before the next scroll is scheduled using `setTimeout`. `setTimeout` is applied to the `gallery.timer` property, which is what we checked for earlier, and 500 milliseconds after the animation finishes the next scroll attempt occurs (since we set the timer for 1,000, which is 500 more than the animation). But which way are we going to scroll? gallery.direction sorts that out for us, like so:

chapter_04/15_iphoto_style_slideshow/script.js *(excerpt)*

```
gallery.direction = function(e,which) {
  var x = e.pageX - which.offset().left;
  gallery.scroll = (x >= gallery.width / 2) ? ">" : "<";
}
```

When the initializing method calls gallery.direction, it passes in two parameters: e for the event that's causing the scroll, and which to hold a reference to the element that triggered the scroll. We'll be diving in to the e parameter in the section called "Event Handler Parameters" shortly, but for now all you need to know is that this parameter allows us to access the coordinates on the page where the event took place. Using this e.pageX, we can calculate the distance from the left-hand edge of the trigger link to the cursor. This number in hand, we use the ternary operator (see the section called "Fading Slideshow") to assign a value to gallery.scroll: ">" if the cursor is right of center, or else "<".

The last method we need to look at is our widget's initializer, gallery.init:

chapter_04/15_iphoto_style_slideshow/script.js *(excerpt)*

```
gallery.init = function() {
  $(gallery.trigger)
    .mouseout(function() {gallery.scroll = false;})
    .mousemove(function(e) {gallery.direction(e,gallery.trigger);})
    .mouseover(function(e) {
      gallery.direction(e,gallery.trigger);
      gallery.slide();
    });
}
```

By now you should be quite accustomed to everything we're doing. gallery.init just chains jQuery methods on the jQuery object selected by gallery.trigger. Let's break that chain down a little.

mouseout sets gallery.scroll to false. This is the property we check to make sure the user wants us to continue scrolling. mousemove calls gallery.direction, which in turn sets `gallery.scroll` as we saw earlier. And lastly, `mouseover` also calls `gallery.direction`, but also adds `gallery.slide` to the mix. By calling `gallery.direction` from the initial mouseover and from any subsequent mouse moves, we ensure that the direction of the scrolling is always properly set.

And there you have it. Add in a `$(document).ready()` to delay the enhancement until the DOM is available, and all you need now are happy site visitors who want to see what your gallery has to offer.

Many of the techniques we employed in building this widget are probably new to you, so you might be feeling a little overwhelmed! In the coming chapters we'll be revisiting them in different forms, and before you know it, they'll be second nature. Before moving on to the next round of changes to StarTrackr!, let's just have a quick look at how we accessed the `mouseover` event's position on the page from within our callback.

Event Handler Parameters

We've seen more than our fair share of event handler callback functions now, but if you look closely at the `mouseover` handler above, you might notice an imposter: e. e is the name we've given to the optional parameter that all jQuery event handlers can receive. We've not seen it until now as it hasn't been required for any of the effects we've implemented so far.

When an event handler is called, jQuery passes in an event object that contains details and data about the event that occurred. The kind of data depends on the kind of event: a `keypress` event will contain information about which key was pressed, a `click` event will contain the location of the click, and so on. jQuery performs some magic on the events so that the same information is available, regardless of which browser the user has.

 Naming the Event Parameter

You certainly don't have to call the event object e—it's just a parameter name, so you can call it whatever you want. The aliases e or `evnt` are fairly standard. People tend to shy away from using `event`, as various browsers respond to `event` as a keyword, so it's best to play it safe and avoid errors.

Anyway, back to the code! The `mouseover` event fires whenever the user moves their mouse over the navigation item. We catch the `e` parameter in our event handler and pass it on to `gallery.direction`. As we've seen, this contains some specific information about the event, such as where it occurred. We use this information to calculate the mouse's horizontal position on the gallery widget:

chapter_04/15_iphoto_style_slideshow/script.js *(excerpt)*

```
var x = e.pageX - which.offset().left;
```

This gives us a number in pixels. We then compare this value to half of the gallery's width. If the number is smaller, we're on the left side; otherwise, we're on the right. This allows us to determine which direction to scroll:

chapter_04/15_iphoto_style_slideshow/script.js *(excerpt)*

```
gallery.scroll = (x >= gallery.width / 2) ? ">" : "<";
```

`pageX` is just one of the many available properties of the event object. We'll be seeing a few more in the next chapter, and there's a full list in the section called "Events" in Appendix A.

Image-ine That!

Milestone time! The widget object we've created, using named variables and functions, is the weapon of choice of a true jQuery ninja! It makes your code readable, concise, and, most importantly, reusable. You've also mastered timers and event objects, which could be equated to flash-bombs and throwing stars, were one feeling particularly metaphorical. There'll be no holding you back soon.

The StarTrackr! site is definitely looking more alive, now that we've added slideshows, lightboxes, and some classy cross-fades. Our client (and his investors) are ecstatic, and he has another series of changes he'd like to see on the site as soon as possible. That's more work for us, which means more jQuery goodness is on the way!

Chapter 5

Menus, Tabs, Tooltips, and Panels

jQuery is certainly a master of the DOM—effortlessly moving things around, animating CSS properties, and manipulating element attributes to help us spice up our static content. But static content is a shrinking part of the Web; more and more fully featured, highly functional, and impressive looking applications are sprouting up every day. This chapter sees us move away from static documents, and into the world of bells and whistles for Rich Internet Applications (RIA).

Our client, specifically the owner-operator of the recently popular StarTrackr! celebrity geotagging and stalking web site, has been reading some business magazines; he's learned the term RIA, and is determined to use it as much as possible. He'd like to see his site move away from simple brochureware and become an online application where users can easily and enjoyably hunt their favorite stars. Which, of course, means we can move onto some really fun stuff.

This chapter is all about the user interface: we'll look at grouping content logically and providing the user with easy access through drop-down menus, tabbed interfaces, sliding panels, tooltips, and accordion controls. With these tools under your belt, you'll be ready to organize even the most complex interface into discrete chunks that are easy and fun to play around with!

Menus

We've tinkered with a few menus already, but they've mostly been simple, top-level navigation panes. In this section we will have a look at applying jQuery to more intricate menu-style navigation controls: collapsible and drop-down menus.

As the StarTrackr! site grows larger (and our client's requests become more elaborate), the navigation structure can grow unwieldy and become potentially confusing to our users. A well-crafted menu allows us to categorize our content structure while minimizing the valuable screen space it consumes.

Expandable/Collapsible Menus

A common feature of vertical site navigation is a submenu system, where links are grouped into similar categories. This makes it easy for the user to find relevant information and, by allowing the top-level categories to be expanded and collapsed, lets us store a large amount of information in a relatively small area. It also looks cool when menus slide open and close shut. A simple and effective expandable menu is very easy to set up; in fact, we learned most of the code required for a menu way back in Chapter 2. We'll start by creating a simple menu, and then add a few extra features to it. Our initial menu will look like the one in Figure 5.1.

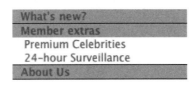

Figure 5.1. Expandable menus

These days (and until the HTML 5 `navigation` tag becomes standard) almost all navigational controls are created using unordered lists. From a semantic standpoint this is perfectly sensible, after all, a navigation menu is just a list of links. For our expandable menu, we'll start off with a set of nested lists:

chapter_05/01_expandable_menus/index.html *(excerpt)*

```html
<ul id="menu">
  <li><a href="#">What's new?</a>
    <ul class="active">
      <li><a href="#">Weekly specials</a></li>
      <li><a href="#">Last night's pics!</a></li>
      <li><a href="#">Users' comments</a></li>
    </ul>
  </li>
  <li><a href="#">Member extras</a>
    <ul>
      <li><a href="#">Premium Celebrities</a></li>
      <li><a href="#">24-hour Surveillance</a></li>
        ⋮
```

Now let's give it a few basic styles so that we're working with a nicer-looking menu:

chapter_05/01_expandable_menus/menus.css *(excerpt)*

```css
#menu, #menu ul {
  list-style-type: none;
  padding: 0;
  margin: 0;
}

#menu li {
  cursor: pointer;
  background: #94C5EB;
  border-bottom: 1px solid #444;
}

#menu li a { text-decoration: none; }

#menu > li > a {
  padding: 2px 10px;
  font-weight: bold;
}

#menu li li {
  cursor: auto;
  border: 0;
  padding: 0 14px;
  background-color: #fff;
}
```

We're using a CSS child selector to style the top-level links differently from the nested ones. This is supported in all modern browsers, but if you require support for Internet Explorer 6, you can simply add a class to your markup and base your styles on that.

Since we'll be reacting to a click event anywhere on the top-level list items (including areas not covered by the anchors), we set a pointer cursor on those elements so that users can easily tell that they're clickable.

As it stands, we have a nice, multilevel menu. All the items are visible, which is a fine behavior for browsers without JavaScript capabilities. Now we can progressively enhance this behavior. First, we hide all of the categories' items:

chapter_05/01_expandable_menus/script.js *(excerpt)*

```
$('#menu > li > ul')
  .hide()
  .click(function(e) {
    e.stopPropagation();
  });
```

We're using the child selector to ensure we avoid accidentally hiding elements that are nested further down the menu structure. This way, if you decide to nest your menu more than one level deep, your code will still function as intended.

You may be wondering about the strange `e.stopPropagation()` line in this block. We'll cover that shortly, but first let's finalize our effect with a `toggle` function to slide the menu up and down:

chapter_05/01_expandable_menus/script.js *(excerpt)*

```
$('#menu > li').toggle(function() {
  $(this).find('ul').slideDown();
}, function() {
  $(this).find('ul').slideUp();
});
```

Run this in your browser and you'll see that we've created a perfectly functional multilevel menu. Before we move on to enhancing it with some additional niceties, let's have a look at what that `stopPropagation` function is doing.

Event Propagation

Event propagation describes the flow of an event through the DOM hierarchy. When an event is fired from an element, any handlers on that element will be given a chance to catch the event. After this processing has occurred, the event is passed further up the DOM tree, giving parent elements a chance to process the event. This makes sense: when you click on a link inside a paragraph, you're *also* clicking on the paragraph itself, so event handlers on both elements should have the chance to react.

The easiest way to understand event propagation is to see it in action. To illustrate this concept we'll set up a quick little experiment. It will consist of the following basic markup: two divs, one inside the other. The outer and inner divs will have ids of outer and inner, respectively:

```
chapter_05/02_event_propagation/index.html (excerpt)
<div id="outer">
  Click Outer!
  <div id="inner">
    Click Inner!
  </div>
</div>
```

Next, we'll add a click handler to each of the div elements, so that when we click on an element an alert will pop up and tell us the element's name:

```
chapter_05/02_event_propagation/script.js (excerpt)
$('div').click(function() {
  alert('Hello from ' + $(this).attr('id'));
});
```

First, click on the outer div: unsurprisingly, you'll see an alert saying "Hello from outer." Now, click on the inner div. You'll see the expected "Hello from inner." But then you'll also see "Hello from outer" … what gives? We only clicked once, so why are we seeing two click events?

As you probably guessed, rather than two click events, it's actually *one* click event happening in *two different places*. The event starts at our inner div and checks to see if there are any event handlers attached to it. It then **bubbles** (or propagates) up to the `div`'s parent element (in this case the outer `div`), and checks to see if there are any event handlers attached that element. The event continues to bubble up the DOM hierarchy until there are no more parents available.

This event bubbling is desirable in many cases; we'll often want to handle the same event at multiple levels of the DOM. For example, if we wanted to set a parent node's class when any children were clicked, it would be far more efficient to add an event handler to the parent node itself than to add a handler to each child. But we still want to be able to attach individual click handlers to any of the children.

On the other hand, it can be undesirable to have an event to bubble up. Sometimes we want the child node to stop the event going any further. As an example, imagine we were making a Whac-A-Mole type game. The game is made up of two parts: a game board and some moles. The moles randomly appear on the screen for a few seconds and then disappear. We might want to attach a handler to each mole to detect a direct hit, and another handler to the game board to detect a miss. With event propagation, we'd end up recording both a hit and a miss as the event bubbled up to our game board.

There are a few techniques available for controlling event propagation. A common JavaScript technique is simply to return `false` from the event handler. This works fine, and is supported across all major browsers. However, jQuery's event system normalizes all events to the W3C standard, which means there's no need to worry about how different browsers treat different edge cases.

To stop event propagation using jQuery we use the `stopPropagation` method, as we did above in our expandable menu code. As we did at the end of the last chapter, we pass our anonymous callback function an `e` parameter to hold the event. Then we simply call `stopPropagation` on that event, and it will cease propagating further up the DOM.

Default Event Actions

Now is probably a good time to discuss another common method for controlling event flow: `preventDefault`. The `preventDefault` command stops the browser from executing the default action that an event would normally perform. Its most common use is stopping a link from loading its target when clicked:

```
$('a').click(function(e) {
  e.preventDefault();
});
```

This code effectively disables every link on the page. It's highly unusual to want to do this to every link, of course, but it's common to override a link's action this way when we're implementing progressive enhancements—such as the lightbox effect we saw in Chapter 4. If JavaScript is unavailable to a particular user, the link will work as normal. But if JavaScript is available, the normal link is replaced with our jQuery functionality.

A common technique left over from the old days of JavaScript development is to simply return `false` from the event handler to prevent the default actions. You need to be aware, though, that using this method in a jQuery handler has the same effect as calling both `preventDefault` and `stopPropagation`.

You can also use the commands `isDefaultPrevented` and `isPropagationStopped` to test whether an event's flow has been modified. As might be implied from their names, these functions will return `true` if the default action has been prevented or the event propagation stopped respectively, and `false` otherwise.

Open/Closed Indicators

Our menu control is functioning as planned, so it's time to abide by the inescapable jQuery law: if it ain't broke, add some bells and whistles to it!

The first tweak we'll implement is the addition of open/closed indicators to the right of the section headings, as shown in Figure 5.2.

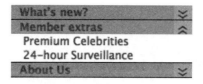

Figure 5.2. Open/closed indicators

You've probably seen this kind of indicator before on the Web (or in desktop applications, for that matter). They usually take the form of small triangles whose direction serves to indicate whether the menu is open or closed. They're extremely helpful, as they provide a hint to the user that there's hidden information to be revealed.

We'll use a CSS sprite to add an indicator to our menu; a single image will contain both the contracted (down-facing) and expanded (up-facing) arrows for our menu sections.

By default, all of the sections are closed, so we show the contracted arrow state in our CSS. In our sprite image the contracted state is aligned to the top, while the expanded state is 20 pixels below the top. We apply this background image to `li` elements inside the menu, and then remove it from deeper nested items:

chapter_05/03_open_closed_indicators/menu.css (excerpt)

```css
#menu li {
  cursor:pointer;
  border-bottom:1px solid #444;
  background: #94C5EB url(arrows.png) no-repeat right top;
}
⋮
#menu li li {
  cursor:auto;
  border:0;
  padding:0 14px;
  background-color:#fff;
  background-image: none;
}
```

With our background image in place, we now need to adjust the CSS sprite's position whenever we toggle a menu item. When the menu item slides down we show the expanded state, and when it slides up we show the contracted state. We'll make clever use of chaining to apply the `css` action before we drill down to find the `ul` to show or hide:

chapter_05/03_open_closed_indicators/script.js (excerpt)

```javascript
$('#menu > li').toggle(function() {
  $(this)
    .css('background-position', 'right -20px')
    .find('ul').slideDown();
}, function() {
  $(this)
    .css('background-position', 'right top')
    .find('ul').slideUp();
});
```

Menu Expand on Hover

For our next trick, we want to make the menu respond to hover events as well as click events. When a user hovers over one of our parent menu items, we'll pause briefly, then expand the menu. Now, you've already seen enough toggle and hover effects to last a lifetime (and don't worry, there's plenty more to come!) so we'll give this one a twist. The jQuery hover event fires the instant you move your mouse over the target item. But for this effect we'll delay the execution so that it only fires if the user hovers for a short while. Otherwise, the control would be virtually unusable, as it would snap open and closed if you so much as grazed it with the mouse.

It's a subtle but important change—and if you try the menu both with and without a delay as follows, you'll notice that the feel of the control is altered dramatically:

```
                          chapter_05/04_menu_expand_on_hover/script.js (excerpt)
$('#menu > li').hover(function() {
  $(this).addClass('waiting');
  setTimeout(function() {
    $('#menu .waiting')
      .click()
      .removeClass('waiting');
  }, 600);
}, function() {
  $('#menu .waiting').removeClass('waiting');
});
```

When the user first mouses over the menu element, we add a class called waiting to the menu item, then set a timer for 600 milliseconds. If the user moves the mouse away from the menu item before the delay concludes, we remove the class.

Once the delay expires it looks for a menu item containing the waiting class (which will only exist if the user hasn't moved the mouse away). If the user is still waiting, we "click" the menu item, causing the effect to fire. This is the first time we've seen the click action used in this way; when called without parameters, it actually fires the click event on the targeted element(s), rather than setting up an event handler. Finally, once we fire the effect we remove the class—so we're back to square one. We also need to modify the click action we defined earlier. As it is, if a user mouses over a menu and then clicks it, the waiting class will cause it to close when the timer goes off. We simply need to add the same `removeClass` call to the click handler.

What we're doing—and we've done this before with earlier effects—is use classes to provide state management. State management is just a fancy way of saying we provide the control with a way of remembering what "state" it is in. We want to remember if the user has moved away from the menu before the delay expires— so we add and remove the `waiting class` appropriately. Using class names for state management is a nifty trick—but it's certainly not the only (or best) way. We've already seen the data functionality provided by jQuery, which is a great way to store simple state information. For larger and more complex controls, we can also integrate state management into the widget's code—as we saw at the end of Chapter 4. As always, the method you use is dependent on the circumstance, and on what feels simplest to you.

Drop-down Menus

If you ever had to code a drop-down menu in the old days of the Web (using what was at the time referred to as DHTML), you'll know just how harrowing an experience it can be. There's an abundance of terrible scripts lingering online from those days but, thankfully, CSS has since stepped in to banish reams of JavaScript spaghetti code to the trash heap. The Suckerfish Drop-down[1] technique, and subsequent derivatives, provide an elegant solution to the problem of drop-down menus.

Suckerfish drop-downs work by carefully styling a list of lists into a drop-down structure, and then hiding the child menu items. The style sheet uses a `:hover` pseudo-selector to trigger the showing and hiding of the child items. This is a perfect JavaScript-free solution; as much as we love JavaScript, we should always aim to use simpler technologies such as CSS when they're suitable.

That said, there are some issues with using pure CSS drop-down menus. Some older browsers are unable to style the `:hover` pseudo selector on non-link elements, and even for those that can, the showing/hiding effect can be a little abrupt. The Suckerfish drop-downs make an excellent base for enhancement: they provide an adequate solution, which can then be improved and streamlined with jQuery. In this example, we'll be adapting the Suckerfish technique to work with browsers that have incom-

---

[1] http://www.alistapart.com/articles/dropdowns

plete support for :hover. We'll also make the drop-down effect a little sleeker with some jQuery animation.

Cross-browser Suckerfish Menus

First, let's set up a simple Suckerfish drop-down as our baseline. We'll be using the same markup we used for the expandable navigation in the section called "Expandable/Collapsible Menus".

The CSS is straight out of the Suckerfish playbook, and will mold the unordered list into a simple horizontal menu. The only additional aspect to pay attention to is the extra class we've attached to the :hover CSS declaration. We'll need this to keep our menu drop-down visible when it otherwise wouldn't be:

chapter_05/05_dropdown_menu/menus.css

```css
#container {
  position: relative;
}

#menu {
  position: absolute;
  top: 0;
  right: 0;
}

#menu, #menu ul {
  padding: 0;
  margin: 0;
  list-style: none;
}

#menu li {
  float: left;
  background: #FFF;
}

#menu a {
  display: block;
  padding: 4px;
  width: 10em;
}
```

```
#menu li ul {
  position: absolute;
  width: 10em;
  left: -999em;
}

#menu li:hover ul, #menu li ul:hover {
  left:auto;
}
```

If you try this on most browsers, you'll be pleasantly surprised: a fully working menu system with no JavaScript! What we want to do now is layer some jQuery on top of this effect so that it functions in older browsers, and animates a bit more smoothly. Our target functionality is illustrated in Figure 5.3.

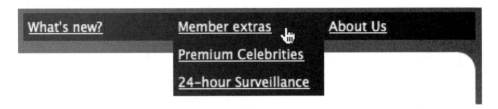

Figure 5.3. Our drop-down menu in action

So how do we replicate this effect using jQuery? "Simple," you might scoff. "Just add a hover action with a slide-down effect." And you'd be right: adding a simple hover function would give us the desired behavior, but there's a problem. What happens when we implement the same functionality in both our CSS and our script? Who wins in the fight between CSS `:hover` and jQuery `hover`? It's messy—they're very evenly matched!

One obvious workaround would be to override the CSS class in our hover event handler. But this will fail, as you're unable (currently) to target pseudo selectors in jQuery to set CSS properties:

```
$('#nav li:hover ul').css('left', '-999px'); // doesn't work!
```

That puts us in a quandary: how can we keep the goodness of Suckerfish CSS menus, but still apply our jQuery enhancements? One solution would be to carefully undo the CSS properties as we hover—but an easier way is to take over the child menu item's CSS properties, regardless of whether we're hovering or not:

```
                                    chapter_05/05_dropdown_menu/script.js (excerpt)
$('#menu li ul').css({
   display: "none",
   left: "auto"
});
$('#menu li').hover(function() {
   $(this)
      .find('ul')
      .stop(true, true)
      .slideDown('fast');
}, function() {
   $(this)
      .find('ul')
      .stop(true,true)
      .fadeOut('fast');
});
```

The first part of this script overrides the CSS we set earlier and hides the submenus using `display: "none"`. When the user hovers over a list item, we find the related child list container and display it. Here we've used `slideDown` and `fadeOut`—but you'll be able to come up with some wacky easing options and CSS background sprites to liven it up. The `stop(true, true)` command, as we saw in the section called "Animated Navigation" in Chapter 3, ensures that the menu will refrain from queuing up animations if we move the mouse around quickly.

The best aspect of this menu control is that when a user visits the site with JavaScript disabled, the Suckerfish drop-downs still work nicely—albeit without the animation effects.

Hover Intent

We've seen a few effects that are triggered by the mouseover event—and you may have noticed that they can sometimes feel a bit too eager to activate. The very instant you pass your mouse over a target element the effect springs to life, even if you're just passing through. This is excellent for making fluid animated effects, but sometimes we're after a different result. With our drop-down menus, the false start can appear unnecessary and distracting. We need a method of delaying the effect until we're sure that the user really wants to activate the target element.

Earlier, we saw a method for achieving this by setting a timer when the user moves over the element. But this has a few side effects. For example, if you have a small timer and a large target area, the user might fail to make it all the way across the element before the timer expires.

Brian Cherne implemented a nice workaround for this issue, in the form of the Hover Intent plugin.[2] Hover Intent has some smarts built into it to calculate the speed of the mouse as it moves across the elements. The effect will only kick in if the mouse slows down enough for the plugin to think the user *intends* to stop there.

Once you've included the plugin, you can use it wherever you'd normally use the hover action. As an example, if we wanted to add a delay to our drop-down menus from the previous section, we just need to replace the command hover with the command hoverIntent:

```
chapter_05/06_dropdown_with_hover_intent/script.js (excerpt)

$('#menu li').hoverIntent(function() {
  ⋮
}, function() {
  ⋮
});
```

The menu will only reveal itself when it thinks a user wants to see it. The best way to experience what this plugin is doing is to compare this example to the previous one, dragging the mouse horizontally across the menu. In our previous example, the menus will slide open in a wave as you move across them; when using hoverIntent, the menus will only slide open when the mouse comes to rest.

As with most plugins, the documentation outlines the handful of options you can specify to fine-tune the effect, so be sure to read through it if you plan on using this functionality.

Accordion Menus

Accordion menus are named after the musical instrument, in the way the expansion of one area leads to the contraction of another. Typically, accordions are fixed so that one—and only one—of the areas must be visible at all times, though some accordions let you collapse an already open area so that all items are hidden.

---

[2] http://cherne.net/brian/resources/jquery.hoverIntent.html

A Simple Accordion

Accordions can be trickier than you'd expect. We saw earlier how a simple expanding and collapsing menu system could be implemented in just a few lines of jQuery code. It's then reasonable for you to assume that adding a constraint (that only one menu element can be open at any time) would be straightforward. Although the basic implementation is indeed quite simple (this is jQuery, after all!), there are some caveats involved in enforcing more complex constraints that you should be aware of.

For this example, we'll be building a simple accordion to group celebrities according to their popularity; this will allow us to save quite a bit of precious screen real estate on the StarTrackr! site. The result we're aiming for is illustrated in Figure 5.4.

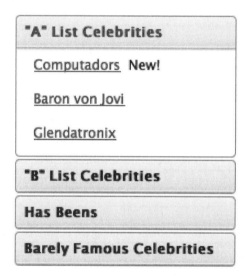

Figure 5.4. A simple accordion control

You can set up an accordion using virtually any structure of HTML markup; all you really need is a set of clearly identifiable headers, each associated with a block of content. For this example, we'll be using a set of nested lists, like this:

```
                          chapter_05/07_simple_accordion/index.html (excerpt)

<ul>
  <li class="active">
    "A" List Celebrities
    <ul>
      <li><a href="#">Computadors</a>  New!</li>
      <li><a href="#">Johny Stardust</a></li>
      <li><a href="#">Beau Dandy</a></li>
    </ul>
  </li>
  <li>
    "B" List Celebrities
    <ul>
      <li><a href="#">Sinusoidal Tendancies</a></li>
      <li><a href="#">Steve Extreme</a></li>
    </ul>
  </li>
  ⋮
</ul>
```

This list markup is an ideal HTML structure for a menu, but there are certainly
other options; you could just as easily use a set of nested divs, with header elements
providing the title of each section. Just about any structure is suitable, as long as
it's consistent and allows you to select all the header triggers and related content.
We've styled the list with some CSS, which you can consult in the sample code
archive.

When our page loads, all of our content areas are visible. By now you should know
what's coming next: we need to hide all of the content, except for our default item:

```
                           chapter_05/07_simple_accordion/script.js (excerpt)

$('#celebs ul > li ul')
  .click(function(e) {
    e.stopPropagation();
  })
  .filter(':not(:first)')
  .hide();
```

We've done this slightly differently than before. In this case we've also pre-empted
an issue that we'll have with event bubbling (covered in the section called "Event
Propagation"). This sort of statement really shows the power of jQuery: we start by

attaching an event listener to every content area, then filter down our selection to exclude the first area, and hide everything that's left.

The `filter` command is a really handy way of narrowing down a selection midstatement. Any elements that don't match the criteria passed to it are discarded from the selection and are no longer affected by subsequent jQuery commands. You can specify the criteria as a selector or as a function (see the note below). We've used filter selectors in the previous example (`:not` and `:first`)—but you can use any jQuery selector to help you find the elements you're after.

`:not` is a neat utility selector, as it selects the opposite of whatever follows it in parentheses. So `$(':not(p)')` will select every element that's not a paragraph, and `$('p:not(.active)')` will select paragraphs without the `active` class.

The opposite of the `filter` method is called `add`. Where `filter` removes elements from the selection, `add` appends new elements to the selection. By combining `filter` and `add`, you can do an awful lot of processing in a single jQuery chain—adding and removing elements as necessary along the way.

Advanced Use of `filter`

Sometimes you'll need to perform filters involving more sophisticated criteria; in these cases you can use a custom function to define your rules. The function is processed for each element in the jQuery selection. If it returns `true`, the element stays in the selection; otherwise, it's scrapped. As an example, let's keep every paragraph element that's either the third in the selection or has the `class active`:

```
$('p').filter(function(index) {
  return index == 2 || $(this).hasClass('active');
});
```

Notice that we have access to the zero-based index of each element in the selection, and that the scope is that of the current element? That's why we can refer to it with `$(this)`. You can include any amount of processing in your criteria function—just be sure to return `true` if you want to hold on to the element.

The code for the accordion effect needs to close any items that are open (as there should only ever be one open at a time), then open the item we clicked on. But there's a problem with this logic: if we click on an item that's already open, it will unnecessarily slide up and down. So first we need to check that the item we clicked on is already open:

chapter_05/07_simple_accordion/script.js *(excerpt)*

```
$('#celebs ul > li').click(function() {
  var selfClick = $(this).find('ul:first').is(':visible'); ❶
  if (!selfClick) { ❷
    $(this)
      .parent()
      .find('> li ul:visible')
      .slideToggle();
  }
  $(this)
    .find('ul:first')
    .slideToggle(); ❸
});
```

Let's break this code down:

❶   We check to make sure if the nested `ul` is visible using the `.is('visible')` construct, and store that result in a variable named `selfClick` (which will be `true` if the user has clicked on a section that's already open).

❷   We use the JavaScript `!` operator in an `if` statement to hide the visible section if it's not the one that was clicked on. `!` means 'not,' so the nested block of code will only be run if `selfClick` is not `true`.

❸   Finally, we toggle the state of the item we clicked on: it slides up if it's open, and down if it's closed.

The way we've coded our solution, it's possible for users to close the open section of the accordion, thus collapsing it entirely. If you'd rather enforce the rule that one item must always remain visible, you could adjust the code so that clicking on the open item will have no effect. This is quite simply done with a little basic JavaScript; if `selfClick` evaluates to `true`, we simply exit the function using the JavaScript `return` keyword:

chapter_05/08_simple_accordion_variant/script.js *(excerpt)*

```
$('#celebs ul > li').click(function() {
  var selfClick = $(this).find('ul:first').is(':visible');
  if (selfClick) {
    return;
  }
  $(this)
    .parent()
    .find('> li ul:visible')
    .slideToggle();
  $(this)
    .find('ul:first')
    .stop(true, true)
    .slideToggle();
});
```

Multiple-level Accordions

Earlier, we saw that you should set up your accordion HTML structure consistently —and here's why! If we've been specific enough with our jQuery selectors, adding another level to the accordion is as simple as including the next level in our event handlers. First of all, we add in the second level of menu items. We use exactly the same structure as the first level, but nest it inside the first level list item:

chapter_05/09_multi_level_accordion/index.html *(excerpt)*

```
<ul>
  <li class="active">"A" List Celebrities
    <ul>
      <li><a href="#">Computadors</a>  New!</li>
      <li>Rising Stars
        <ul>
          <li><a href="#">Johny Stardust</a></li>
          <li><a href="#">Beau Dandy</a></li>
        </ul>
      </li>
      <li>Falling Stars
        <ul>
          <li><a href="#">Kellie Kelly</a></li>
          <li><a href="#">Darth Fader</a></li>
            ⋮
```

For our single-level accordion, we attached our accordion code to all of the first-level children of the root list by using this code: `$('#accordion > li').click(…)`. As the structure of our nested list is exactly the same as before, we just need to apply the same code to the nested elements, which we can accomplish simply by adding them to the selector:

chapter_05/09_multi_level_accordion/script.js *(excerpt)*

```
$('#accordion > li, #accordion > li > ul > li').click(…);
```

If you follow that selector chain you'll see that we're adding the accordion code to the correct list items. We could have just added it to every list item, but it may lead to strange behavior with nested content, depending on your HTML structure. The resulting menu is shown in Figure 5.5.

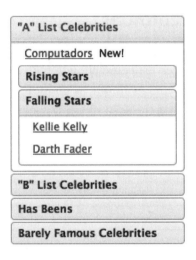

Figure 5.5. A multiple-level accordion menu

If you want to add more levels to the accordion, just repeat this process again. If the long selectors get out of hand, you could add an extra class to the root of each level; any more than a few levels, though, and perhaps there are more appropriate controls to better present your information, rather than accordions (see Chapter 8).

jQuery UI Accordion

As we've seen, it's easy to create a fairly complete accordion control from scratch using jQuery. However, the jQuery UI library also contains an accordion control, which includes an impressive range of options. These include changing icons, triggering on mouseover, and reacting in specific ways to the accordion's containing element (for example, you can choose to let the content areas have a fixed height or an auto height). An example of the jQuery UI accordion, using the Sunny theme, is shown in Figure 5.6.

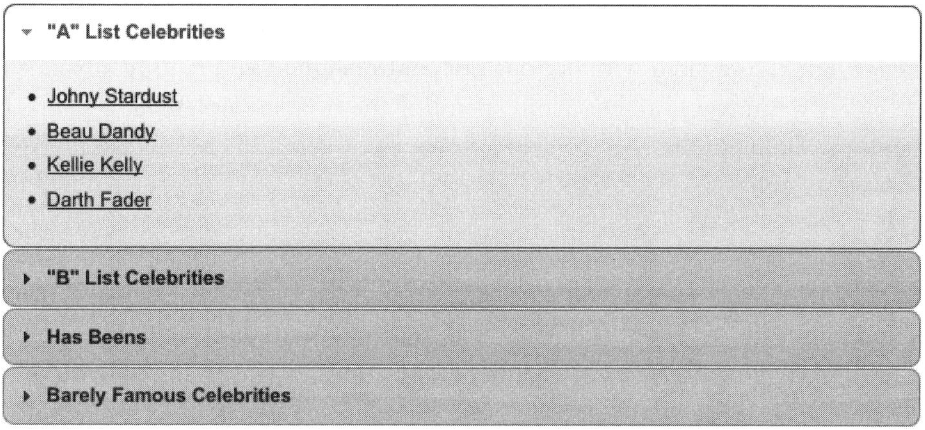

Figure 5.6. jQuery UI accordion control, with the Sunny theme

Like our custom accordion, the markup for the jQuery UI accordion requires pairs of headers and content elements. By default, it assumes that the headers are link tags and that the content immediately follows them; however, it will be confused if the content includes links, so it is usually best to specify a selector to help it determine which part of your content is the title:

```
chapter_05/10_jquery_ui_accordion/script.js (excerpt)
$('#accordion').accordion({header: 'h3'});
```

This is all the code you'll need to turn your content into a fully functional accordion, as long as the h3's next sibling is the content pane you want to hide or show.

The accordion also provides functionality to programmatically interact with the control. For example, you can open a particular content pane using the `activate` option, along with the index of the pane you want to open. To open the third pane (remember, indexes start from zero), you'd write the following:

```
                                    :chapter_05/10_jquery_ui_accordion/script.js (excerpt)

$("#accordion").accordion('activate', 2);
```

There are many other options available for configuring and interacting with the accordion, and these are well documented on the jQuery UI site.[3]

Using the jQuery UI control comes at a significant cost in terms of file size and bandwidth use compared with our custom control—but if you require advanced functionality and would rather avoid spending the time to implement it yourself, it can be a viable option.

Tabs

Tabs provide a way to group content logically, and have become a staple of many desktop applications' interfaces. They're also common on the Web, if you count top-level navigation elements styled to *look* like tabs. However, in the world of JavaScript, tabs are generally used to break content into multiple sections that can be swapped in order to save space.

Basic Tabs

Our simple tabs have all the content of the page preloaded—all we need to do is hide and show as required. If you've been following this book from the beginning, you can probably take a good guess at how to approach this.

We'll break the tabs control into two components: the tab navigation, and a content area. This lets us have an acceptable solution for browsers that are without support for JavaScript: a simple list of anchor links to elements on the page. It might look less spiffy than our cool tabs, but it's perfectly functional and provides access to all the same content. First, we'll set up our tab contents as a simple collection of div elements:

```
                                    chapter_05/11_simple_tabs/index.html (excerpt)

<div id="info">
  <p id="intro">
    Welcome to <strong>StarTrackr!</strong> the planet's premier …
```

---

[3] http://jqueryui.com/demos/accordion/

```
  <p id="about">
    StarTrackr! was founded in early 2009 when a young …
  </p>
  <p id="disclaimer">
    Disclaimer! This service is not intended for the those …
  </p>
</div>
```

Next, we need to create our tab navigation bar. As with so many controls and effects, it's the overall illusion that's important. An unordered list of links will do nicely, but we'll style them to look tab-like:

chapter_05/11_simple_tabs/index.html (excerpt)

```
<ul id="info-nav">
  <li><a href="#intro">Intro</a></li>
  <li><a href="#about">About Us</a></li>
  <li><a href="#disclaimer">Disclaimer</a></li>
</ul>
```

We've styled the links with CSS to have a tab-like appearance, but there are dozens of different ways of accomplishing this, so use whatever you're familiar with or what seems most sensible. We've opted for extremely basic styles, since what we want to focus on is the functionality.

The first task we'll do (after our document's ready) is hide all of the tabs except the first one—this will be our default tab. We could do this by hiding all the panes, and then showing the first one, like this:

```
$('#info p').hide().eq(0).show();
```

But this makes jQuery do more work than is necessary; we want to avoid hiding a tab only to show it again straight away. Instead, we can be more specific with our selector; we can combine filters to select everything except the first element:

chapter_05/11_simple_tabs/script.js (excerpt)

```
$('#info p:not(:first)').hide();
```

The important point is that once the page loads, only one tab content pane is displayed to the user. The code to switch tabs is straightforward, and quite similar to the other hide/show controls we've built so far:

```
chapter_05/11_simple_tabs/script.js (excerpt)

$('#info-nav li').click(function(e) {
  $('#info p').hide();
  $('#info-nav .current').removeClass("current");
  $(this).addClass('current');

  var clicked = $(this).find('a:first').attr('href');
  $('#info ' + clicked).fadeIn('fast');
  e.preventDefault();
}).eq(0).addClass('current');
```

There's one peculiar aspect worth pointing out: to select the content pane corresponding to the clicked link, we're joining the `href` attribute of the link directly to our selector using the JavaScript + operator. This only works because anchor links use the hash symbol (#) to identify their targets, and jQuery also uses the hash symbol to select elements by id. This is pure coincidence, but it's very fortunate for us as there's no need to parse the text or use regular expressions to create our selector.

After we've attached the click handler, we filter our navigation list to just the first element using the `eq` selector and add the `current` class to it. In our example the first tab is the default tab; if you want a different tab to be first, you need to change the `0` (as it's a zero-based index) to the one you'd prefer.

jQuery UI Tabs

While our basic tab solution provides a good foundation for us to build on, we're by no means the first people to attempt to build a tabbed content pane using jQuery. Enough people have demanded tabbed interfaces for the jQuery UI library to include a very feature-rich tab widget as part of its control collection.

Before you throw away our basic tabs in favor of the shiny jQuery UI tabs, think about what you want your tabs to do. With the jQuery knowledge you've acquired so far you should have no problems implementing many of the features yourself

—tasks like changing tabs on mouseover instead of on click, programmatically changing tabs, or collapsing a tab's content when you double-click on the tab itself.

One feature that would take us significantly more work to implement (at least for the moment) is the ability to load content via Ajax. We'll be looking at Ajax in a lot more detail in Chapter 6, but for the meantime we can have a look at the simplest possible use of it: loading content from the server into our page without refreshing.

By now you're probably accustomed to including jQuery UI functionality. Make sure you build a download that includes the Tabs component, then include the CSS and JavaScript files into your HTML. You can have a look at what our jQuery UI tabs will look like in Figure 5.7.

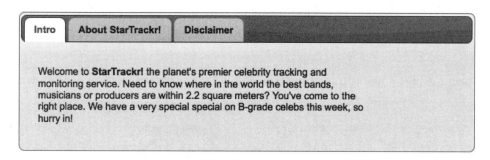

Figure 5.7. jQuery UI tabs

With the UI library and CSS styles in place, adding the content is easy. Content loaded via Ajax has no requirement for a container to be preset—the plugin automatically generates the required DOM elements:

```
chapter_05/12_jquery_ui_tabs/index.html (excerpt)

<div id="info">
  <ul id="info-nav">
    <li><a href="#intro">Intro</a></li>
    <li><a href="about.html">About StarTrackr!</a></li>
    <li><a href="disclaimer.html">Disclaimer</a></li>
  </ul>
  <div>
    <p id="intro">
      Welcome to <strong>StarTrackr!</strong> the planet's premier …
    </p>
  </div>
</div>
```

As we did before, we first create a tab navigation list. For static content, you need to specify an anchor name that corresponds to the id of the element containing the related content (#intro in our example). The next two tabs are our Ajax tabs; they simply point to HTML files on the server (or in our case, on the hard disk). In a real web application, they'd point to server-side scripts that generate dynamic content; for the sake of illustrating how jQuery UI's Ajaxy tabs work, we'll stick with a few static HTML files. These can contain whatever content you'd like to load into your tabs.

The functionality we'll implement will degrade gracefully in the absence of Java-Script; those tabs will simply act as links to the referenced files. When JavaScript is enabled, however, jQuery will load the content of the target page into the tab content pane without refreshing the page. There's no need to worry about it pulling in the whole HTML page—it's smart enough to only include the content between the opening and closing <body> tags.

To turn the above markup into an Ajax-enabled tab interface, all you need to write is:

chapter_05/12_jquery_ui_tabs/script.js (excerpt)

```
$('#info').tabs();
```

Try it out in your browser to confirm that it works. If this is not "Write less, do more," we don't know what is!

Tab Options

The tab control comes with reams of customization options that you can find on the jQuery UI tab demo page.[4] We'll explore a few of the juicy ones now:

---

[4] http://jqueryui.com/demos/tabs/

```
                       chapter_05/13_jquery_ui_tab_options/script.js (excerpt)

$('#info').tabs({
  event: 'mouseover',
  fx: {
    opacity: 'toggle',
    duration: 'fast'
  },
  spinner: 'Loading...',
  cache: true
});
```

As part of the control's initialization, we've passed a JavaScript object containing a collection of options: `event`, `fx`, `spinner`, and `cache`. The `event` option lets you choose the event that changes tabs—here we've replaced the default `click` with `mouseover`. To change tabs now, the user need only hover over the desired tab.

Next, we've added some animation options to specify a fast fade transition when we switch between tabs. The `fx` option works exactly like the `animate` command, letting you tweak the transition in whichever way you need.

The last two options are for our Ajax tabs. `spinner` specifies the HTML to display while the content is being loaded. With all your pages sitting on your local machine, you're likely to never see this text—but you'll certainly notice the delay (and therefore the `spinner` text) when you put your pages up on a real web server. It's called `spinner` as it's often used to display an animated GIF image of a spinning icon, which is meant to indicate loading and almost always named **spinner.gif**.

The `cache` option instructs the browser to hold on to a copy of the tab content after it's loaded. This way, if a user is clicky on your tabs—switching repeatedly back and forth—the browser won't need to download a fresh copy of the data each time.

Tab Control Methods

There are also a host of methods for interacting with the tabs programmatically. You can add, remove, and reload tabs, and change the open tab automatically. For example:

```
                       chapter_05/14_jquery_ui_tab_control/script.js (excerpt)

$('#info').tabs().tabs('rotate', 3500);
```

The first `tabs` call sets up our tab pane, and the second one instructs jQuery to cycle through the tabs every 3,500 milliseconds (or 3.5 seconds). There's a lot more you can do with your tabs, so have a look at the documentation to see what's possible.

The last item we'll have a look at is selecting a tab programmatically. You can find the currently selected tab by using the selected option:

```
$('#tabs').tabs('option', 'selected');
```

Of course, you can also set the current tab. This is handy if you want links in your content to simply change the open tab rather than linking to a new page. For this example, we've inserted a link to the About Us page in the content of the first tab. We can hijack that link and have it open the About Us tab instead:

```
chapter_05/14_jquery_ui_tab_control/script.js (excerpt)

$("#info p a[href=about.html]").click(function() {
  $('#info').tabs('select', 1);
  return false;
});
```

Panels and Panes

Panels and panes are nothing more than controls that just hold other controls! When used correctly they help organize a page into logical areas, minimizing complexity for the user. This lets seasoned users take advantage of all your site or application's features without having your newbies drown in a sea of buttons and widgets. Panels are most effective when they provide contextual tools and controls that users can work with while documents are open or in focus.

Slide-down Login Form

One increasingly popular method of reducing visible clutter is a hidden menu that rests at the very top of the screen. A small button or link reveals to the user that more information is available. Clicking the button causes a panel to slide into view, and moving away from the panel causes it to slide right back.

A convenient and practical space saver for sure, but what kind of information should be stored there? The most popular use for slide-down panels is to display the login fields for the site. Most users know that these features are generally displayed to the top right of a site's browser window, so a well-placed icon or link will catch the attention of those looking to log in. The login form we'll create can be seen in Figure 5.8.

Figure 5.8. Slide-down login form

This will be an easy addition to our site, as we already know most of the jQuery commands that will be involved. We'll throw some quick CSS styles on the control, but, as always, it's up to you to style it in a way that's consistent with your site. Then comes the by-now-familiar refrain—hide the form on pageload, then capture the click event to toggle it into and out of sight:

```
chapter_05/15_login_panel/script.js (excerpt)
$('#login form').hide();
$('#login a').toggle(function() {
  $(this)
    .addClass('active')
    .next('form')
    .animate({'height':'show'}, {
      duration:'slow',
      easing: 'easeOutBounce'
    });
}, function() {
  $(this)
    .removeClass('active')
    .next('form')
    .slideUp();
});
```

The only difference between this code and the expandable menu from the beginning of the chapter is that here we're using a CSS class to control the position of our background image, rather than the jQuery `css` action. Because these classes are only really used when JavaScript is available (as otherwise we'll be presenting a control that's always open), neither solution is necessarily better, and the one you choose will depend more on your preference.

This was a bit too easy, so we'll finesse it a touch. If our login form were to submit via Ajax (without triggering a page refresh), we'd want the panel to disappear after the form was submitted. Actually, even if we're loading a new page, having the menu slide up after clicking is a nice flourish:

```
                                    chapter_05/15_login_panel/script.js (excerpt)

$('#login form :submit').click(function() {
  $(this)
    .parent()
    .prev('a')
    .click();
});
```

We start by capturing the `click` event on the form's submit button, and then move back up the DOM tree looking for the containing element. We could just perform our hide here, but given that we've already written code to handle the hiding in our original handler, we can just step back through the DOM using the `prev` method, and click on our hide/show link.

Sliding Overlay

Translucent sliding overlays have been popping up all over the place of late: from message dialogs, to shopping cart summaries, to navigation controls, and more. The reason for their popularity is simple: they look incredibly cool—like the highly questionable interfaces from action movie computer scenes—except that they're actually useful!

The most important factors to consider in the creation of the sliding overlay are where you want the contents to slide from, and how the overlay will be triggered. The choices will affect how the user interacts with the control and how they expect it to act. This type of control is fairly new to the Web—so there are no conventions you need to adhere to—but you can look for analogies on the desktop for how they should perform. Perhaps you'll create a version of it that actually sets some rules!

For example, you might like to include a content panel that slides out when the user moves the mouse close to the edge of the page—like the auto-hide taskbar or dock on many operating systems. Or perhaps moving over the bottom edge of the content area could cause a **Next/Previous** control to slide into view.

Our overlay will be triggered by moving the mouse over a Shopping Cart link. Mousing over the link will cause a menu to slide down from under the header, over the page, informing the user of the number of items currently in the shopping cart, and providing links to checkout or view the cart. As illustrated in Figure 5.9, the shopping cart icon that acts as the trigger is located in the top-right corner of the content area.

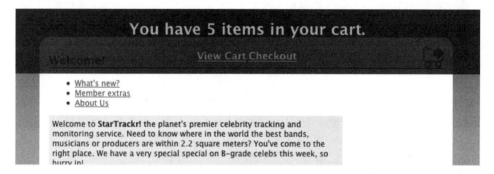

Figure 5.9. A sliding shopping cart overlay

As always, styling provides the real base of our effect. This will determine what our trigger will look like, and where our sliding commences. Our trigger will be absolutely positioned in the top-right corner of the page contents:

```
                                    chapter_05/16_sliding_overlay/panel.css (excerpt)
.cart a {
  position: absolute;
  width: 32px;
  height: 32px;
  right: 15px;
  top: -10px;
  background: transparent url(shoppingcart.png) no-repeat 0 0;
  text-indent: -9999px;
}
```

```
.cart a:hover, .cart-hover {
  background-position: 0 -32px;
}

#overlay {
  position: absolute;
  width: 100%;
  height: 100px;
  top: 0;
  left: 0;
  color: #fff;
  background-color: #000;
  display: none;
  text-align: center;
}

#overlay a {
  font-size: 130%;
  font-weight: bold;
}
```

Because the overlay will only be triggered by jQuery, it stands to reason that it should be added to the page markup with jQuery as well. The overlay is set up to be 100% width of the page, and have a height of 100 pixels. We want the overlay to slide down from the top, so we set the top position to 0. Of course, we also hide it so that it's absent from the page when it loads.

The first step is to add the overlay to the markup. We will give it a hover handler, because when it slides into the page we want it to remain visible for as long as the user keeps the mouse over it. We give it a class of active as long as it's open, and use that class to determine when it needs to be closed. When the user mouses away from it, we remove the class, and set a timer, which will look for an overlay without the class class and close it after a little less than a second. This way, if the user re-opens the overlay while the timer is running, the timer method will do nothing:

```
                                    chapter_05/16_sliding_overlay/script.js (excerpt)

$('<div></div>')
  .attr('id', 'overlay')
  .css('opacity', 0.65)
  .hover(function() {
    $(this).addClass('active');
  }, function() {
    $(this).removeClass('active');
    setTimeout(function() {
      $('#overlay:not(.active)').slideUp(function() {
        $('a.cart-hover').removeClass('cart-hover');
      });
    }, 800);
  }).appendTo('body');
```

We're using the `opacity` CSS property to make our overlay semi-transparent. `opacity` values range from 0 to 1, with 1 being completely opaque and 0 being invisible.

 Accessibility

Be careful when creating semi-transparent controls that there's sufficient color contrast between your content and the background. Maybe it's easy for you to read, but always consider that some of your visitors may have less than perfect vision. When in doubt, err on the side of caution, with higher contrasts than you think are necessary.

Now let's add the event listener to our trigger link:

```
                                    chapter_05/16_sliding_overlay/script.js (excerpt)

$('.cart a').mouseover(function() {
  $(this).addClass('cart-hover');
  $('#overlay:not(:animated)')
    .addClass('active')
    .html('<h1>You have 5 items in your cart.</h1>
➥<a href="#">View Cart</a> <a href="#">Checkout</a>')
    .slideDown();
});
```

There's a new filter in our selector here: `:animated`, which allows us to select elements that are currently being animated (or, as in this case, combined with the `:not` filter to select elements which are not mid-animation.) We add some static markup to our overlay, but in a real application, you'd want to obtain the number of cart items in order to display it here.

We are also adding a class to the trigger link to style it, as its hover style would otherwise switch off when the overlay came between it and the cursor.

Of course, this is only one example of this sort of functionality; you can likely think of many others. Transparency is remarkably easy to manipulate in jQuery, and really makes interface components feel a lot slicker.

Tooltips

A tooltip is an interface component that appears when a user hovers over a control. They're already present in most browsers; when you provide a `title` attribute for a link or an `alt` attribute for an image, the browser will usually display it as a tooltip when the user hovers over that element.

JavaScript tooltips have a bit of a bad rap. They tend to be implemented in an obnoxious manner, acting more like an ad popup than a useful information tool. However, there are situations in which a tooltip can provide just the right touch to your application, helping to inform your users in a contextual fashion without cluttering the rest of your interface.

First, we'll have a go at replacing the browser's default tooltips with ones we can style and animate. Then we'll look at extending this to create a much more versatile tooltip, which can contain HTML and be attached to any element on the page.

Simple Tooltips

Tooltips typically appear when the user hovers over a hyperlink—to provide additional information about where the link will take them. Of course, there'll be other places you'll want to use tooltips, but this is a good place to start. We'll look at replacing the browser's default tooltips with our own custom-styled, animated ones, as illustrated in Figure 5.10.

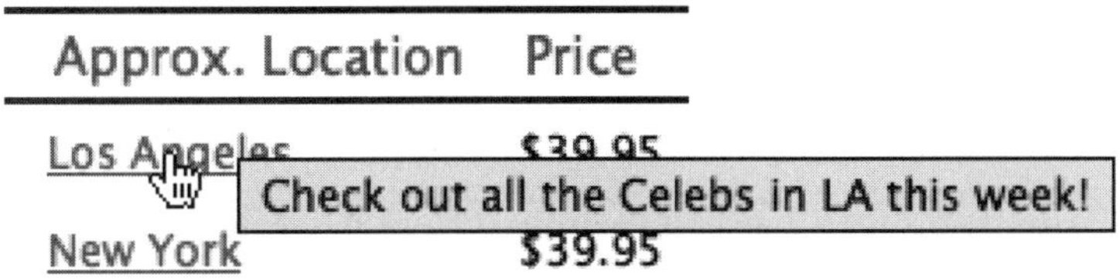

Approx. Location	Price
Los Angeles	$39.95
New York	$39.95

Figure 5.10. Our custom tooltips

For our simple control, we'll use the `title` attribute of the links. This is great for our ever-vigilant efforts to maintain acceptable functionality for users without JavaScript support; depending on their browser, they'll most likely see the text as a basic browser tooltip:

```
chapter_05/17_simple_tooltips/index.html (excerpt)

<a href="#" title="Check out all the … ">New York</a>
```

Using the `title` attribute can be a bit limiting: you're unable (technically or reliably) to have HTML nested inside your tooltip, and you'll need to be careful with special characters that might break the tag. There are a few alternate techniques for storing the tooltip's text. We'll have a look at another method when we make our advanced tooltip—but it's important to note that any method will have upsides and downsides, and you'll need to decide which is best in each particular circumstance.

Being able to style the tooltip is the main reason for implementing a custom control in the first place—so go nuts with your styles! However, for our example, we'll define some very basic styles for our tooltips:

```
chapter_05/17_simple_tooltips/tooltips.css (excerpt)

.tooltip {
  display: none;
  position: absolute;
  border: 1px solid #333;
  background-color: #ffed8a;
  padding: 2px 6px;
}
```

The tooltip control is positioned absolutely, which will allow us to move it around as required. Next, we'll set up some stubs for our code to sit in, which lets you see the general structure: a simple `hover` function, followed by a chained `mousemove` function. We want the tooltip to turn on and off with the `hover` event, and update its position whenever the mouse is moved:

chapter_05/17_simple_tooltips/script.js *(excerpt)*

```
$('.location').hover(function(e) {
  // Hover over code
}, function() {
  // Hover out code
}).mousemove(function(e) {
  // Mouse move code
});
```

Starting with the overall structure and then filling in the details is a great way to plan out your code, ensuring you know what's going on before diving in. It helps when writing code to always have a contextual understanding of where that piece sits in the larger picture.

Let's start filling in those stubs. The hover over code is the most interesting, so we'll start with that. Notice that we're passing the optional parameter `e` into the hover code. This is important, as we'll need to access the X and Y coordinates of the event in order to position the tooltip:

chapter_05/17_simple_tooltips/script.js *(excerpt)*

```
// Hover over code
var titleText = $(this).attr('title');
$(this)
  .data('tipText', titleText)
  .removeAttr('title');

$('<p class="tooltip"></p>')
  .text(titleText)
  .appendTo('body')
  .css('top', (e.pageY - 10) + 'px')
  .css('left', (e.pageX + 20) + 'px')
  .fadeIn('slow');
```

First we need to grab the `title` from the link, which will be the text we want our tooltip to display.

The next part of the code is a touch peculiar: it saves the tooltip text using the `data` method that we saw in the section called "Smarter Scrolling with the `data` Action" in Chapter 4. We need to do this because we'll be removing the `title` from the link, in order to prevent the browser from displaying its default tooltip that will conflict with our custom one. By storing the text using the `data` command, we can recover and replace the link title later.

We now have everything we need to create our tooltip control. We'll create a new paragraph element with a `class` of `tooltip`, in order to hook into the styles we created earlier. Then we use the `text` method to set the tooltip's contents. We *could* use `html` instead of `text` here, but according to W3C standards, the `title` attribute should not contain HTML. The advanced tooltip we'll be looking at shortly will allow us to include HTML, but for the moment we'll stick with plain text.

A Question of Style

We could've specified the paragraph's `id` with jQuery like this: `$('<p></p>').attr('id', 'tooltip')`. Likewise, we could've used JavaScript string concatenation to populate the element's content: `$('<p>' + titleText + '</p>')`. Both methods result in the same DOM objects, and they're both fairly clear and readable, so it's up to your personal coding style whether you prefer doing more with jQuery chaining or with plain JavaScript.

After we add our new node to the page (using `appendTo`) we set a few inline styles, using the event object (`e`) to obtain the position where we need to place the tooltip. `pageX` and `pageY` are properties of the event object that allow you to find out where the event took place on the page. This can be tremendously useful in a lot of different situations; you'll often find yourself needing to position an element on the screen based on an event which just fired:

chapter_05/17_simple_tooltips/script.js (excerpt)

```
// Hover out code
$(this).attr('title', $(this).data('tipText'));
$('.tooltip').remove();
```

The hover out code couldn't be simpler: we just reverse what we did in the hover over code, restoring the `title` attribute and removing the tooltip:

```
                                    chapter_05/17_simple_tooltips/script.js (excerpt)

// Mouse move code
$('.tooltip')
  .css('top', (e.pageY - 10) + 'px')
  .css('left', (e.pageX + 20) + 'px');
```

Finally, we need to respond to mouse movement by updating the tooltip's location. This way the tooltip will follow the mouse around, just like the browser's built-in tooltips do. And presto! We've replaced the default tooltips with our own, and we're fully in control of their appearance and animation.

Advanced Tooltips

It's good to know how to build a simple tooltip, but we also know that we can do better. For more sophisticated tooltips, which can include other markup (such as images or links) inside the content, we'll need to move them from the `title` attribute into our actual markup. We'll hide them with CSS, then reveal and position them using jQuery as required. The final effect is illustrated in Figure 5.11.

Figure 5.11. Our advanced tooltip

Our tooltip markup will consist of two nested `span` elements, which will sit inside the element we want to use to trigger the tooltip. This may occasionally require some creativity with your markup, but helps us to position the tooltip, as we can give it an absolute position offset from the parent element. It also helps us handle triggering events, since, if the user moves the mouse over the tooltip, it will still be over the triggering element, so no additional `hover` event handling is required.

Here's an example of the tooltip markup:

```
                        chapter_05/18_advanced_tooltips/index.html (excerpt)
<p>
  Welcome to
    <strong>StarTrackr!
      <span class='tooltip'>
        <span><a href='#'>Legal Disclaimer</a></span>
      </span>
    </strong> the planet's premier celebrity tracking …
</p>
```

When we're done, the tooltip will look great and will contain a link to the disclaimer page. But let's not hang around; we've considered a few tooltip methods, so let's drive straight in.

As we'll see when we start writing the code, our tooltip will be quite clever, positioning itself on whichever side of the target element that has enough room for it to be displayed. In order to make a cool text-bubble graphic work in this context, we'll need four different bubbles: above-left, above-right, below-left, and below-right. We'll be using a single sprite for each of the tooltip's four possible states, as illustrated in Figure 5.12.

Figure 5.12. Our tooltip sprite

These tooltips require some fairly complex jQuery code. We'll go over it bit by bit, but don't worry if you have trouble understanding all of it right now. There's a bit of a leap from writing quick two- or three-line scripts which replace and highlight content on the page to writing a more complex UI widget. At the beginning of the next chapter, we'll have a look at some of the ways we can try to minimize complexity and keep our code readable, even as it becomes longer and more involved.

For the moment, try to focus on seeing the bits of jQuery you already know employed in a larger context; this should give you an idea of how you can go about combining small pieces of logic into a larger picture that performs really impressively.

Our first task is to create a TT object that will contain all our code. We set a `delay` variable at the top of the object (this will make it easier to modify the configuration of the widget without hunting through the code to find where this variable was set):

chapter_05/18_advanced_tooltips/script.js (excerpt)

```
var TT = {
  delay: 600,
```

Then we add a function called `setTips`, which we'll run when the page loads or is resized. This function will find all the tooltips on the page and determine their position by looking at their parent elements. It will also set up a `hover` event on each of them so that they're displayed on mouseover. Here's the hover event:

chapter_05/18_advanced_tooltips/script.js (excerpt)

```
setTips: function() {

  $('.tooltip').parent().hover(function() { ❶
    // store the tooltip being hovered
    TT.current = $(this); ❷
    TT.timer = setTimeout(function() { ❸
      // find the tooltip,
      TT.current.find(".tooltip").fadeIn('fast');
    }, TT.delay);
  }, function() {
    // on mouseout, clear timer and hide tooltip
    clearTimeout(TT.timer); ❹
    $(this).find(".tooltip").fadeOut('fast');
  }).attr("title", ""); // clear the title to stop browser tooltips
```

That's a fairly dense block of code, so let's see if we can make some sense of what's happening:

❶ We've attached the `hover` event to the parent of the tooltip `span`. If you look back at the markup, you'll see this is correct: we put the tooltip inside the element we want to attach it to.

2 We store a reference to that parent element inside a variable. What's unusual here is that we're using a property of our `TT` object instead of a global variable. We'll come back to this in the next chapter, but for now just know that it's much the same as writing `var current = $(this);`.

3 We're using the familiar `setTimeout` function, except that this time we're saving the timer to a variable. This is so we can turn it off by name if we need to. We're accessing the delay property we set before as the second parameter for `setTimeout`. As we've seen, this is how long the browser will wait before displaying the tooltip.

4 When the user mouses off the target, we want to stop the timer so that the tooltip will stay hidden after the delay expires. We do this with the JavaScript `clearTimeout` method, passing in the reference to our timer.

Okay, so now that our hover handler is set up, we need to determine the position of each of our tooltips. We'll use `each()` to loop over them, but first we'll grab the height and width of the screen. If we were to do this *inside* the loop, jQuery would need to calculate those values once for each tooltip, even though they're always the same. By storing the values outside the loop, we avoid this wasteful calculation and improve the performance of our script:

```
                                chapter_05/18_advanced_tooltips/script.js (excerpt)

var screenWidth = $(window).width();
var screenBottom = $(window).scrollTop() + $(window).height();

$(".tooltip").each(function() {
  // grab the containing element
  $container = $(this).parent();

  // give it relative position if required
  if ($container.css("position") != 'absolute'
     && $container.css("position") != "fixed") { ❶
    $container.css({position: 'relative'});
  }

  var totalHeight = $container.height() + $(this).outerHeight(); ❷
  var width = $(this).outerWidth();
  var offset = $container.offset();

  // now we get the position the tip
  var top = $container.height(); // default placement ❸
  var left = 0;
```

This part of the code should be a little easier to understand. We loop over each
tooltip on the page, and first store a reference to the container element just to avoid
having to write $(this).parent() over and over. Notice that the variable name
starts with $: this is just to help us remember that the variable contains a jQuery
selection. Here's a breakdown of the contents of the loop:

❶   We check to see if the parent element has position: absolute; or position:
    fixed;. It has to be positioned, since we'll be using position: absolute; to
    offset the tooltip from it. If it already has absolute or fixed, we'll leave it that
    way. If it doesn't, though, we'll give it position: relative;.

❷   We need to know the total combined height of both the tooltip and the parent
    element, so we store that in a variable to use later.

❸   By default, we give the tooltip a top position equal to the height of the container.
    This means it will appear directly *below* the container (since it is offset from
    the top by exactly the container's height).

Logical Operators

In JavaScript, when you're testing for values in an `if` statement, you can use the `&&` operator to mean *and*. So in the above example, the contents of the `if` block will only execute if *both* conditions (on either side of `&&`) are met.

You can also write `||` (two pipe symbols) to mean *or*. If we'd used that instead of `&&` above, the contents of the `if` block would execute if *either* condition was met.

This is good work so far! We're almost done, but we need to fix one small problem: what if the tooltip's position takes it off the screen? If the target element is right at the bottom of the screen, and we want the tooltip to appear below it, the tooltip will remain unseen!

It's time for a little collision detection. We need to find out if the tooltip is hitting either the bottom or right edge of the screen. Let's have a look at how we accomplish this:

chapter_05/18_advanced_tooltips/script.js (excerpt)

```
// re-position if it's off the right of the screen
if (offset.left + width > screenWidth) {
  left = 0 - width + 42;
  $(this).addClass('left');
} else {
  $(this).removeClass('left');
}

// re-position if it's off the bottom of the screen
if (offset.top + totalHeight > screenBottom) {
  top = 0 - $(this).outerHeight();
  $(this).addClass('above');
} else {
  $(this).removeClass('above');
}
```

We check to see if the tip's horizontal or vertical offset, plus its width or height, is greater than the width or height of the screen (which we calculated earlier). If it is, we modify the `top` or `left` property respectively, and assign a class that we'll use to display the appropriate part of our background image sprite.

The final (and easiest) step is to use the `css` action to assign the calculated `top` and `left` properties to the tips:

chapter_05/18_advanced_tooltips/script.js *(excerpt)*

```
$(this).css({
  "top": top,
  "left": left
});
```

We'll call our `setTips` method on document-ready, and also each time the window is resized, to ensure that our tips are always adequately positioned:

chapter_05/18_advanced_tooltips/script.js *(excerpt)*

```
$(document).ready(function() {
  TT.setTips();
});

$(window).resize(function() {
  TT.setTips();
});
```

With that code in place, we just need to add some CSS to position our background sprite appropriately, based on the classes we assigned:

chapter_05/18_advanced_tooltips/tooltip.css *(excerpt)*

```
span.tooltip.left {
  background-position: 100% 0;
}

span.tooltip.left span {
  padding: 15px 0 0 17px;
}

span.tooltip.above {
  background-position: 0 100%;
}

span.tooltip.above span {
  padding: 13px 0 0 12px;
}
```

```
span.tooltip.above.left {
  background-position: 100% 100%;
}

span.tooltip.above.left span {
  padding: 13px 0 0 17px;
}
```

 IE6 Support

Although jQuery does a fantastic job of handling cross-browser issues in our JavaScript code, it's not so good for our CSS. The above style rules rely on chaining several `class` selectors together. This will confuse Internet Explorer 6, which will only see the last `class` in any style rule. Moreover, our PNG image relies on alpha-channel transparency for the tooltip's drop shadow, and this is also unsupported by IE6.

Over the last few years, several major sites (including YouTube and Facebook) began phasing out support for IE6. This doesn't mean that they totally ignore this browser, rather that they accept that IE6 users will receive a degraded experience (perhaps similar to what visitors without JavaScript will see).

For our tooltip example, we could use conditional comments[5] to target some styles specifically to IE6 and provide it with the same tooltip functionality—except using a flat background image without a thought-bubble style or a drop shadow. This way, the background position would be inconsequential, and the PNG issue solved.

And there you have it! The final tooltip not only waits to see if you really meant for it to display, but it also shifts its position to make sure it's fully visible whenever it does display! Because we've avoided linking this code to anything specific on our page, it's easy to reuse this script on any other page—you just need to include a few spans with a `tooltip class`, and you're off to the races. This is an important lesson: you should always try to structure your code in such a way that you can reuse it later. This will save you work in the long run, and give you more time to experiment with cool new functionality instead of rebuilding the same old widgets every time you need them.

---

[5] http://reference.sitepoint.com/css/conditionalcomments/

Order off the Menu

Whew! That was a hard sprint to the finish line. Over the course of this chapter, we've ramped up our jQuery know-how and used it to move beyond simple hiding and revealing, and well into the territory of the true UI ninja. You've learned how to reduce complexity on the screen by packaging up links and widgets into collapsing menus, accordions, panels, and tooltips.

In the next chapter, we'll look at reducing complexity in our code, and then tackle what's ostensibly the most important part of jQuery: Ajax!

6

Construction, Ajax, and Interactivity

Throughout the preceding chapters we've wowed and dazzled our client with a cornucopia of visual effects and optical magic tricks, giving his site a lifelike appearance. Unfortunately, our client is becoming savvy: as well as wanting his pages *looking* Web 2.0, he wants them *acting* Web 2.0 as well. And having pages act Web 2.0 means one thing: Ajax!

And not just a little bit—he wants the works: inline text editing, Twitter widgets, endlessly scrolling image galleries … he wants StarTrackr! to have more Ajax-enabled bells and whistles than Facebook, Flickr, and Netvibes combined.

That's fine by us. Implementing client-side Ajax functionality is easy, especially with jQuery as our framework. But these cool new features come at a cost of increased complexity. Some simple tasks (such as loading in a snippet of HTML) are no problem—but as we start to tackle the business of creating advanced Ajax components, the risk of making a mess of unmaintainable spaghetti code grows large. So before we jump into the deep end, we'll review some ways we can manage complexity, and write well-behaved code that will impress our peers.

Construction and Best Practices

JavaScript is a wonderful language. Don't let anyone tell you any different. Its historically poor reputation stems from years of misunderstanding and misuse: an almost infinite collection of inline scripts, displaying little regard for good coding practices like encapsulation and reuse. But the past few years have ushered in a new era for this underdog of the Web. Developers have begun to respect (and conquer) the language, and the result has been some great code libraries—including our favorite, jQuery.

jQuery has greatly simplified the process of dealing with Ajax and the DOM, but it hasn't changed the benefits of writing nice clean JavaScript code. There's no need for us to become masters of JavaScript—but there are a few steps we should take to ensure we're writing the kind of code that will make future developers and maintainers of our projects want to buy us a beer.

Cleaner jQuery

We've done a fairly good job of steering clear of any involved JavaScript code—that's a testament to how good jQuery is at doing what it does. But as our jQuery components and effects grow more complex, we need to start thinking about how to best structure our code. Once again we should remember that, under the hood, jQuery is just JavaScript—so it'll serve us well to steal a few best practices from the world of JavaScript. We already saw a bit of this kind of code organization when we built our advanced tooltip script at the end of Chapter 5. Now let's reveal the whys and hows of writing cleaner jQuery code.

Code Comments

Just like HTML and CSS, JavaScript provides you with a way to comment your code. Any line that you begin with two slashes (//) will be ignored by the browser, so you can safely include explanations about what your code is doing. For example, in this snippet the first line will be ignored, and only the second will be processed as code:

```
// Assign the value '3' to the variable 'count':
var count = 3;
```

If you need to write comments which stretch over multiple lines, you can begin them with /* and end them with */. For example:

```
/* An example of
   a multiline
   comment
*/
var count = 3;
```

Comments go a long way to making your code reusable and maintainable: they help you see at a glance what each line or section is doing when you revisit code you wrote months ago.

Map Objects

We've been dealing with key/value pair objects since all the way back in Chapter 2. We use them to pass multiple options into a single jQuery action, for example:

```
$('p').css({color:'green', padding:'3px'});
```

They aren't special jQuery constructs—once again, it's just plain old JavaScript—but they're great for encapsulating data to pass around in your own functions and widgets. For example, if you pull data out from some form fields, you can package them up into key/value mapped pairs that you can then process further:

```
var id = $('input#id').val();
var name = $('input#name').val();
var age = $('input#age').val();

var data = {
  type: 'person',
  id: id,
  name: name,
  age: age
}
```

With the data all wrapped up, we're able to easily pass it around and use it however we like. To access any one of an object's values, we simply need to type the object's name, followed by a period (.), followed by the key associated with that value we wish to access. For example, given the data object defined above, if you wanted to check to see if the `type` property contained the string `'person'`, and alert the `name` property if so, you'd write:

```
if (data.type == 'person') {
  alert('Hello ' + data.name);
}
```

Namespacing Your Code

Even the nicest of libraries still lets you write the nastiest of spaghetti code—and jQuery is no exception. Sorting through 20 pages of `hover` and `toggle` commands will end up driving you crazy, so to save your sanity you'll want to group logical chunks of code together.

We already had a go at doing this in the section called "Advanced Tooltips" in Chapter 5—and if you go back and have a look at that example, you'll notice that almost all of the code is wrapped up in an object named `TT`. This object is much the same as the `data` object above (and all the object literals we've been working with so far), except that it also contains *functions*, as well as static variables.

So when we wrote `setTips: function() { … }`, we were assigning that function to the `setTips` *property* of the `TT` object. Once that's done, we can write `TT.set-Tips()` to execute the function. Now every function we write that has to do with tooltips can be contained inside `TT`. Because the only object we're declaring in the global scope (more on this in a second) is `TT`, we can rest assured that none of our functions or variables will conflict with other JavaScript code on the page. We refer to this technique as **namespacing**, and refer to all our `TT` variables and methods as being part of the `TT` **namespace**.

Our namespace object can be given any name so long as it's a valid variable name. This means it can start with a dollar sign, underscore, or any alphabetical character—lowercase or uppercase.

Additionally, the more unique, short, and helpful the name is, the more successful it will be. We're looking to avoid clashes in function names, so making namespaces that are likely to clash will only escalate the problem.

`TRKR` would be a good choice for StarTrackr! It's short, helpful in that it alludes back to our site name, and fairly unique.

Here's what we're looking to avoid. Say you have a function named `exclaim`:

```
function exclaim () {
  alert("hooray");
}
exclaim();// hooray
```

It's not especially inspired as function names go, but there you have it. Trouble is, some third-party code that you want to put in your site also has a function named `exclaim`:

```
function exclaim () {
  alert("booooo");
}
exclaim();// booooo
```

Now, when you expect the alert to show "hooray," you instead see a disheartening "booooo." Rather than simply picking another function name and risking the same result, let's put our method inside the `TRKR` namespace:

```
var TRKR = {};

TRKR.exclaim = function () {
  alert("hooray");
};
```

There's no limit now to what we can do with the methods and properties of our namespace:

```
var TRKR = {};
TRKR.namespaces = "cool";
TRKR.boolean = true;
TRKR.pi = 3.14159;
TRKR.css = {
  "color": "#c0ffee",
  "top": 0
};
TRKR.exclaim = function () {
  alert("hooray");
};
```

Now we can still let out a buoyant "hooray," but there's much less chance of other code stepping on our toes:

```
TRKR.exclaim (); // hooray
TRKR.namespaces; // "cool"
exclaim(); // boooooo
```

Namespacing code this way also means that it can be easily reused on other pages. All we need to do is plunk the TRKR object down in another page, and we'll have access to all our juicy functions. Now that's quality code!

Once you've set up your namespace, you can either add your properties one by one after declaring the object, as we did above, or you can include them all inside the object literal, like this:

```
var TRKR = {
  namespaces: "cool",
  boolean = true,
  pi = 3.14159,
  css = {
    "color": "#c0ffee",
    "top": 0
  },
  setup: function() {
    TRKR.one = 1;
    ⋮
  },
  exclaim: function() {
    alert("hooray");
  }
};
```

This code block results in exactly the same namespace object as the one we saw before, and it's up to you which you prefer. Most of the code you'll encounter in the remainder of the book will make use of namespacing, whenever it's appropriate.

Scope

In programming, **scope** refers to the area of code where a defined variable exists. For example, you can define a variable as global by declaring it outside of any loops or constructs. Global variables will be accessible from anywhere in your code.

Likewise, a variable that you declare inside a construct (such as a function or an object) is said to be local to that construct.

This seems simple, but it can become messy when we start defining callback methods for our Ajax requests, because the callback will often be run in a different context than the one where it was defined. So if you try to refer to this in a callback, expecting it to point to your widget namespace, you'll be unpleasantly surprised: it might be undefined, or it might refer to something else entirely. For example:

```
var WIDGET = {};
WIDGET.delay = 1000;
WIDGET.run = function() {
  alert(this.delay); // 1000 … good!
  $(p).click(function() {
    alert(this.delay) // undefined! bad!
  });
};
```

When a p tag is clicked, our event handler runs in a different context than the widget object itself. So this.delay will most likely not exist (and if it does, it's a different variable to what we wanted anyway!). There are a few ways we can deal with this, but without being too JavaScripty, the easiest way is to store the widget's scope in a variable:

```
var WIDGET = {};
WIDGET.delay = 1000;
WIDGET.run = function() {
  alert(this.delay); // 1000 … good!
  var _widget = this;
  $(p).click(function() {
    alert(_widget.delay) // 1000 … yes!
  });
};
```

By setting _widget to point to this *in the context of the widget*, we'll always be able to refer back to it, wherever we are in the code. In JavaScript, this is called a **closure**. The general convention is to name it _this (though some people also use self). If it's used in a namespacing object, it's best to name it with an underscore (_), followed by the widget name. This helps to clarify the scope we're operating in.

Client-side Templating

Most of the menus and effects we've seen so far have contained static content. Of course, most menu text is unlikely to change, but as we explore Ajax-enabled widgets, the need to inject and replace text dynamically becomes more of an issue. This brings us to the problem of templating: where do you put the markup that will structure the content you're inserting into your pages?

There are a number of ways you can approach this issue. The simplest is to replace the entire contents of the pane every time it's displayed—say, via the `html` action. Whenever we need to update a content pane, we replace its entire contents with new markup, like so:

```
$('#overlay').html("<p>You have " + cart.items.length +
➥" items in your cart.</p>");
```

Data Sources

Throughout our discussion of templating we'll be assuming that the content we need to update is coming from some fictitious JavaScript data source (like `cart.items` in the above example). The format of your data source is likely to vary widely from project to project: some will be pulled in via Ajax, some injected directly via a server-side language, and so on. Evidently those parts of the code will need to be adapted to your needs.

Directly writing the HTML content is fine if we only have a small amount of basic markup—but for more elaborate content it can quickly lead to a nasty mess of JavaScript or jQuery string manipulation that's difficult to read and maintain. You will run into trouble if you try to build complex tables via string concatenation.

One way of circumventing this problem is to provide hooks in your HTML content, which can be populated with data when required:

```
<div id='overlay'>
  <p>You have <span id='num-items'>0</span> items in your cart.</p>
  <p>Total cost is $<span id='total-cost'>0</span></p>
</div>
```

We've now added a few container fields to the HTML. When an update of the data is required, we use jQuery to update the text of the containers:

```
$(this).find('#num-items').text(cart.items.length);
$(this).find('#total-cost').text(cart.getTotalCost());
```

This is much nicer than our first attempt: it leaves all the markup in the HTML page where it belongs, and it's easy to see what the code is doing.

There's one other (very handy) option for managing markup that will be manipulated by jQuery. When you're working with applications that return a list or grid of results—say, an item list for a shopping cart—you can include an element that acts as a template for each item, and simply copy that element and edit its contents whenever you need to add a new item.

Let's put this into practice by doing a bit of work on the StarTrackr! shopping cart. We'd like to be able to add and remove items using jQuery. The items sit in an HTML `table`, and we'd prefer to avoid writing out whole table rows in our jQuery code. It's also difficult to use placeholders, as we're unaware of how many items there will be in the cart in advance, so it's unfeasible, simply prepare empty table rows waiting for jQuery to populate them with content.

Our first task is to create an empty row with `display:none;` to act as our template:

chapter_06/01_client_side_templating/index.html (excerpt)

```
<table id="cart">
  <thead>
    <tr>
      <th>Name</th>
      <th>Qty.</th>
      <th>Total</th>
    </tr>
  </thead>
  <tr class="template" style="display:none;">
    <td><span class="item_name">Name</span></td>
    <td><span class="item_qty">Quantity</span></td>
    <td><span class="item_total">Total</span>.00</td>
  </tr>
</table>
```

Next we'll create a helper function that does the templating for us. This keeps the code centralized, making it easy to maintain when the template changes. The `template` function accepts a jQuery selection of a table row, as well as a cart item (an object containing the item name, quantity, and total price). The result is a filled-in template ready to be inserted into our HTML document:

chapter_06/01_client_side_templating/script.js *(excerpt)*

```
function template(row, cart) {
  row.find('.item_name').text(cart.name);
  row.find('.item_qty').text(cart.qty);
  row.find('.item_total').text(cart.total);
  return row;
}
```

So for each new row of data, we need to copy the template, substitute our values, and append it to the end of the table. A handy way to copy a selected element is via the `clone` method. The `clone` method creates a copy of the current jQuery selection. Once you have cloned an element, the selection changes to the new element—allowing you to insert it into the DOM tree:

chapter_06/01_client_side_templating/script.js *(excerpt)*

```
var newRow = $('#cart .template').clone().removeClass('template');
var cartItem = {
  name: 'Glendatronix',
  qty: 1,
  total: 450
};
template(newRow, cartItem)
  .appendTo('#cart')
  .fadeIn();
```

The template class is removed—because it's not a template anymore! We then set up our cart item (in a real example this data would come from the server, of course), and then use our `template` method to substitute the data into the row. Once the substitution is complete, we add the row to the existing table and fade it in. Our code is kept simple and all our markup stays in the HTML file where it belongs.

Are there other templating techniques around? Oh yes, dozens! For very high-level requirements you might need to investigate alternatives, but the methods detailed above are common for most sites and are likely to be all you'll need.

Browser Sniffing (... Is Bad!)

Browser sniffing is fast becoming a relic of the past, and is punishable by unfriend-ing—or unfollowing—or whatever the Web equivalent of death is. This is hard for many people to believe or accept, because we've done browser sniffing for so long, and because it seems so much easier than the alternative (which we'll look at shortly). **Browser sniffing**, if you've been lucky enough never to have encountered it, is the process of using JavaScript to figure out which version of which web browser the user is browsing with. The idea is that once you know this information, you can work around any known bugs that exist in the browser, so your page renders and functions correctly.

But this technique has become far too unreliable: old browsers are updated with patches, new versions are released, and completely new browsers are introduced —seemingly every day! This means that workarounds in your code can (and will) break or become redundant, and you'll have to become a walking encyclopedia of browser bugs.

Now, having said this, there are a couple of functions in jQuery (albeit holding on for dear life) that assist with browser sniffing.

`$.browser` has a few flags for determining if the current user's browser is Internet Explorer, Safari, Opera, or Mozilla. Sometimes you'll be unable to avoid using this to work around pesky cross-browser bugs.

`$.browser.version`, on the other hand, is a deprecated action that you should try to avoid (though it's likely to remain in the library for compatibility). It reports the current version of the user's browser. With these commands you can execute condi-tional code, like so:

```
if ($.browser.mozilla && $.browser.version.substr(0,3)=="1.9") {
    // Only do this code in Firefox with version 3 (rv 1.9)
}
```

Relying on browser revision numbers and vendor names, though, is just asking for trouble down the road. You want to avoid fixing old code, especially when you could be writing shiny new code, so perhaps it's time to talk about the alternative to browser sniffing …

Feature Detection

The reason browser sniffing has been exiled is that it targets the symptom, instead of the cause of the trouble. For example, Internet Explorer has no direct support for the `opacity` CSS property. Before we make use of `opacity` in our code, we could test to see if the user is using Internet Explorer and act accordingly. But the issue isn't really Internet Explorer: the issue is `opacity` itself!

To replace browser detection, jQuery has introduced the `$.support` method to report on the abilities of the user's browsers. Instead of asking, "Is the user's browser Internet Explorer?" you should now ask, "Does the user's browser support the `opacity` style?" like so:

```
if (!$.support.opacity) {
  // Doesn't support opacity: apply a workaround
}
```

The beauty of this approach is that if new browsers emerge in the future which also have no support for the `opacity` style, or if Internet Explorer suddenly *starts* supporting it, your old code will still work perfectly.

There are a dozen or so properties you can test for besides opacity. For example: `$.support.boxModel` returns `false` if a browser is in quirks mode, `$.support.leadingWhitespace` returns `true` if a browser preserves leading whitespace with `innerHTML`, and so on. Make sure you check the full list in Appendix A if your project requires it.

Ajax Crash Course

Where once "Ajax" was the buzzword *du jour*, today it's merely another tool in our web development arsenal—a tool we use to provide seamless and natural page interactions. Ajax can be a bit finicky to implement ... unless you're using jQuery!

What Is Ajax?

The term Ajax was coined in 2005 as an acronym for Asynchronous JavaScript and XML. Many people found the term problematic, as they were already doing Ajax-like work but without always using the technologies mentioned in the acronym. Eventually the term has settled down to simply mean almost any technique or technology that lets a user's browser interact with a server without disturbing the existing page.

The non-Ajax method of interacting with a server is the familiar model we're accustomed to on the Web: the user clicks a link or submits a form, which sends a request to the server. The server responds with a fresh page of HTML, which the browser will load and display to the user. And while the page is loading, the user is forced to wait ... and wait.

Ajax lets us fire requests from the browser to the server without page reload, so we can update a part of the page while the user continues on working. This helps us mimic the feel of a desktop application, and gives the user a more responsive and natural experience.

As Ajax runs on the browser, we need a way to interact dynamically with server. Each web browser tends to supply slightly different methods for achieving this. Lucky for us, jQuery is here to make sure we don't have to worry about these differences.

We've seen armfuls of jQuery functions for manipulating the DOM, so you might be worried about the barrage of documentation you'll need to absorb to write killer Ajax functionality. Well, the good news is that there are only a handful of Ajax functions in jQuery—and most of those are just useful wrapper functions to help us out.

Loading Remote HTML

We'd better make a start on some coding—the StarTrackr! guy is growing cranky, as it's been a while since we've given him an update and there's yet to be any Ajax gracing his site. We'll put a quick Ajax enhancement up for him using the easiest of the jQuery Ajax functions: `load`.

The `load` method will magically grab an HTML file off the server and insert its contents within the current web page. You can load either static HTML files, or dynamic pages that generate HTML output. Here's a quick example of how you use it:

```
$('div:first').load('test.html');
```

That's a very small amount of code for some cool Ajax functionality! This dynamically inserts the entire contents (anything inside the <body> tags) of the **test.html** file into the first `div` on the page. You can use any selector to decide where the HTML should go, and you can even load it into multiple locations at the same time.

 Which `load`?

Be careful—there are a couple of disparate uses for the `load` keyword in jQuery. One is the Ajax `load` method, which we've just seen, and the other is the `load` event, which fires when an object (such as the window or an image) has finished loading.

Enhancing Hyperlinks with Hijax

Let's move this goodness into StarTrackr! then. We're going to wow our client by setting up a host of pages containing key celebrities' biographies. The main page will include a bunch of standard hyperlinks to take you to the biography pages. Then, with our new Ajax skills, we'll intercept the links when a user clicks on them, and instead of sending the user to the biography page, we'll load the information below the links.

This is a great technique for loading external information; as well as our home page loading snappily, any users who visit our site without JavaScript will still be able to visit the biography pages as normal links. Progressively enhancing hyperlinks in this manner is sometimes called **hijax**, a term coined by Jeremy Keith (you hijack the hyperlinks with Ajax, get it?).

To start on our site, we're going to need some HTML to load in. Keeping it nice and simple for now, we'll construct pages consisting of just a heading and a description:

chapter_06/02_hijax_links/baronVonJovi.html (excerpt)

```
<body>
  <h1>Baron von Jovi</h1>
  <p id="description">
    It's a little known fact that Baron von Jovi …
  </p>
</body>
```

We'll require one HTML page per celebrity. If you had millions of entries, you'd probably want to avoid coding them all by hand—but you could load them from a database, passing a query string to a server-side script to load the correct page. We only have a few featured celebs, so we'll do it the long way.

Limitations of the `load` Function

For security reasons, the content you load must be stored on the same domain as the web page from which your script is running. Web browsers typically do not let you make requests to third-party servers, to prevent **Cross-site Scripting** attacks —that is, evil scripts being maliciously injected into the page. If you need to access content hosted on a different domain, you may need to set up a server-side proxy that calls the other server for you. Alternatively, if the third-party server can deliver JSONP data, you could have a look at the jQuery `getJSON` function. We'll be looking into this function very shortly.

Once we have our catalog, we'll insert a regular old list of links into the StarTrackr! page. We should then be able to click through to the correct biography page:

---

chapter_06/02_hijax_links/index.html *(excerpt)*

```html
<ul id="biographies">
  <li><a href="barronVonJovi.html">Baron von Jovi</a></li>
  <li><a href="computators.html">The Computadors</a></li>
  <li><a href="darthFader.html">Darth Fader</a></li>
  <li><a href="moFat.html">Mo' Fat</a></li>
</ul>
<div id="biography">
  Click on a celeb above to find out more!
</div>
```

We've added an extra `div` underneath the list. This is where we'll inject the response from our Ajax calls. The next step is to intercept the links—and do some Ajax:

---

chapter_06/02_hijax_links/script.js *(excerpt)*

```javascript
$('#biographies a').click(function(e) {
  var url = $(this).attr('href');
  $('#biography').load(url);
  e.preventDefault();
});
```

First, we select all the links inside the unordered list, and prevent the default event from occurring (which would be to follow the link and load the target page). We grab the original destination of the link (by retrieving the `href` attribute of the link we clicked on), and pass it onto the `load` function.

This code works perfectly, but injecting the entire contents of the page turns out to be a bit problematic. Our new content contains `<h1>` tags, which should really be used to give the title of the entire page, instead of a small subsection. The problem is that we don't necessarily want to load the entire page via Ajax, just the bits we're interested in. And once again, jQuery has us covered …

Picking HTML with Selectors

The `load` action lets you specify a jQuery selector as part of the URL string. Only page elements that match the selector will be returned. This is extremely powerful, as it lets us build a complete and stand-alone web page for our regular links, and then pull out snippets for our Ajax links.

The format for using selectors with `load` is very simple: you just add the selector string after the filename you wish to load, separated with a space:

```
$('#biography').load('computadors.html div:first');
```

The selector you use can be as complex as you like—letting you pick out the most interesting parts of the page to pull in. For our StarTrackr! biographies, we'd like to display the information contained in the description section. We'll modify the code to look like this:

chapter_06/03_load_with_selector/script.js (excerpt)

```
var url = $(this).attr('href') + ' #description';
```

Be sure to include a space before the hash, to separate it from the filename. If you run this version, you'll see that now only the description `div` is loaded in. We will have a proper look at adding loading indicators very soon, but until then you can code up a quick and dirty solution: just replace the target element's text with "loading …" before you call `load`. Again, with your files sitting on your local machine, you'll never see the loading text, but it's good to know how to do it:

chapter_06/03_load_with_selector/script.js (excerpt)

```
$('#biography').html('loading…').load(url);
```

There you have it! Ready to show the client. But since it only took us 15 minutes, perhaps we should look into the `load` function's nooks and crannies a little so we can spruce it up even more.

 ## The Entire Page Is Still Loaded

You might think that specifying a selector could be a sneaky way to reduce the bandwidth of your Ajax calls. It doesn't work that way, unfortunately. Regardless of whether or not you add a selector, the entire page is returned, and then the selector is run against it!

Advanced `loading`

There are a few additional tweaks you can make to your `load` calls if you need to. A common requirement is to specify some data to pass along to the server; for example, if you had a search function that returned information based on a query string, you might call it like this:

```
$('div#results').load('search.php', 'q=jQuery&maxResults=10');
```

The second parameter passed to `load` is called `data`. If you pass in a string (as we did above), jQuery will execute a `GET` request. However, if you instead pass an object containing your data, it will perform a `POST` request.

Additionally, we can perform processing when a request has finished by supplying a callback function. The callback function will be passed three parameters: the response text (the actual data), a string containing the status of the response (fingers crossed for success), and the full response object itself:

```
$('div#result').load('feed.php', function(data, status, response) {
  // Post-processing time!
});
```

The `data` and `callback` parameters to the request are optional, as are the parameters to the callback function itself. This allows you to use syntax as simple or as complex as you require when calling `load`.

Prepare for the Future: `live` and `die`

You have the all-important Ajax component running—so it's time to show the client. He's excited. "This is great stuff!" he bellows. "Oh, oh! Can you also make it so the background is highlighted when you move your mouse over the biography?"

"Sure thing," you say. "That's just a two-second job …" and you scribble out some simple jQuery below your Ajax code:

```
$('p#description').mouseover(function() {
  $(this).css('background-color','yellow');
});
```

"There you go," you say, confidently. But as you refresh the page, you notice that this code fails to work! Why? If you think about it, it makes sense: we're attaching the event handler to the `p#description` element when the document loads, but when the document first loads there's no `p#description` element! We're adding it dynamically with Ajax later on. What to do?

We *could* work around this problem by only adding the mouseover event in the callback function of our Ajax code, but there's a nicer way: the `live` method. `live` lets you bind a handler in a manner similar to what we've been doing so far—except that it works for all current *and future* matched elements. That's quite amazing; jQuery will remember your selection criteria, and if it sees a match on any new elements that you add, it will attach the event handler!

The syntax is a little different than for regular events, but `live` is a fantastically powerful feature when using Ajax (or indeed, any time you plan on adding new elements to the page dynamically). To fix up our example above, we'll rewrite the mouseover event using the `live` method:

chapter_06/04_live_event_handler/script.js *(excerpt)*

```
$('#description').live('mouseover', function() {
  $(this).css('background-color', 'yellow');
});
```

 `live` like Jive or `live` like Give?

The `live` function has a corresponding `die` event—so you might be wondering how to pronounce "live"? *Live* like *jive* or *live* like *give*? After many heated internal debates, we turned to good old-fashioned research, and we can reveal that the answer is ... *live* like *jive*!

With this code running, whenever a new element is added that matches `#description`, our event handler code will be attached. To use `live`, you specify the event you'd like to handle, and the function you'd like to run when the event is fired. If you want to stop the event from occurring later on, you need to unbind it with the `die` method:

```
$('p#description').die('mouseover');
```

The mouseover event handler will be removed, and will no longer be attached to new elements matching the selector.

 Named Functions

If you attach a named function (rather than an anonymous function) with live, you can remove individual functions by specifying their name as a second parameter to die: $('#el').die('click', myFunction);. This way, any other handlers that you have bound to the element will continue to run.

Fetching Data with $.getJSON

"Now that you have all this Ajax stuff running," says the client, in an alarmingly offhand manner, "could you just add a list of the latest Twitter comments about celebrities at the top of the page? My investors are coming around this afternoon, and I promised them we'd have Web 2.0 mashup stuff to show them. That should be easy, shouldn't it? I mean, you already have Ajax working … Thanks."

A few years ago, the term **mashup** was coined to describe applications or sites which grab data from multiple third-party web sites and squish it together in a new and (with any luck) interesting way. Many web site owners recognized the benefit of opening up their data for people to play with, and opened up XML feeds that programmers could access. This type of open data source is generally referred to as an **API**, or Application Programming Interface; it's a way for developers to programmatically access a site or application's data. However, XML is a bulky format, and one which is difficult to parse on the client side.

Recently, **JSON** (JavaScript Object Notation, usually pronounced like "Jason") has become a popular format for data interchange in Ajax applications. JSON is a lightweight alternative to XML, where data is structured as plain JavaScript objects. No parsing or interpretation is required—it's ready to go in our scripts!

jQuery provides us with a fantastic method for fetching JSON data: $.getJSON. This basic version of this method accepts a URL and a callback function. The URL is a service that returns data in JSON format. If the feed is in the JSONP format, you're able to make requests across domains. As an example, let's grab a list of web pages that were recently tagged with "celebs" on the social bookmarking web site delicious.com:[1]

chapter_06/05_getJSON/script.js *(excerpt)*

```
$.getJSON(
  'http://feeds.delicious.com/v2/json/tag/celebs?callback=?',
  function(data) {
    alert('Fetched ' + data.length + ' items!');
  });
```

Where did that URL come from? We found it by reading the documentation on the site's API help page.[2] Every site will have different conventions and data formats, so it's important to spend some time with the API docs!

A Client-side Twitter Searcher

But why are we wasting time on Delicious? We have a Twitter stream to incorporate, and we need to do it quick smart. Following the API link from the Twitter home page[3] will lead us to the information we need to get this show on the road. We'll use the search URL to return the JSON data for recent public tweets about celebrities:

chapter_06/06_twitter_search/script.js *(excerpt)*

```
var searchTerm = "celebs";
var baseUrl = "http://search.twitter.com/search.json?q=";
$.getJSON(baseUrl + searchTerm + "&callback=?", function(data) {
  $.each(data.results, function() {
  $('<div></div>')
    .hide()
    .append('<img src="' + this.profile_image_url + '" />')
    .append('<span><a href="http://www.twitter.com/'
      + this.from_user + '">' + this.from_user
      + '</a> ' + this.text + '</span>')
    .appendTo('#tweets')
    .fadeIn();
  });
```

---

[1] http://delicious.com
[2] http://delicious.com/help/api
[3] http://apiwiki.twitter.com/

The search results are returned in the form of an object containing a `results` array. We iterate over each of the array items using jQuery's `$.each` helper method. This function will execute the function we pass to it once for each item in the initial array. For each item we create a new `div` containing the user's profile picture, a link to their profile on Twitter, and the text of the celebrity-related tweet. The result: a cool Twitter display in just a few lines of code!

 Working with JSON

If you've tried a few `getJSON` calls to remote servers, you might have noticed that the data returned requires a bit of work to decipher. You'll (mostly) have to figure it out for yourself. Different services have API documentation of varying quality and clarity. Sometimes it will provide you with examples, but at other times you'll be left on your own. One way to examine an API's data structure is to type the API URL directly into your web browser and inspect the resulting JSON directly.

The jQuery Ajax Workhorse

If you were feeling particularly adventurous and hunted down the `load` function in the jQuery core library source code, you'd find that sitting snuggly at the bottom of the function would be a call to the `$.ajax` method. In fact, if you were to investigate any of jQuery's Ajax functions, you'd find it's the same with all of them!

All of jQuery's Ajax functions are simply wrappers around the `$.ajax` method, each designed to provide you with a simple interface for a specific type of task. By having these helper methods and additional functionality, jQuery gives you an Ajax Swiss Army knife that strikes the perfect balance between power and ease-of-use.

The `$.ajax` method is the heart of jQuery's Ajax abilities and is the most powerful and customizable Ajax method available to us. Being the most complex in jQuery's arsenal, it can take a while to conquer, but it's well worth the effort; this is the creature you'll be spending most of your Ajax time with.

Use the Source, Luke!

If you've made it this far in your jQuery quest, you should be bold enough to have a peek at the JavaScript that makes up your library of choice. Even if you struggle to understand everything that's going on, it's often helpful to see broadly what the underlying code is doing—it can sometimes help you discover functionality that you might have missed if you only read the documentation. Make sure you're looking at the non-minified version, though, otherwise you'll see nothing but gibberish!

The syntax used with the `$.ajax` method is more complex than the others we've encountered so far, because you need to spell out everything you want it to do: it will take nothing for granted. It's still fairly straightforward to use, though. Here's a simple `GET` request:

```
$.ajax({
  type: 'GET',
  url: 'getDetails.php',
  data: { id: 142 },
  success: function(data) {
    // grabbed some data!
  };
});
```

We specify the request type, the URL to hit, and a success callback wherein we can manipulate the data. Easy. The complexity emerges from the number of possible options you can provide. There are over 20 available options, ranging from error callbacks, to usernames and passwords for authentication requests, to data filter functions for pre-processing returned information ... You'll only need some of these options most of the time—most common functionality uses just a few. But we'll be putting a bunch of the options to good use in the coming sections and chapters, so they'll become quite familiar to you. A full reference of all the options available can be found in Appendix A.

Common Ajax Settings

Oftentimes you'll want to apply several of the same settings to multiple Ajax calls in the same script. Typing them out at length each time would grow tedious, so jQuery allows you to specify global settings with the `$.ajaxSetup` action:

```
$.ajaxSetup({
  type: 'POST'
  url: 'send.php',
  timeout: 3000
});
```

This sets the defaults for further Ajax calls, though you can still override them if you need to. By specifying the common defaults for the page, we can dramatically simplify the code required to actually send a request:

```
$.ajax({
  data: { id: 142 }
});
```

This call will send a POST request to send.php, which will time out if it takes longer than 3,000 milliseconds. Some settings are unable to be set via the $.ajaxSetup method; error, complete, and success callback functions, for example, should be handled with the global Ajax events described in the next section.

Loading External Scripts with $.getScript

Cramming desktop-style functionality into our web apps is great, but suffers a downside: as our applications become larger, download time increases proportionately. And the fickle public have better things to do than just sit around twiddling their thumbs waiting for our masterpieces to unveil themselves—and will go elsewhere. We need our application to be as snappy as possible. And, unsurprisingly, jQuery is here to give us a helping hand.

The $.getScript function will load and execute a JavaScript file via Ajax. How does this help us out? Well, if we plan carefully, we can load a minimal amount of our code when the page loads and then pull in further files as we need them. This is particularly useful if we require any plugins that have a sizeable footprint, but regardless of size you should try to delay the loading of your code until it's absolutely necessary.

By way of example, let's load in the Color plugin we saw in the section called "Color Animation" in Chapter 3 from the jQuery plugin repository:

```
$.getScript('http://view.jquery.com/trunk/plugins/color/
➥jquery.color.js', function() {
  $('body').animate({'background-color': '#fff'}, 'slow');
});
```

GET and POST Requests

Finally, jQuery packs in a couple of helper functions for performing GET and POST requests. These are simple wrapper functions around the $.ajax method, but are more convenient to use; just select a URL and any data you want to push—and off you go!

The two calls are almost identical, with the only difference being the HTTP request type: $.get will perform a GET request and $.post will perform a POST request. Both requests accept the same parameters, which (besides the URL) are all optional:

```
$.get(url, data, callback, dataType);
$.post(url, data, callback, dataType);
```

The data parameter should contain any data that needs to be sent to the server. As with the $.ajax function, the callback we specify will be passed the response data and status. The type parameter lets you specify the data type that will be passed on to the callback function; this can be xml, html, script, json, jsonp, or text, but it's unlikely you'll ever need to use this parameter. Here's what these methods look like in action:

```
$.get("getInfo.php", function(data) {
  alert("got your data:" + data);
});

$.post("setInfo.php", {id: 2, name: "DJ Darth Fader"});
```

Yes, they're very easy and convenient, but beware! The $.get and $.post methods are supposed to be for quick, one-off requests. The callback function only fires when everything goes hunky-dory—so unless you're watching with a global event handler (which we'll cover in the next section), you'll never know if a call fails. In some situations that's totally acceptable: perhaps you're just intermittently pinging a service, in which case $.get is a fine solution. But for most production-level functionality, you're just going to have to get used to the more complex $.ajax method!

jQuery Ajax Events

When making Ajax requests with jQuery, a number of events are fired. These can be handled anytime we'd like to do some extra processing—perhaps adding a "loading" message when a request begins and removing it when it concludes, or handling any errors that may have occurred.

There are two types of Ajax events in jQuery: local and global. Local events apply only to individual Ajax requests. You handle local events as callbacks, just as you do with any of the other events we've seen. Global events are broadcast to any handlers that are listening, and so present a great way to implement functionality that should apply to all requests.

As an example, jQuery defines an `error` local event and an `ajaxError` global event. The `error` event can be handled for an individual request, whereas `ajaxError` can handle an error that occurs in any request. Local events are handled inside the `$.ajax` call, like this:

```
$.ajax({
  url: "test.html",
  error: function() {
    alert('an error occurred!');
  }
});
```

Global events, on the other hand, are generally attached to the DOM node where you'd like to show a response to the user. For instance, you may have a `div` element for displaying your Ajax error messages:

```
$("#msg").ajaxError(function(event, request, settings) {
  $(this).html("Error requesting page " + settings.url + "!");
});
```

Whenever any Ajax call from the page fires an error, this handler will be called. We're interested in more than just errors though: there are a bunch of other interesting events we can hook into if we need to. They're all structured as above, and most have a corresponding local and global version—so you can choose the granularity with which you handle them.

The `success` (local) and `ajaxSuccess` (global) events let us know when an event has completed successfully. The `complete` (local) and `ajaxComplete` (global) events tell us when an Ajax request has concluded, regardless of its success or failure. You will only receive either a `success` or `error` event for each request—but you'll always receive a `complete` event.

The `beforeSend` (local) and `ajaxSend` (global) events let us react just before an Ajax request is sent into the world. And finally, the `ajaxStart` and `ajaxStop` global events occur when an Ajax request fires and no others are already running, and when all requests are finished, respectively.

We'll be looking at some practical uses for these events in the coming examples of Ajax interactivity.

Interactivity: Using Ajax

Phew! There was a lot to cover in reaching this point, but we've arrived. We know how to nicely structure our ideas in JavaScript, and we're ready to wield our shiny new AJAX tools. It's time to pull up the client's requirements list and put our skills to the test!

The client is fully focused now. He's confident that StarTrackr! will become one of the biggest photo-sharing sites in the world. Accordingly, he's done some business analysis on his competitors and has determined that the biggest problem with most photo sites is that they aren't primarily concerned with celebrities. StarTrackr! is way ahead of the field here—in fact, it has thousands of photos already uploaded by users from around the world. To capitalize on his company's strengths he wants to engage the site's community in organizing the collection.

Ajax Image Gallery

The first step to launching StarTrackr! into the photo-sharing space is to display some pictures on the home page. Our initial version is intended as a proof of concept to show the client how the gallery might look. It will grab random images via Ajax and display them in a container. Every few seconds, it will go and grab some more.

The trickiest part of playing with Ajax is talking to your back-end coders about data formats. You'll need to sit down and come to an agreement on what the data you're sending and receiving should look like. Will the server send XML, JSON, or some custom text format? What fields do you need to pass to the server to update the database? How do you specify empty fields? Will there be any success or error messages sent back?

Our service returns half a dozen random image names every time we call it. We have a particularly lazy developer who insists on giving us a simple, pipe-delimited string of image names. A sample response might look like this:

```
computadors.jpg|night_out.jpg|mr_speaker.jpg|dj_snazzy_jeff.jpg
```

Many web frameworks will now happily return XML or JSON responses for you to consume, but when working with hand-rolled APIs, it's certainly not uncommon to receive plain-text delimited messages that you'll have to manipulate and convert into usable data. In this case, we'll use JavaScript to split the string on the pipe symbol: `data.split('|');`. This will give us an array of image names to work with.

Our gallery is just a bunch of image tags inside a containing `div` element, so the styling is up to you. The starting HTML is as simple as:

chapter_06/07_ajax_image_gallery/index.html *(excerpt)*

```
<div id="gallery"></div>
```

Next, we create a `GALLERY` object literal that will act as our widget namespace. We'll need to define a few constants: a selector for the gallery, the URL for our image service, and a delay time (in milliseconds) for rotating our images. We'll also stub out a couple of methods that will form the backbone of the gallery:

chapter_06/07_ajax_image_gallery/script.js *(excerpt)*

```
var GALLERY = {
  container: "#gallery",
  url: "getImages",
  delay: 5000,
  load: function() {
    // Load our data
  },
  display: function(image_url) {
    // Process the data
  }
};
```

Onto the good part: filling in the guts of the Ajax loader. The first task we'll tackle is store a reference to the GALLERY object itself—because when our Ajax callback methods run, the scope will be changed and this will no longer refer to GALLERY. We saw in the section called "Scope" that this is simply a matter of storing the current scope in a variable, so we can retrieve it later: var _gallery = this;.

For the sample code, we're using a simple text file called **getImages** to substitute for our server-side functionality; it contains an example of the kind of response we'd expect to receive from the server. Note that Internet Explorer will refuse to execute Ajax requests targeting the local file system for security reasons. For testing purposes, therefore, it's best if you use another browser. Of course, if you have access to a server, you should use that instead of a local file!

We could grab our data with the $.get helper method, but our gallery is going to become more complex rather quickly, so we'll be needing the advanced features of the $.ajax function. We set up our callback using the success option. The callback will split the data into an array, with each element containing a reference to an image:

chapter_06/07_ajax_image_gallery/script.js *(excerpt)*

```
load: function() {
  var _gallery = this;

  $.ajax({
    type:"get",
    url: this.url,
    success: function(data) {
      var images = data.split('|');
      $.each(images, function() {
        _gallery.display(this);
      });
    }
  });
}
```

Going Loopy

The `$.each` utility function is a nice jQuery way of looping through JavaScript object and array elements—just pass it the array and a callback function for each element. The callback function also accepts an optional parameter that provides you with the index of the element in the original array, if you need it.

With a collection of filenames in hand, we now need to create the `img` tags and append them to the document. We could do this in the `success` callback of our load function, but our widget will quickly become confusing if we just throw all our functionality into one big bucket like this. A nicer approach is to separate the loading code from the displaying code. That's why we created the `display` stub earlier—it accepts our image URL and adds a new image to the gallery's containing element:

chapter_06/07_ajax_image_gallery/script.js (excerpt)

```
display: function(image_url) {
  $('<img></img>')
    .attr('src', 'images/' + data)
    .hide()
    .load(function() {
      $(this).fadeIn();
    })
    .appendTo(this.container);
}
```

The load we call here isn't `GALLERY.load`; it's the regular jQuery `load` event. So when the image tag has finished loading its source, we perform a `fadeIn`.

We've set up our gallery widget, but we've yet to set it in motion. All that's required is a `GALLERY.load()` call once our document is ready:

chapter_06/07_ajax_image_gallery/script.js (excerpt)

```
$(document).ready(function() {
  GALLERY.load();
});
```

Randomizing the Images

Fire this up in your browser and you'll see your new Ajax gallery in full swing! Well, sort of … it's really just a static set of images being loaded separately from the main page. That is not very *Ajaxy*! Ideally, we'd like to ping our server at regular intervals to rotate the images at random.

Not so Random

Because we're faking a server response with a static text file, the images won't be random: the same six images will load every time. If you have a little server-side know-how, it should be a simple task to build a quick script to serve up random images.

There's another problem with our current gallery: if you load the page without JavaScript, you'll see an Image Gallery section with no images in it. Ideally, we'd like some static images to be there by default, and then replace them with Ajax if JavaScript is available.

If we first solve the problem of periodically replacing the images, we should also be set up to replace an initial batch of static images, so let's look at that first. We'll need to set a timer that will call our loading function every few seconds.

The timer could be set in a few different places, each with a slight variation in effects. We'd like to set it so that requests occur a set amount of time after the previous set has finished loading. If we set a constant delay between requests (say, with the `setInterval` function), a slow network response might cause some images to be displayed for a very short amount of time before being replaced by the next set.

We could avoid this by starting the timer after we process the last set. Perhaps we should start our timer in the `success` callback? Think about that for a second: what would happen if a request was unsuccessful? Our `success` callback would never fire, so we'd never set up our timer and never reload new images.

The solution is to handle the `complete` event in our `$.ajax` call. We saw in the section called "Ajax Crash Course" that `complete` is called whenever a request concludes, regardless of success or failure. That seems like a perfect place to set our timer:

```
chapter_06/08_ajax_image_gallery_improved/script.js (excerpt)
complete: function() {
  setTimeout(function() {
    _gallery.load();
  }, _gallery.delay);
}
```

The setTimeout function waits for the delay period to expire before calling our GALLERY.load method again. But our display method simply appends images to the gallery's containing element, so every call will just add another stack of images to the page. That's going to get out of hand quite quickly! It will obviously be necessary to clear the existing images before we add the new ones. Again, there are few spots where we could do this; the start of the success method is a good candidate, but we could also experiment with other places.

For our effect, we'd like to fade out the images slowly as soon as the next set is requested. This gives us a nice wash of images fading in and fading out over time. The local beforeSend event is our friend here. It gives us a chance to react before the user's request is sent off to the server:

```
chapter_06/08_ajax_image_gallery_improved/script.js (excerpt)
beforeSend: function() {
  $(_gallery.container)
    .find('img')
    .fadeOut('slow', function() {
      $(this).remove();
    });
}
```

All we'll do is grab the current set of images and slowly fade them out. When the callback method of the fadeOut function fires (indicating that the fade is done), we'll remove the images from the page. The next set of images can now happily take their place.

This also solves our progressive enhancement problem. Now that our gallery widget is removing existing images from the page before loading new ones, we can safely add a set of static images to our HTML page for visitors without JavaScript.

If we showed this cool gadget to the client in its current state, he'd find it hard to believe that it was really using Ajax, because there's no animated spinning GIF image! We'd better add one before he comes around ...

Adding a Spinner

A spinner is an animated image used to show the user that work is in progress on the page; it usually indicates that an Ajax request is underway and we're waiting for the server to respond.

Because the spinner is a JavaScript-dependent feature, it should be added to the page using JavaScript. Often a page will begin with one or more spinners spinning, to show the user that additional information is being loaded. When the loading is done, the spinner is removed. But a common practice among some web developers is to include the image in the HTML or CSS code. This creates a problem: if users have JavaScript disabled, they're greeted with a page full of spinning GIFs, leaving them wondering if anything is happening at all! The rule should always be: if you're going to remove it with JavaScript, you should add it with JavaScript!

You can be fairly flexible with exactly how you create your spinner. We'll be setting it as the background image of a block-level element, but you could just as easily include it as an `img` tag. Here's the CSS:

```
                     chapter_06/09_ajax_gallery_with_spinner/script.js (excerpt)
#spinner{
  height: 100%;
  background: transparent url(spinner.gif) no-repeat center center;
}
```

Our old images are being removed in the `beforeSend` event, before the Ajax request is sent off. That sounds like a perfect spot to start our spinner spinning, so that users will never see a blank, empty page. The new element stretches over the entire gallery display area—and our spinner is centered horizontally and vertically:

```
                    chapter_06/09_ajax_gallery_with_spinner/script.js (excerpt)
$('<div></div>')
  .attr('id', 'spinner')
  .hide()
  .appendTo(gallery.container)
  .fadeTo('slow', 0.6);
```

All good things must come to an end, so after the Ajax call is done we need to eliminate the new element. The optimal place for us to do that is in the `complete` handler, to ensure that we remove the spinner no matter what the outcome of the request. Preceding the removal with a slow fade seems like a nice touch:

```
                    chapter_06/09_ajax_gallery_with_spinner/script.js (excerpt)
$('#spinner').fadeOut('slow', function() {
  $(this).remove();
});
```

 Simulating Server Latency

If you have your code running on a local server, your requests are often going to be answered very quickly—far quicker than the time it takes to see your fading animations in action. Most server-side languages have a method to "sleep" for a given amount of time before returning. For example, in PHP you can use `sleep(4);` to wait for four seconds before continuing. This can help make your testing a bit more realistic.

Global Progress Indicator

We could add individual spinners to every part of the page that will be affected by Ajax requests, but in the end our page is going to contain a whole bunch of Ajax interactions which are all centered around the same widget. We might as well add a global spinner that sits on top of our widget, and let this serve as an indicator for all Ajax events. Whenever any Ajax requests commence, the spinner will be displayed. When all requests have completed, it stops.

Let's start by adding a place for our progress indicator to go. (Although you could add and remove it dynamically as we did earlier, our global element will be used so often that we'll leave it on the page.) We'll also add a class that we'll attach and remove from the element at the appropriate times:

```
chapter_06/10_global_event_handlers/gallery.css (excerpt)

.progress {
  background: #fff url(progress.gif) no-repeat center right;
}
```

Then we register the global Ajax event handlers `ajaxStart` and `ajaxStop`. Remember, the `ajaxStart` method is run when an Ajax request occurs and no other requests are currently running, and `ajaxStop` is fired after all requests have finished.

How does jQuery know?

Internally, the number of Ajax requests in progress is tracked by a counter. You can access this counter at any time via the `$.active` property. This will return a numeric value containing the number of currently working Ajax requests.

Here are our global handlers:

```
chapter_06/10_global_event_handlers/script.js (excerpt)

$('#ajaxInProgress')
  .ajaxStart(function() {
    $(this).addClass('progress');
  })
  .ajaxStop(function() {
    $(this).removeClass('progress');
  });
```

Set up the Progress Indicator First

There is one gotcha to look out for when you're loading content via Ajax when your page loads. You'll need to define your global handlers *before* you do your initial requests, otherwise they'll miss the events being fired.

Endless Scrolling

Ajax allows us to grab more content from the server whenever we want. At some stage, someone realized that this meant paginating data was no longer absolutely necessary; instead of scrolling to the bottom of the page and hitting a **Next** link, we could just load in more content automatically.

This kind of endless scrolling is a technique that's gaining popularity as a way of displaying large amounts of data: images, comments, RSS feeds, emails … but it has its detractors.

Endless scrolling can easily be misused; you need to gauge your needs and decide if it's appropriate. You must ensure that the interaction makes sense to the user and feels natural to use. For StarTrackr!, an endless scroll works, as the images are more like a random stream of pictures, and the users are unconcerned with the scale of the data; there's no need for them to know they're on picture 10 of 1037, for example.

Before we get underway on the second phase of our Ajax gallery, we will need to remove the setTimeout call from the complete event handler. We want the user to be in control now, instead of the timer.

The first requirement for an endless scrolling component is, unsurprisingly, a scroll bar. We'll display one by setting overflow:auto on our gallery container and reducing its width a little.

We've added a couple of new methods to our GALLERY object: an init() function for performing some necessary setup code, and a checkScroll() method which will be called whenever the scroll event fires:

```
chapter_06/11_endless_scrolling/script.js (excerpt)
init: function() {
  var _gallery = this;
  $(this.container).scroll(function() {
    _gallery.checkScroll();
  });
  this.load();
},
```

We keep a local reference to the gallery object again, so it's available inside our event handler.

As you might remember from Chapter 3, the scroll event will notify us anytime the user moves the scroll bar:

chapter_06/11_endless_scrolling/script.js *(excerpt)*

```
checkScroll: function() {
  var gallery_div = $(this.container);
  if (gallery_div[0].scrollHeight - gallery_div.height() -
➥gallery_div.scrollTop() <= 0) {
    this.load();
  }
}
```

Our `checkScroll` function looks a bit complex at first, but there's really little to it. We're going to be messing around with the gallery's containing object quite a bit in this function, so we store a reference to it to avoid running the same selector over and over. (This would lead to a significant performance hit—especially as jQuery will generate lots of events whenever the user scrolls the scroll bar.)

Next, we do some math to determine whether the scroll bar has hit the bottom yet. For this we'll need to break out of jQuery for a bit and deal with some plain old JavaScript. The `scrollHeight` property is a nonstandard JavaScript property that's nonetheless supported by all major browsers. It tells us the total scrollable height of an element, unlike `height`, which only tells us how much vertical space the element occupies on the page. In order to access it, we need to pull the raw DOM node from the jQuery object; the shortcut for this is `[0]`.

By subtracting the element's height and the current scrolling position from this `scrollHeight` property, we'll determine how far from the bottom of the element the user is scrolled to. If this equals `0`, the scroll bar is resting at the bottom, and we can load the images.

But what happens if the user starts scrolling up and down like a crazy person? Will we start firing off requests willy-nilly? We sure will! And as the requests start returning, our code will start adding in images—lots of them! That may be a little inappropriate for our gallery control, so as a final touch let's build in a small safeguard.

We'll add a Boolean property to our `GALLERY` object called `running`. When we're about to load some data, we'll first check that the `running` variable is set to `true`. If it is, this means an Ajax call is currently underway, and we won't start another one: we'll just `return`. If it's `false`, we'll go ahead with our call, but first set it to `true`.

Finally, when the request is over (successful or not), we reset the `running` variable to `false`, ready to start all over again:

```
                                    chapter_06/11_endless_scrolling/script.js (excerpt)

var GALLERY = {
  running: false,
  ⋮
  load: function() {
    // Don't call if we're already running!
    if (this.running) {
      return;
    }
    this.running = true;

    var _gallery = this;
    $.ajax({
      ⋮
      complete: function() {
        _gallery.running = false;
      }
    });
  }
};
```

Keeping Context

So far we've been ensuring we can access the gallery object by storing it in a variable, with `var _gallery = this;`. But if you're comfortable with keeping track of any scope changes yourself then there is a nicer way: the `ajax` action has an option called `context` that allows you to set the scope and avoids the need to keep a local reference:

```
var GALLERY = {
  url: "getImages",
  load: function() {
    $.ajax({
      type:"get",
      url: this.url,
      context: this,
      success: function(data) {
        // "this" now refers to the GALLERY object!
        alert('loaded ' + this.url);
      }
    });
  }
};
```

This makes your code neater and shorter—but you have to be aware that the scope is being modified by jQuery in the function callbacks. Other code (such as the `$.each` loop which displays the images) will still obey the regular JavaScript scope rules, so for those you'll still have to keep your own reference. The `context` option doesn't have to be a custom object as shown above—it can also be a jQuery or DOM object:

```
$("<div>").attr("id", "result").appendTo("body");
$.ajax({
  type: "get",
  url: "GetResults.html",
  context: $("#result"),
  success: function(data) {
    // "this" now refers to the #result element
    $(this).html(data);
  }
});
```

Handling Errors

Error handling in Ajax is often left in the "we'll do it at the end" basket. But it's a basket that's seldom emptied. There are a few reasons for this. One is that proper error handling can be tricky to implement. Another is that errors might appear to occur infrequently—especially when we're developing on a local network. As a result, it can sometimes feel like time spent on developing error handling is wasted.

Nothing could be further from the truth! Errors happen—all the time. You know this is true, because you've seen hundreds of them, on web sites and in desktop applications. How your application recovers from problems is key to the overall impression your users will take away from your site.

One of the most common types of error that the end user will experience is when an Ajax interaction starts ... but never ends. This will often be experienced as an eternally spinning, animated GIF. It's a torturous position to be in: Is the page still working? Should I wait just a minute longer? Has my data really been submitted, and if I refresh will it send it all again? Sometimes this will be caused by a JavaScript error (usually when unexpected data is returned), but more often than not, it is because the developer failed to implement any timeout handling.

jQuery includes a simple method for handling timeouts—so there's no excuse for leaving this step out. Like many of the Ajax options, you can specify both local and global level settings, so you can tailor your error handling to your application. To set a global timeout for all requests, use the $.ajaxSetup method and set the timeout property. Let's set ours to 20 seconds:

```
$.ajaxSetup({
  timeout: 20000
});
```

If you have some requests that you expect (or need) to come back faster, you can override the global timeout in the request itself:

```
$.ajax({
  timeout: 4000,

  ...
});
```

It's all well and good to see that your request has timed out—but what are you supposed to do about it? jQuery will give us a fairly good clue as to what went wrong. The error event fires whenever something goes wrong—and this includes when your timeout delay expires.

The handler we specify for this event will receive the XmlHTTPRequest object and a status message that we can use to determine the cause of the error; timeout, error (for HTTP errors, such as everyone's favorite, 404), and parsererror (which would indicate improperly formatted XML or JSON) are values you might see.

You can choose to react differently to different errors, but typically you'll want to simply try the request again. We'll use the `setTimeout` function to wait for a second before sending another request (you might need to add some code to make your server sleep for the duration of the timeout, in order for an error to occur):

chapter_06/12_ajax_error_handling/script.js *(excerpt)*

```
var GALLERY = {
  delay: 1000,
  ⋮
  load: function() {
  var _gallery = this;
  $.ajax({
    type:"get",
    url: this.url,
    ⋮
    error: function(xhr, status) {
      setTimeout(function() {
        _gallery.load();
      }, _gallery.delay);
    }
  }
});
```

Any errors that arise from the `load` operation will fire the error code, which will call `load` again … over and over until it succeeds. Is that a good idea? Probably not! If it has failed ten times in a row, it would seem unlikely to suddenly work the eleventh time around, so at some point we're going to have to throw up our hands and say, "That's it!"

So to finesse this a little bit, we'll make a couple of changes: first we'll add a counter variable, which we'll call `attempts`. Secondly, we're going to be modifying the delay time on each request (we'll see why soon), so we need to add a new method to reset everything to the initial values:

```
chapter_06/12_ajax_error_handling/script.js (excerpt)

var GALLERY = {
  delay: 1000,
  attempts: 3,
  reset: function() {
    this.delay = 1000;
    this.attempts = 3;
  },
  ⋮
}
```

The reset method will be called whenever a request successfully completes, or when we give up entirely because of too many errors. And with the new properties in place we can be a bit savvier with our retrying:

```
chapter_06/12_ajax_error_handling/script.js (excerpt)

error: function(xhr, status) {
  if (_gallery.attempts-- == 0) {
    // Sorry. We give up.
    _gallery.reset();
    return;
  }
  setTimeout(function() {
    _gallery.load();
  }, _gallery.delay *= 2);
}
```

 Increment and Decrement

In JavaScript, if you follow a numeric variable with - - or ++, the variable will be decremented or incremented by 1, respectively. This is a handy shortcut for the - = and += operators we've already seen.

Every time there's an error, we decrement the attempts variable. If we make it all the way down to 0, we give up retrying. Also, we've made a subtle change to the delay time in the setTimeout function: we double the length of the delay on each attempt to call the load method. So on the first error we wait for one second, on the second error two seconds, and if that call also fails, we wait four seconds. This is known as **exponential backoff**, and is a handy way to decrease the frequency of our requests when there's a real problem; if a user's internet connection has dropped, there's no sense pinging away madly waiting for it to come back up.

Code for Errors First!

Error handling can seem like a real pain, and the chances of it being skipped are great indeed! One way to give error handling a fighting chance of making it into your next project is by coding the error cases first. The bonus with this approach is that if you do it well, you're more likely to catch less obvious issues with your other code, so you can end up saving time in the long run.

Even these few simple steps are going to save the day in the majority of cases, but there's a lot more we could do with error handling. For example, you could take advantage of the global `ajaxError` handler to implement some general handlers for your pages, respond differently to different types of errors, or provide error messages to let your users know that something has gone wrong.

Image Tagging

Displaying the images is one thing, but our primary objective in Ajaxifying StarTrackr! is to begin gathering data from the community. Tagging has proven itself a great way to build up a collection of metadata that relates to your content. It works by letting users add words that they think describe the item they're looking at. If a lot of people use the same words, you can be fairly confident there's a correlation between the two. This in turn can help other users browse your site for content that's relevant to them.

Consuming XML

You've had a chat with your developer, and told him that you need some additional fields returned from the data service. He offered a solution that involved indicating rows with pipe delimiters, fields with semicolons, attributes wrapped in curly brackets and tildes, and …

Luckily you know a couple of Jedi mind tricks, and with a swift wave of your hand convinced him that XML was the format he was looking for.

Although JSON is the up-and-coming golden boy of data interchange formats on the Web, you're still going to find a lot of web services that spit out XML. XML is more mature than JSON, so there are more libraries around for the back-end folks to work with. And although JSON is much easier to play with (since it's essentially a JavaScript object ready to go), jQuery makes manipulating XML data a breeze. We've been told that the data we'll be receiving looks like this:

```xml
<?xml version="1.0" encoding="UTF-8"?>
<celebs>
  <celeb id="421">
    <name>Johnny Stardust</name>
    <image>johnny_200.jpg</image>
  </celeb>
  <celeb id="422">
    <name>Kellie Kelly</name>
    <image>kellie_200.jpg</image>
  </celeb>
</celebs>
```

Now that we have our data, we need to update our initial implementation to make use of it. For our first pass we just split the filenames and iterated over each of them using $.each. But now our requirements are a little more complex. We're receiving XML nodes and we need to extract the information we require from them. The good news is that jQuery lets us deal with XML documents exactly the same way we deal with the DOM!

This means we can use all the jQuery actions we already know to traverse the DOM and pick out what we're interested in. For example, we can use find() to search for nodes by name, and next and prev to traverse siblings:

chapter_06/13_consuming_xml/script.js *(excerpt)*

```javascript
success: function(data) {
  $(data)
    .find('celebs')
    .children()
    .each(function() {
      var node = $(this);
      var id = node.attr('id');
      var name = node.find('name').text();
      var image = node.find('image').text();
      _gallery.display({'id': id, 'image': image, 'name': name});
    });
}
```

We loop over each `celeb` node and extract its ID, name, and image URL, which we then combine into an object literal and pass to our `display` method. (This is why JSON is so handy: it already comes packaged up as a JavaScript object!)

We next have to amend the `display` function itself to accept our new data object rather than a simple text string. Our `data` object has some additional information that we'll need to access when it comes time to load the tags, namely an ID, which we'll pass to the tag service. We'll store that value in the `img` tag itself, via the jQuery `data` function.

Now that we have access to a celebrity's name in our data, we can also fix an accessibility and standards-compliance issue with our previous code: we can add an `alt` attribute to our images, containing the celebrity's name:

```
                                    chapter_06/13_consuming_xml/script.js (excerpt)
display: function(dataItem) {
  $('<img />')
    .attr({
      src: '../../images/' + dataItem.image,
      alt: dataItem.name
    })
    .hide()
    .data('id', dataItem.id)
    .load(function() {
      $(this).fadeIn();
    })
    .click(function() {
      CELEB.load($(this).data('id'));
    })
    .appendTo('#gallery');
}
```

Being able to augment DOM nodes with data is tremendously useful; we can now know easily which ID we need to load tag data for inside the `click` handler. Once we have the ID we're ready to move on to the next stage of the image tagging feature: grabbing and displaying the tag data itself.

We could lump this logic in to the `GALLERY` widget, but now we're dealing with a whole new context. Instead, we'll separate it out into a new `CELEB` widget to keep it nice and readable:

```
var CELEB = {
  url: 'celebs.json',

  load: function(image_id) {
    var _celeb = this;
    $('#details input').attr('disabled', 'disabled');
    $.getJSON(
      this.url,

      function(data) {
        $('#details input').removeAttr('disabled');
        _celeb.display(data);
      });
  },

  display: function(data) {
    $('#id').val(data.id);
    $('#name').val(data.name);
    $('#tags').val(data.tags.join(" "));
  }
}
```

Thankfully our developer is now sold on the JSON idea, and has set up a JSON data service to allow us to grab the tag information. This consists of an ID, a name, and an array of tags for us to display.

We use `$.getJSON` to fetch the data—but this lacks a `beforeSend` or `complete` event handler we can react to in order to give the user some visible feedback that a request is occurring. What we'll do instead is disable the form fields before we send the request, and re-enable them when the data comes back, using the `attr` method to set the `disabled` attribute.

Once the data comes back, we pass it to the `display` function and populate the fields. Yet another successful Ajax implementation! Of course, with our simulated JSON response, the celebrity name and tags will be the same no matter which image you click. But you can try changing the contents of **celebs.json** to simulate different server responses.

Sending Form Data

All this displaying of data is great—but if we want to reap some of the benefits of user-generated content and build up a loyal celebrity-obsessed community, we'll have to start moving some data in the other direction!

Naturally jQuery can help us out with this—we just need to collate our data into a form that can be sent. We could read all of the field values and concatenate them into a string—which would be quite cumbersome, really—or create an object that holds all the key/value pairs from the form. The latter would be a little less painful, but there's one more sneaky trick up jQuery's magic Ajax sleeve: you can easily collate data from a form, ready to send, with the `serialize` method.

The `serialize` method sucks up `input` fields that have a `name` attribute attached to them. Therefore, if you want to take advantage of this feature, you'll need to ensure that your fields are named:

chapter_06/14_sending_form_data/index.html *(excerpt)*

```
<form>
  <input type="text" name="name" />
  <input type="text" name="tags" />
  <input type="hidden" name="id" />
  <input type="button" value="update" />
</form>
```

With our markup appropriately set up, we need only call `serialize` on a jQuery selection of the form itself:

```
var form_data = $("form").serialize();
```

Serializing the data converts it into the typical query string format containing the field name and value separated by ampersands:

```
name=Kellie+Kelly&tags=b-grade+has-been+rich&id=8
```

And if you'd rather have your data in a more organized format, you can use the oddly named `serializeArray` action. It's oddly named as it returns an object (not an array) containing the key/value pairs of all the form fields.

Let's take it for a spin:

```
                          chapter_06/14_sending_form_data/script.js (excerpt)

update: function() {
  var form_data = $('form').serialize();
  $.post(this.set_url, form_data, function() {
    $('#status').text('Update successful!');
  });
}
```

The `$.post` method is certainly easy to use! But, as we mentioned earlier, there's no way of knowing if something went wrong—so there's no way we could tell the user about it. You're better off replacing that call with our new friend `$.ajax`. That way, as well as adding an "Update Successful!" message, we can also add error messages and attach a `class` for a spinner too:

```
                          chapter_06/14_sending_form_data/script.js (excerpt)

$.ajax({
  type: "POST",
  url: this.url,
  data: form_data,
  beforeSend: function() {
    $('#ajaxDetails').addClass('progress');
  },
  error: function() {
    $('#status').text('Update failed—try again.').slideDown('slow');
  },
  success: function() {
    $('#status').text('Update successful!');
  },
  complete: function() {
    $('#ajaxDetails').removeClass('progress');
    setTimeout(function() {
      $('#status').slideUp('slow');
    }, 3000);
  }
});
```

The last little interesting tidbit we added was a `setTimeout`, which runs in the complete event handler to slide away the message after a few seconds. To tie this all together, we simply call this update method when the Submit button is clicked:

```
                                    chapter_06/14_sending_form_data/script.js (excerpt)
$('#update').click(function() {
  CELEB.update();
});
```

This works nicely, and looks sharp—a job well done. Of course, as with the previous examples, our mock server is unable to respond to the data being sent and update the tags in a database. If you want to verify the data being sent, you can open up the Console tab in Firebug (which we discussed in the section called "Troubleshooting with `console.log`" in Chapter 4). Every Ajax request your page fires will show up in this display, and you can inspect the contents of each request, as shown in Figure 6.1.

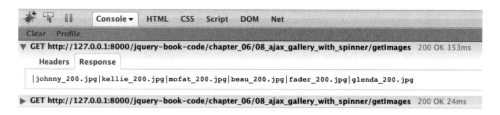

Figure 6.1. Inspecting Ajax requests with Firebug

Ajax Ninjas? Check!

Our client is going bananas. There's no way we can shut him up about it. But hey, it's been a fairly impressive effort on our part: a fully functional, stable, dynamic image gallery and image tagger without doing a single page refresh. And we barely broke a sweat. But there's still plenty more we can do!

Ajax (as we know it) started life as a buzzword and quickly became overhyped and misunderstood. Now that the hype has died down, we can all appreciate Ajax for the nifty tool it is. Thanks to jQuery, it's a tool that's extremely easy to wield—and a tool that's extremely easy to become addicted to. With the growing number of cool third-party JSON APIs and mashup tools becoming available, there seems to be no limit to what you can accomplish with a little ingenuity!

Chapter 7

Forms, Controls, and Dialogs

In its infancy, the Web was a read-only medium. Discontent with a nearly infinite collection of linked documents, early web developers wanted more; specifically, they didn't just want people to *read* their web pages about their cats—they wanted them to sign their guest books and tell them how great their cats were. HTML forms gave us a feedback mechanism that would eventually give rise to the enormous and complex web-based applications that we have today.

JavaScript stepped in to help simple HTML form elements emulate many of the more sophisticated and interactive input controls found in desktop applications, but the code has often been unwieldy and bloated. jQuery allows us to simplify control creation and lets us concentrate on turning our ideas into functioning controls quickly and elegantly.

And it's lucky for us that it's quick! Our client is keen to build on the fancy Ajax controls we've built for him. Now that he has his buzzword-compliant features, he concedes that he probably should have first fixed up some of the forms on the site, which now look painfully 1999 in comparison. He wants "some inline editing, fancy form validation messages, cool dialog boxes, and everything—*everything*—should be drag and droppable, like it's a web site from the future!" Fortunately for us, jQuery lets us build web sites from the future.

Forms

HTML forms are old. And a bit clunky. And browsers vary wildly in how they deal with them. Yet, thanks to JavaScript, these forms have become the basis for some amazingly cool web applications. As always, if JavaScript can do it, jQuery can make it fun!

We know the drill by now: form elements are DOM elements, so jQuery is great at manipulating them. But form elements aren't your typical DOM elements, so there are a handful of special jQuery tricks for dealing with them more specifically. We've seen quite a few of them throughout the book so far—but now it's time to focus on them a little more closely.

Simple Form Validation

Form validation is essential, even if it often seems boring. However, proper, well-designed and implemented forms can make or break how your users perceive your site. Who hasn't had the experience of giving up on a web site because of a particularly frustrating form?

 Server-side Form Validation

Client-side form validation with jQuery should *only* be used to assist your users in filling out a form, and should *never* be relied upon to prevent certain types of data being sent to the server. Users with JavaScript disabled will be unhindered by your jQuery validation, so they can submit any values they want. Because of this, if there's any security risk from users submitting malicious data through your forms, that data needs to be thoroughly validated on the server side.

Although jQuery avoids dealing with the nitty-gritty of form validation, it does provide some convenient methods for accessing and setting form values—and that's half the battle! You can select form fields like any other element, but there are some extra filters to make your code more efficient and readable.

The :input filter, for example, selects all elements that are inputs, select boxes, textareas, or buttons. You'd use it as you would any filter. Here's how we'd give all of our form elements a lovely lemon chiffon background:

```
$('#myForm:input').css('background-color', 'lemonchiffon')
```

If you want to be more choosy about which elements you're selecting, there are a number of more specific form element filters: :text, :password, :radio, :checkbox, :submit, :button, :image (for image buttons), and :file. And remember, you're free to apply multiple filters in a single selection.

Furthermore, there are some additional filters that let you select form elements based on their state and value. The :enabled and :disabled filters will fetch elements based on their disabled attribute, and :checked and :selected help you find radio buttons, select box items, and checkboxes that are checked or selected.

 :checked and :selected in Conditional Logic

These filters are particularly helpful when you need to perform different actions depending on the checked or selected state of a checkbox or radio button. For example, you can check to see if a box is checked with
if($(this).is(':checked')).

After you've selected your elements, it's time to find their values so you can validate them against your requirements. We've already used the val function enough to know what it does: it returns the value of a form field. We can now perform some simple validation—let's test to see if any text boxes in a form are empty:

chapter_07/01_simple_validation/script.js (excerpt)

```
$(':submit').click(function(e) {
  $(':text').each(function() {
    if ($(this).val().length == 0) {
      $(this).css('border', '2px solid red');
    }
  });
  e.preventDefault();
});
```

Fill out one or two of the text inputs, and try submitting the form; any input you leave blank will be highlighted in red.

The `val` action works for select boxes and radio buttons too. As an example, let's alert the radio button value when the user changes the selection:

chapter_07/02_radio_buttons/script.js *(excerpt)*

```
$(':radio[name=sex]').change(function() {
  alert($(this).val());
});
```

This `change` event is fired whenever a value in a form has changed. For checkboxes, select boxes, and radio buttons, this occurs whenever the value changes from its current value. For a text `input` or `textarea`, it fires whenever a user changes the element's value—but only when the focus is moved away from the element. This is a great way to implement some simple inline validation.

Let's revisit our simple validation example, except that this time we'll test for empty fields whenever the user moves to the next field. For this, we'll need to capture the `blur` event, which fires whenever a form field loses focus. This is perfect for inline validation:

chapter_07/03_simple_inline_validation/script.js *(excerpt)*

```
$(':input').blur(function() {
  if ($(this).val().length == 0) {
    $(this)
      .addClass('error')
      .after('<span class="error">This field must … </span>');
  }
});
$(':input').focus(function() {
  $(this)
    .removeClass('error')
    .next('span')
    .remove();
});
```

We're just checking that the fields are filled in, but any type of validation can be implemented in this way. You can check for a minimum or maximum number of characters, or a specific format using regular expressions, or check that a password confirmation field matches the original password field.

Avoid Over-validating!

One important point to consider when designing form validation: keep it simple! The more rules you add, the more likely you'll have forgotten an edge case, and wind up frustrating some of your users. Offer hints, sample inputs, and guidance, instead of rules that will prevent users from submitting the form if their postal code is formatted differently to what you expected!

The submit Event

We also can hook into the submit event, which is fired when the form's submitted. This is a better technique than listening for a click event on the submit button, as it will also fire if the user submits the form by pressing the **Enter** key. If you return false from the submit event handler, the form will not be submitted. In our example below, we'll check all of the text boxes in the form. If any are left empty, we'll pop up a message, and focus on the offending element:

```
                                          chapter_07/04_submit_event/script.js (excerpt)
$("form").submit(function() {
  var error = false;
  $(this).find(":text").each(function() {
    if ($(this).val().length == 0) {
      alert("Textboxes must have a value!");
      $(this).focus();
      error = true;
      return false; // Only exits the "each" loop
    }
  });
  if (error) {
    return false;
  }
  return true;
});
```

With all of these raw, form-based tools at your disposal you can easily add validation to your forms on a page-by-page basis. If you plan your forms carefully and develop a consistent naming standard, you can use jQuery to generalize your validation so that it can apply to many forms.

But—as we've already seen—there are an enormous number of edge cases to consider when designing form validation. If you need really bulletproof validation and would rather spend your time designing the user interaction, perhaps you should consider the Validation Plugin.

Form Validation with the Validation Plugin

Building your own inline validation system can be a daunting endeavor; you need to know regular expressions to be able to verify that an email address or phone number is valid, for example. The Validation plugin solves a lot of these problems for you, and lets you add sophisticated and customizable inline validation to most forms with minimal effort.

We'll stop short of going over every option available for use with this plugin here (that would fill a whole chapter!), but we'll look at the most common ones.

Let's start with the form. To illustrate as many of the different validation options, we'll go with a sign-up form that includes password and password confirmation fields:

chapter_07/05_validation_plugin/index.html (excerpt)

```html
<div id="signup">
  <h2>Sign up</h2>
  <form action="">
    <div>
      <label for="name">Name:</label>
      <input name="name" id="name" type="text"/>
    </div>
    <div>
      <label for="email">Email:</label>
      <input name="email" id="email" type="text"/>
    </div>
    <div>
      <label for="website">Web site URL:</label>
      <input name="website" id="website" type="text" />
    </div>
    <div>
      <label for="password">Password:</label>
      <input name="password" id="password" type="password" />
    </div>
    <div>
```

```
      <label for="passconf">Confirm Password:</label>
      <input name="passconf" id="passconf" type="password" />
    </div>
    <input type="submit" value="Submit!" />
  </form>
</div>
```

To use the Validation Plugin, we simply need to call `validate` on a selection of our form, passing it any options we want to use. The most important option is `rules`, which is where you need to define rules used to validate the users' input:

chapter_07/05_validation_plugin/script.js *(excerpt)*

```
$('#signup form').validate({
  rules: {
    name: {
      required: true,
    },
    email: {
      required: true,
      email: true
    },
    website: {
      url: true
    },
    password: {
      minlength: 6,
      required: true
    },
    passconf: {
      equalTo: "#password"
    }
  },
  success: function(label) {
    label.text('OK!').addClass('valid');
  }
});
```

There are a considerable number of predefined validation rules available, and of course you can define your own. You'll need to consult the documentation to learn about all of them. Here we've used `required`, `email`, `url`, `minlength`, and `equalTo`.

`required` marks a field as required, so it will be flagged as an error if it's empty. `email` and `url` validate the format of the field; emails must contain an @, URLs must begin with http://, and so on. Inside the `rules` object, we define an object for each form field, named after the field's `id`. `minlength` is self-explanatory (and, as you'd expect, there's a corresponding `maxlength`). Finally, `equalTo` allows us to specify a jQuery selector pointing at another form field, the contents of which will be checked against the current field to see if they're the same.

The Validation plugin will add a new `label` element after each form field to contain the error message; by default this will have a `class` of `error`, so you're free to style it in as stern a fashion as you'd like.

By default, the plugin will only display a message if a field's value is invalid. User research has shown, however, that users complete forms more quickly and confidently if they're also provided with feedback for *correct* entries. That's why we're using the `success` callback to set the value of the message `label`, and giving it a `class` to style it with a nice green check mark. `success` is passed the message element itself, so you can manipulate it in any way you'd like. Our sample form is illustrated mid-completion in Figure 7.1.

Figure 7.1. Inline validation with the Validation plugin

It's also possible to customize the error messages themselves, and it's worth noting that there are a number of localized variants in the **localization** folder of the plugin directory.

This example is just the beginning of what's possible with the Validation plugin. Make sure you consult the documentation and the examples in the plugin's demo folder to explore all the available features.

Maximum Length Indicator

Our client wants to limit the feedback form content field to 130 characters. "Like Twitter?" you ask. "Why would you want to do that?" He rambles off a spiel about targeted feedback and attention span and … but we know he just wants to copy Twitter. The "remaining characters" count is another feature making a comeback these days, though the idea of setting a limit on the length of input is as old as computers themselves.

By displaying the remaining characters next to the form field, users have clear expectations of how much they can type.

We'll set a `class` of `maxlength` on the `textarea` we want to target with this effect. Then, in our script, we append a `span` after it and add a new kind of event handler:

```
chapter_07/06_max_length_indicator/script.js (excerpt)

$('.maxlength')
  .after("<span></span>")
  .next()
  .hide()
  .end()
  .keypress(function(e) {
    // handle key presses;
  });
```

After we append the span, the `textarea` is still the selected element. We want to modify the new `span`, so we move to it with the `next` action. Then we hide the `span`, but now we need to go back to our form element to add an event handler, so we use the `end` action. The `end` action moves the jQuery selection back to where it was before the last time you changed it. In our example, `hide` doesn't change the selection, but `next` does. So when we call `end`, the selection moves back to the state it was in before we called `next`.

Now that we're back on the form element, we attach a `keypress` event handler. As you might expect, this event fires whenever a key is pressed. Here we can check whether another character is still allowed—and prevent the user from adding more characters if it's not:

chapter_07/06_max_length_indicator/script.js *(excerpt)*

```
var current = $(this).val().length;
if (current >= 130) {
  if (e.which != 0 && e.which != 8) {
    e.preventDefault();
  }
}
```

Now comes the meat of the effect: we grab the value of the element and use the JavaScript `length` property to give us its length. If the current number of characters is greater than the maximum length, we'll prevent the key press from registering by using the `preventDefault` action of the event.

When handling a `keypress` event, the event has a `which` property corresponding to the ASCII code of the key pressed. Note that we've allowed the **delete** (ASCII code 0) and **backspace** (ASCII code 8) keys to function regardless of the number of characters. If we didn't do this, the user could paste in a response that exceeded the limit—yet be unable to delete any characters to make it fit:

chapter_07/06_max_length_indicator/script.js *(excerpt)*

```
$(this).next().show().text(130 - current);
```

The last task to do is display the number of remaining characters in the `span` we created. We move to the next element, make sure it's visible, and display the results of our simple calculation to indicate how many more characters are allowed.

Form Hints

A nice trick to decrease the amount of space a form takes up on the page is to move the label for a form field *inside* the input itself. When users move their focus to the field, the label magically vanishes, allowing them to start typing. If they leave the field empty and move away, the original label text appears back in its place.

This technique is only appropriate for short and simple forms. In larger forms, it's too easy for users to lose track of what each particular field is for in the absence of visible labels. This can be a problem if they need to revisit or change values they've already entered.

That said, for simple forms like login or search forms, where most users are very familiar with what each field is for, it can be a great way to save space and streamline your interface. Looking at Figure 7.2, you could probably come up with a good guess of how to implement the effect yourself. The only tricky part is how to return the default value to the input when the user moves on without entering anything into it.

Figure 7.2. Form hints

If you guessed that we'd do it using the `data` action, you'd be correct. We'll store the default value in the data for each clearable item—and if the value is still empty when the user leaves, we'll restore it from there:

```
                              chapter_07/07_form_hints/script.js (excerpt)
$('input.clear').each(function() {
  $(this)
    .data('default', $(this).val())
    .addClass('inactive')
    .focus(function() {
      $(this).removeClass('inactive');
      if ($(this).val() == $(this).data('default') || '') {
        $(this).val('');
      }
    })
    .blur(function() {
      var default_val = $(this).data('default');
      if ($(this).val() == '') {
        $(this).addClass('inactive');
        $(this).val($(this).data('default'));
      }
    });
});
```

We need to go through each element and save the default value when the document loads. Then we keep track of the focus and blur events that will fire whenever the user moves into or out of our inputs. On focus, we test if the value of the text box is the same as our default text; if it is, we clear the box in preparation for the user's input.

On the way out, we check to see if the text box is empty, and if it is we put the original value back in. We add and remove a class as we go; this allows us to style the form fields differently when they're displaying the hint. In our example, we've simply made the text color a little lighter.

Check All Checkboxes

With text inputs firmly under our control, it's time to move on to other form controls. We'll start off with a bugbear of StarTrackr's users: there's too much checkbox ticking required when filling in the various celebrity information forms. This is resulting in skewed data, bored users, and inaccurate reports on celebrities. Our client has asked that each category of statistic have a "check all" box, so that the user can toggle all of the checkboxes off or on at once.

Knowing the jQuery form filters makes this task a walk in the park. We just have to select all checkboxes in the same group, and check or clear them. The way we group checkboxes together in HTML forms is by giving all of the related items the same name:

chapter_07/08_check_all/index.html (excerpt)

```html
<div class="stats">
  <span class="title">Reason for Celebrity</span>
  <input name="reason"
    type="checkbox" value="net" />Famous on the internet<br/>
  <input name="reason"
    type="checkbox" value="crim" />Committed a crime<br />
  <input name="reason"
    type="checkbox" value="model" />Dates a super model<br />
  <input name="reason"
    type="checkbox" value="tv" />Hosts a TV show<br />
  <input name="reason"
    type="checkbox" value="japan" />Big in Japan<br />
  <hr />
  <input class="check-all"
    name="reason" type="checkbox" /><span>Check all</span>
</div>
```

We've given the last checkbox the special `class` of `check-all`. This box will act as our master checkbox: when it is checked or unchecked, our code springs to life. First, we construct a selector string that will select all of the checkboxes with the same name as the master checkbox. This requires gluing a few strings together, to end up creating a selector that looks like `:checkbox[name=reason]`.

We then set all of the related checkboxes to have the same checked value as our master checkbox. Because our code is running after the user has changed the value, the `checked` property will reflect the new state of the checkbox—causing all of the related items to be either selected or deselected accordingly:

chapter_07/08_check_all/script.js (excerpt)

```javascript
$('.check-all:checkbox').change(function() {
  var group = ':checkbox[name=' + $(this).attr('name') + ']';
  $(group).attr('checked', $(this).attr('checked'));
});
```

Performance Issues

If your page is large, trawling through every DOM node looking for checkboxes can be slow. If you're noticing pages becoming unresponsive, you might want to investigate the `context` parameter of the jQuery selector, which limits where jQuery will hunt for your selections. We'll cover the `context` parameter in Chapter 8.

Inline Editing

Inline editing (aka edit in place) was one of the first effects that truly showed Ajax's power to create naturally helpful controls. The first time you used an inline edit box you were amazed; every time after that it was unnoticeable—it just worked like it should work.

There are a number of ways you can recreate the effect. The easiest way is to disguise your form fields as labels: remove the borders, give them the same background color as your page, and add borders back in when the users focuses on it! This is a great cheat, and means your form acts just like a regular one (because it is). However, this can be tricky to accomplish, and require a lot of extra markup and styles if you want many different parts of the page to be editable.

As a result, a more common approach is to allow the editing of non-form elements: paragraph tags and title tags, for example. When the user clicks on the tag, the contents are replaced with a text box or `textarea` that the user can interact with. When the task is complete, the original tags are replaced with the new content.

We'll use classes to mark content as being editable. For simple one-liners, we'll use `input` elements (by assigning the class `editable`), and for longer passages we'll use textareas (which we'll give the `class` name `editable-area`). We'll also be sure to assign each element a unique `id`. This is so we can send the data to the server for updating in the database, and reload the new data on the next pageload:

chapter_07/09_inline_editing/index.html *(excerpt)*

```html
<h3 id="celeb-143-name" class="editable">Glendatronix</h3>
<p id="celeb-143-intro" class="editable-area">
  Glendatronix floated onto the scene with her incredible debut …
</p>
```

To make it work, we need to capture a few events. The first is the `hover` event, to add an effect so the user can see that the element is editable (we'll go with a tried and tested yellow background color).

We also want to capture the `click` event—which will fire when the user clicks on the editable content—and the `blur` event, which signifies the end of editing:

chapter_07/09_inline_editing/script.js (excerpt)

```
$(".editable, .editable-area")
  .hover(function() {
    $(this).toggleClass("over-inline");
  })
  .click(function(e) {
    // Start the inline editing
  }).blur(function(e) {
    // End the inline editing
  });
```

When the user clicks an editable area, our code kicks in. First, we grab a reference to the element that was clicked and store it in the `$editable` variable (to prevent us having to reselect it every time). We'll also check for the `active-inline` class with `hasClass`. If the element already has the `active-inline` class, it's already an edit box. We'd rather not replace the edit box with another edit box:

chapter_07/09_inline_editing/script.js (excerpt)

```
// Start the inline editing
var $editable = $(this);
if ($editable.hasClass('active-inline')) {
  return;
}
```

Next up, we want to grab the contents of the element—and then remove it. To obtain the contents we'll just save the `html` data to a variable … but we'll also use the `$.trim` method to remove whitespace from the start and end of the content string. This is necessary because, depending on how your HTML is laid out, the string could have extra carriage returns and line spaces that we want to prevent showing up in the text box.

Then we add our `active class`, which serves the dual purpose of indicating that editing is in process, and providing a hook for our styles. Finally, we clear out the current element with the `empty` action. This command is similar to `remove`, except that calling `empty` on an element will result in all of its *children* being removed, rather than the element itself:

chapter_07/09_inline_editing/script.js (excerpt)

```
var contents = $.trim($editable.html());
$editable
  .addClass("active-inline")
  .empty();
```

Chaining with `empty` and `remove`

It's important to remember that any jQuery actions you chain after a `remove` or `empty` command will be applied to the removed selection and *not* the selection that you had before you removed the elements. The reasoning behind this is that if you simply threw away the elements, they'd be lost forever. This way you have the option to keep them around, process them, or store them for future use.

Finally, it's time to insert our brand-new text box or `textarea`. We will check for the `editable class` to determine which kind of form element we need to append (remember that we indicated multiline content with `editable-area`). We set the new element's value with the contents of the elements we removed, and append it to the target element:

chapter_07/09_inline_editing/script.js (excerpt)

```
// Determine what kind of form element we need
var editElement = $editable.hasClass('editable') ?
  '<input type="text" />' : '<textarea></textarea>';

// Replace the target with the form element
$(editElement)
  .val(contents)
  .appendTo($editable)
  .focus()
  .blur(function(e) {
    $editable.trigger('blur');
  });
```

You might be curious about the use of the `trigger` function. It's simply a different way to cause an event to fire (so, in this example, we could also have used the `$editable.blur()` syntax we've already seen). The trigger action is more flexible than its shorter counterpart—but for now we'll just stick with the basic usage.

`trigger` is being used in this example for clarity: to show whoever is reading the code that we want to manually fire an event. In this case we're just passing on the event; the `input` was blurred, so we tell the original element that it's time to finish editing. We could manage all of this inside the `input` box's `blur` event handler, but by delegating the event like this, we avoid nesting our code another level (which would make it harder to read). It also makes sense to let the original element deal with its own logic.

The counterpart to `trigger` is `bind`. `bind` lets us add event handlers to an object. Sound familiar? So far we've been binding events by using shorthand convenience methods like `click`, `hover`, `ready`, and so on. But if you pop the hood, you'll see that internally they all rely on `bind`.

The `bind` action takes a string containing the name of the event to bind, and a call-back function to run. You can also bind multiple events to an item in a single call by wrapping them in an object. For example, our code attached three separate events to `.editable` and `.editable-area` elements: `click`, `hover`, and `blur`. If you wanted to, you could rewrite that with the `bind` syntax:

```
$('.editable, .editable-area').bind({
  hover: function(e) {
    // Hover event handler
  },
  click: function(e) {
    // Click event handler
  },
  blur: function(e) {
    // Blur event handler
  }
});
```

Let's return to our example; with the editing over, we can go back to our default state. We'll grab the value from the form element, and send it to the server with `$.post`, putting a "Saving ..." message in place as we do so. When the POST is done, we eliminate the message and replace it with the updated value. As with the Ajax functionality we saw in the previous chapter, we're faking a server-side response with an empty **save** file. In a real world application, you'd want to check that the changes had actually been saved to the database by checking the response data:

chapter_07/09_inline_editing/script.js *(excerpt)*

```
.blur(function(e) {
  // end the inline editing
  var $editable = $(this);

  var contents = $editable.find(':first-child:input').val();
  $editable
    .contents()
    .replaceWith('<em class="ajax">Saving … </em>');

  // post the new value to the server along with its ID
  $.post('save',
    {id: $editable.attr('id'), value: contents},
    function(data) {
      $editable
        .removeClass('active-inline')
        .contents()
        .replaceWith(contents);
    });
});
```

There are two new jQuery functions in this block of code, but both of them are fairly self-explanatory. `contents()` returns the entire contents of a DOM node, which can include other DOM elements and/or raw text, and `replaceWith()` swaps whatever you've selected with whatever you pass to it. Be careful when using the latter method; in our example we know that `contents()` will only return one element—but if it returned multiple elements, each of those elements would be replaced with the same loading message!

Autocomplete

We've appeased the client—he's having a blast playing with the inline edit fields over in the corner. While we have a few minutes up our sleeves until his next request, let's really impress him by having the "last known whereabouts" field of the celebrity form autocomplete from a list of major cities. The resulting functionality is illustrated in Figure 7.3.

We'll use the Autocomplete plugin from the jQuery plugin repository. It's a full-featured and stable plugin that provides exactly the functionality we need, with minimum weight.

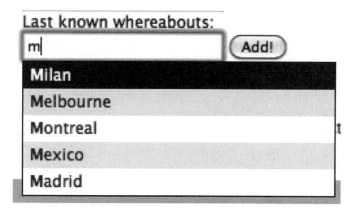

Figure 7.3. Autocompleting "last known whereabouts" field

Firstly, we need the plugin. Head over to the repository and grab it,[1] have a quick look at the examples, then include it your page.

We'll also need to set some CSS styles. There's an example CSS file included with the plugin, so you can gain some idea of the `class`es that are added. We've used several of these styles to give our drop-down suggestion list a standard appearance.

The Autocomplete plugin attaches itself to a `select` box. We're applying it to the location field in our simple form:

chapter_07/10_autocomplete/index.html *(excerpt)*

```
<label for="location">Last known whereabouts:</label>
<input type="text" id="location"/>
```

Now let's see what the Autocomplete plugin can do for us. By default, it requires a local collection of data stored in an array; this is perfect for us, as we want to source our data from an HTML list on the page:

[1] http://docs.jquery.com/Plugins/Autocomplete

```
                                chapter_07/10_autocomplete/script.js (excerpt)
var cities = ['New York', 'Melbourne', 'Montreal', 'London' … ];
$('#location').autocomplete(cities,{
  autoFill: true,
  selectFirst: true,
  width: '240px'
});
```

We've simply passed in a JavaScript array, but Autocomplete also allows us to pass in a URL, in which case it will retrieve the list of potential values via Ajax. Autocomplete will expect a plain-text return comprising one value per line, which should be easy to obtain after a quick chat with your back-end developers!

The above code is enough to get it up and running, but we can also specify a bunch of options. `autoFill` gives us a nice type-ahead effect (filling out the text box with the currently suggested completion), `matchContains` will cause it to match substrings of words, rather than just the first letters, and so on. There's a lot you can fine-tune, so it's worth having a quick study of the options list.

The Autocomplete plugin also fires the `result` event when the user chooses an option. It will give us the name of the tag that was selected as the second parameter passed to our event handler (after the event object). For example, this would alert the selected option when it's selected:

```
$('#location')
  .autocomplete(cities)
  .result(function(event, selection) {
    alert(selection);
  });
```

Very simple, but very funky. And the client is still playing with the last toy we built for him! Perhaps we're a bit too good at playing with form elements, and better return to the to-do list!

Star Rating Control

Building a large celebrity-stalking community is our client's primary goal; he's starting to realize that the users of his site are becoming his product—a product he can start to sell to advertisers. Keen to explore this possibility, he wants to increase user engagement, and help his users feel important. He has to look after his product, after all. We've thought about this a bit, and tossed him a star rating idea—after all, people love nothing more than to express their feelings through the assignment of gold stars. Our control will appear as shown in Figure 7.4.

Figure 7.4. Star rating control

The basis for our star rating control is a radio button group; it's perfect, as the browser enforces a single selection from the group. You can select the range that you want the user to choose from, simply by adding the correct number of buttons:

```
chapter_07/11_star_ratings/index.html (excerpt)

<div class="stars">
  <label><input id="rating-1" name="rating" type="radio" value="1"/>
➥1 Star</label>
  <label><input id="rating-2" name="rating" type="radio" value="2"/>
➥2 Stars</label>
  <label><input id="rating-3" name="rating" type="radio" value="3"/>
➥3 Stars</label>
  <label><input id="rating-4" name="rating" type="radio" value="4"/>
➥2 Stars</label>
</div>
```

The hard part, of course, is replacing these radio buttons with our star control. You can try to grapple with styling the HTML controls with only CSS, but it will be much easier and more flexible if you split the control into two parts: the underlying model that stores the data, and the shiny view with stars. The model, in this case, is the original HTML radio button group. Our plan of attack is to hide the radio buttons, and display a list of links that we've added via jQuery, styled to look like stars. Interacting with the links will switch the selected radio button. Users without JavaScript will simply see the radio buttons themselves, which is fine by us.

For the stars themselves, we will again rely on CSS sprites. This way our control will only be reliant on a single image (shown in Figure 7.5), which saves on HTTP requests and makes it easier for our graphic designers to edit.

Figure 7.5. Star CSS sprite image

Our CSS will apply the CSS sprite image to the links we create that represent half-stars. To move between the different image states, we just need to update the `background-position` property:

```
                               chapter_07/11_star_ratings/stars.css (excerpt)
.stars div a {
  background: transparent url(../../css/images/sprite_rate.png)
➥0 0 no-repeat;
  display: inline-block;
  height: 23px;
  width: 12px;
  text-indent: -999em;
  overflow: hidden;
}

.stars a.rating-right {
  background-position: 0 -23px;
  padding-right: 6px;
}

.stars a.rating-over { background-position: 0 -46px; }

.stars a.rating-over.rating-right { background-position: 0 -69px; }
```

```
.stars a.rating { background-position: 0 -92px; }

.stars a.rating.rating-right { background-position: 0 -115px; }
```

We've decided to make the user select a rating out of four stars, rather than the usual five. Why? User psychology! Offer a person a middle road and they'll take it; by having no middle we make the users think a bit more about their selection. We achieve better results, and we'll be better able to present users with the best content (as chosen by them)!

But four is a limited scale—that's why we want to allow for half-star ratings. This is implemented via an optical illusion—you probably noticed that our star images are chopped in half. Our HTML will contain eight radio buttons, and they'll each be worth half a star. There's two parts to the code for transforming our eight radio buttons into four stars. First, the `createStars` function will take a container with radio buttons and replace it with star links. Each star will then be supplemented with the proper event handlers (in the `addHandlers` method) to let the user interact with the control. Here's the skeleton of our `starRating` object:

chapter_07/11_star_ratings/script.js *(excerpt)*

```
var starRating = {
  create: function(selector) {
    $(selector).each(function() {
      // Hide radio buttons and add star links
    });
  },

  addHandlers: function(item) {
    $(item).click(function(e) {
      // Handle star click
    })
    .hover(function() {
      // Handle star hover over
    },function() {
      // Handle star hover out
    });
  }
}
```

The create method iterates through each container matching the selector we pass in, and creates a list of links that act as a proxy for the radio buttons. These links are what we'll style to look like stars. It will also hide the original form elements, so the user only sees our lovely stars:

chapter_07/11_star_ratings/script.js *(excerpt)*

```
$(selector).each(function() {
  var $list = $('<div></div>');
  // loop over every radio button in each container
  $(this)
    .find('input:radio')
    .each(function(i) {
      var rating = $(this).parent().text();
      var $item = $('<a href="#"></a>')
        .attr('title', rating)
        .addClass(i % 2 == 1 ? 'rating-right' : '')
        .text(rating);

      starRating.addHandlers($item);
      $list.append($item);

      if ($(this).is(':checked')) {
        $item.prevAll().andSelf().addClass('rating');
      }
    });
```

We start by creating a container for the new links (a div element); we'll be creating one new link for each of the radio buttons we're replacing. After selecting all the radio buttons with the :radio selector filter, we take each item's rating and use it to create a hyperlink element.

 Conditional Assignment with Modulus

For the addClass action, we're specifying the class name conditionally with a ternary operator (see the section called "Fading Slideshow" in Chapter 4), based on a bit of math. As we've done earlier in the book, we're using the modulus (%) operator to determine whether the index is even or odd. If the index is odd, we'll add the rating-right class; this makes the link look like the right side of a star.

Once our link is ready, we pass it to the `addHandlers` method—this is where we'll attach the events it needs to work. Then, we append it to the list container. Once it's in the container, we see if the current radio button is selected (we use the `:checked` form filter). If it's checked, we want to add the `rating class` to this half-star, and to all of the half-stars before it. Any link with the `rating class` attached will be assigned the gold star image (which will allow users to see the current rating).

To select all of the elements we need to turn gold, we're going to enlist the help of a couple of new jQuery actions: `prevAll` and `andSelf`. The `prevAll` action selects *every* sibling before the current selection (unlike the `prev` action, which only selects the immediately previous sibling). For our example, we want to add the `class` to the previous siblings *and* the current selection. To do so, we apply the `andSelf` action, which simply includes the original selection in the current selection. Now we have all of the links that will be gold, so we can add the `class`.

 Other Traversal Methods

You might have guessed that, along with `prevAll`, jQuery provides us with a `nextAll` method, which grabs all of an element's siblings occurring *after* it in the same container. jQuery 1.4 has also introduced two new companion methods: `prevUntil` and `nextUntil`. These are called with a selector, and will scan an element's siblings (forwards or backwards, depending on which one you're using) until they hit an element that matches the selector.

So, for example, `$('h2:first').nextUntil('h2');` will give you all the elements sitting between the first `h2` on the page and the following `h2` in the same container element.

If you pass a second parameter to `prevUntil` or `nextUntil`, it will be used as a selector to filter the returned elements. So, for example, if we had written `nextUntil('h2', 'div')`, it would only return `div` elements between our current selection and the next `h2`.

After doing all this hard work, we can now add the new list of links to the control, and get rid of the original buttons. Now the user will only interact with the stars:

chapter_07/11_star_ratings/script.js (excerpt)

```javascript
// Hide the original radio buttons
$(this).append($list).find('input:radio').hide();
```

The control looks like it's taking shape now—but it doesn't do anything yet. We need to attach some event handlers and add some behavior. We're interested in three events. When users hover over a star, we want to update the CSS sprite to show the hover state; when they move away, we want to revert the CSS sprite to its original state; and when they click, we want to make the selection gold:

chapter_07/11_star_ratings/script.js *(excerpt)*

```
$(item).click(function(e) {
  // React to star click
})
.hover(function() {
  $(this).prevAll().andSelf().addClass('rating-over');
},function() {
  $(this).siblings().andSelf().removeClass('rating-over');
});
```

The `hover` function is the easiest: when hovering over, we select all of the half-stars before—including the current half-star—and give them the `rating-over class` using `prevAll` and `andSelf`, just like we did in the setup. When hovering out, we cover our bases and remove the `rating-over` class from all of the links. That's hovering taken care of.

Now for the click:

chapter_07/11_star_ratings/script.js *(excerpt)*

```
// Handle Star click
var $star = $(this);
var $allLinks = $(this).parent();

// Set the radio button value
$allLinks
  .parent()
  .find('input:radio[value=' + $star.text() + ']')
  .attr('checked', true);

// Set the ratings
$allLinks.children().removeClass('rating');
$star.prevAll().andSelf().addClass('rating');

// prevent default link click
e.preventDefault();
```

The important part of handling the `click` event is to update the underlying radio button model. We do this by selecting the correct radio button with the `:radio` filter and an attribute selector, which searches for the radio button whose value matches the current link's text.

With the model updated, we can return to messing around with the CSS sprites. First, we clear the `rating class` from any links that currently have it, then add it to all of the links on and before the one the user selected. The last touch is to cancel the link's default action, so clicking the star doesn't cause it to fire a location change.

Controls

That takes care of our client's primary concern: form usability. Now we can start doing some of the really fun stuff. jQuery and jQuery UI are the perfect tools for moving beyond the primitive HTML form controls we all know and accept. Once we leave the stuffy confines of the Web's ancient history behind, we find that the ability to create amazing new controls is limited only by our imagination. After all, there should be more ways to interact with a web site than entering some text in a box!

Date Picker

Our client wants to add a "CelebSpotter" section to the site, where his users will be able to report celebrity spottings. Of course, they'll need to report the date and time of the spotting. Early tests of this functionality showed that users were often confused by the date format they were required to enter. This problem was partially offset by adding sample data and format hinting, but the client wants to take it further and add a fancy date picker to the form.

If you've ever sat down and created a reasonably functional date picker in JavaScript, you'd be inclined to avoid ever doing it again. It's a lot of hard work for a control that's, in the end, just a date picker. Mind you, date pickers are crucially important controls that can be insanely frustrating when done wrong. The problem is that because they're so involved, there are a lot of places for them to go wrong. Fortunately for our sanity, jQuery UI contains a highly customizable and fully-featured date picker control that lets us avoid many of the potential pitfalls of building one ourselves. An example of this control is shown in Figure 7.6.

Figure 7.6. jQuery UI date picker control

We'll start with the input field currently being used for the date:

chapter_07/12_date_picker/index.html *(excerpt)*

```
<input type="text" id="date" />
```

If you're just looking for the basic date picker, the jQuery code can be no more complicated than a single line:

```
$("#date").datepicker();
```

The date picker is triggered when the `input` box receives `focus`, and slides into view with the current month and day selected. When the text box loses `focus`, or when a date is selected, it disappears. Sure, it looks very nice, and works with the jQuery smoothness we expect—but what does it offer us over and beyond competing date pickers? (Remember, just because you're using jQuery, it doesn't mean you should ignore other suitable JavaScript components.)

The date picker component in jQuery UI is feature-packed. Packed! It is fully localizable, can handle any date formats, lets you display multiple months at once, has a nifty date range mechanism, allows configurable buttons, is keyboard navigable (you can move around with **ctrl** + arrow keys), and more.

All told, there are over 50 options and events available to you to tweak—almost every tiny aspect of the date picker! To make the calendar you see in Figure 7.6, we've used just a few of them:

chapter_07/12_date_picker/script.js *(excerpt)*

```
$('#date').datepicker({
  showOn: 'button',
  buttonText: 'Choose a date',
  buttonImage: 'calendar.png',
  buttonImageOnly: true,
  numberOfMonths: 2,
  maxDate: '0d',
  minDate: '-1m -1w',
  showButtonPanel: true
});
```

The `showOn` lets us choose when the calendar will pop up. The available options are `'focus'` (when the text box receives focus), `'button'` (a button is added next to the text box, which users can click to open the calendar), or `'both'` (which allows for both options). To use an icon for the button, we've specified a `buttonImage`. We also set `buttonImageOnly` to `true`; this means that only the image will be displayed, rather than a standard form `button`.

Next up, we've set the `numberOfMonths` to 2—this means the user will see two months worth of days at the same time. You can even specify an array instead of an integer; for example, `[3, 3]` will show a 3x3 grid of months!

The `maxDate` and `minDate` options let you set the range within which the user can select a date. You can specify a JavaScript date object, or you can use a string to dictate relative dates. The latter option is usually easier, and that's what we've done here. We've set the `maxDate` as 0—which means today's date. The `minDate` we've set as -1m -1w so the user can only select a date that is up to one month and one week in the past. You can plus or minus as much time as you need: `y` for year, `m` for month, `w` for week, and `d` for day.

 Date Validation

You may have set a maximum date for the date picker, but users are still able to select a date outside of that range—they can enter it into the text box manually. If you must ensure that dates are within a given range, you need to be performing validation on the server side! The date ranges you specify in the date picker options are to assist your users in picking valid options; that way, they avoid submitting a form that contains frustrating errors.

Date Picker Utilities

The jQuery UI library also provides a few date picker utilities for globally configuring the date pickers, as well as making it easy to play with dates.

The $.datepicker.setDefaults method accepts an object made up of date picker settings. Any settings that you specify will be applied to all date pickers on the page (unless you manually override the defaults). For example, if you want every date picker to show two months at a time:

```
$.datepicker.setDefaults({
  numberOfMonths: 2
});
```

The remaining utility functions are for manipulating or assisting with dates and date formats. The $.datepicker.iso8601Week function accepts a date and returns the week of the year it's in, from 1 to 53. The $.datepicker.parseDate function extracts a date from a given string; you need to pass it a string and a date format (for example, "mm-dd-yy"), and you'll receive a JavaScript date object back. Finally, the $.datepicker.formatDate does the opposite. It will format a date object based according to the format you specify—which is great for displaying dates on screen.

Sliders

Our client wants his visitors to be able to find the celebrities they're looking for quickly and easily. He also recognizes that many of his clients will be looking for celebrities whose location information falls in a particular price range, so he wants us to add a price range filter to the site. This is a perfect opportunity to introduce another great jQuery UI component: slider!

We'll start with a basic form, consisting of two select boxes: one for the maximum price, and one for the minimum price. Then we'll call on jQuery UI to add a fancy slider to control the values of those boxes. The end result is illustrated in Figure 7.7.

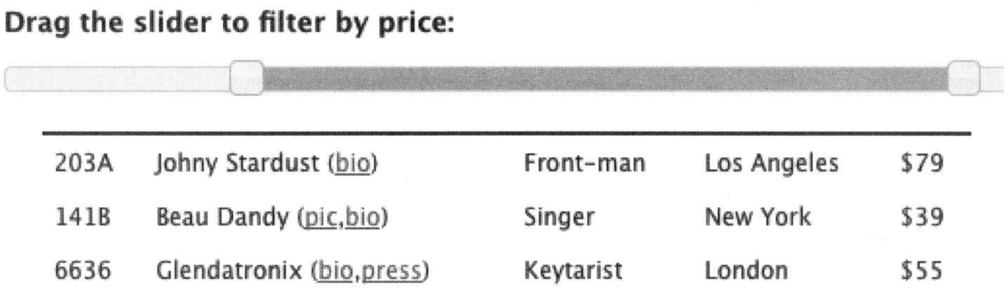

Drag the slider to filter by price:

203A	Johny Stardust (bio)	Front-man	Los Angeles	$79
141B	Beau Dandy (pic,bio)	Singer	New York	$39
6636	Glendatronix (bio,press)	Keytarist	London	$55

Figure 7.7. A jQuery UI slider

Let's have a look at the basic markup:

```
                              chapter_07/13_sliders/index.html (excerpt)
<div id="price-range">
  <form>
    <label for="min">Minimum Price:</label>
    <select id="min">
      <option value="0">0</option>
      <option value="10">10</option>
      <option value="20">20</option>
      ⋮
      <option value="80">80</option>
      <option value="90">90</option>
    </select>
    <br/>
    <label for="max">Maximum Price:</label>
    <select id="max">
      <option value="10">10</option>
      <option value="20">20</option>
      <option value="30">30</option>
      ⋮
      <option value="100">100</option>
    </select>
  </form>
</div>
```

Now for a look at the code. When the page loads, we first grab the current maximum and minimum values in the `select` boxes. Then we initiate our slider by calling the `slider` method on a newly created empty `div`:

```
var max = $('#max').val();
var min = $('#min').val();

var rangeSlider = $('<div></div>')
  .slider({
    min: 0,
    max: 100,
    step: 10,
    values: [min, max],
    range: true,
    animate: true,
    slide: function(e,ui) {
      $('#min')
        .val(ui.values[0]);
      $('#max')
        .val(ui.values[1]);
      showCelebs();
    }
  })
  .before('<h3>Drag the slider to filter by price:</h3>');

$('#price-range').after(rangeSlider).hide();
```

Whoa! That's a lot of options. Let's see if we can break them down: `min` and `max` are the minimum and maximum values of the slider, respectively. `step` is the amount by which the slider increments. `values` is used for specifying the default value of the slider. Because we've specified an array of two values, the slider bar will have two handles, each with a separate value. Here we're using the values from the `select` lists that we grabbed earlier, so that the slider will always match up with the data in those boxes.

`range` and `animate` are helpful options when creating a slider with more than one handle, as we're doing here: `range` indicates that the area between the handles should be styled differently, usually with a shadow or a different color. This option can also be set to `min` (in which case the area between the minimum and the first handle will be shaded) or `max` (which will shade the area between the last handle and the maximum). `animate` simply tells jQuery to animate the handle's position smoothly if the user clicks elsewhere on the bar, rather than simply jumping there.

Finally, `slide` allows you to specify an event handler that will run whenever the user moves the handles on the slider. The event handler can accept an optional `ui` parameter that allows you to access some of the slider's properties; here we're using the `values` property to adjust the values of our select boxes. We also call `showCelebs`, a custom method in which we'll show or hide celebrities, depending on whether their prices fall within the chosen range.

It's also possible to capture the `change` event, which is very similar to the `slide` event, except that it will also fire if the slider's values are modified programmatically (`slide` only fires when the user interacts directly with the slider).

The jQuery UI slider component will create a horizontal slider by default—but if you want a vertical one you can specify `orientation: 'vertical'`.

We've used `before` and `after` to add a title to our slider and affix it to the page, and we've also hidden the original `select` boxes. Try this now, and you'll see a nicely themed slider that you can play with, and which will adjust the values of the `select` boxes.

In order to make it filter the celebrities, we simply need to implement the `showCelebs` method:

```
                                    chapter_07/13_sliders/script.js (excerpt)

function showCelebs() {
  var min = $('#min').val();
  var max = $('#max').val();
  $('.data tr').each(function() {
    var price = parseInt($(this).find('td:last').text().
➥substring(1));
    if (price >= min && price <= max) {
      $(this).fadeIn();
    } else {
      $(this).fadeOut();
    }
  });
}
```

We extract the values of the select boxes, then cycle through each row in the celebrities table, and hide or show it depending on whether or not the price is within the selected range. The only tricky part here is a bit of JavaScript string processing, required to extract the price from the row text; we use `substring(1)` to extract everything from the first character on (which will conveniently strip the prices of their dollar signs). Then we use `parseInt` to turn the string into a number.

We'll also call `showCelebs` on document-ready, so that the list is prefiltered based on the default values in the form.

This works entirely as expected, and allows users to easily and visually filter celebrities based on their desired price range. Sliders are a great UI widget precisely because they're so intuitive: users will know how to use them without being told. You can probably come up with a few other controls that could benefit from being *sliderized*!

Drag and Drop

Dragging and dropping is coming of age. It's always been there in the background, but has felt out of place (and therefore detrimental to a good user experience) next to the mundane text boxes and radio buttons that make up a typical form. But that was the olden days, with olden day forms. Today, if done well, drag and drop can augment forms in a highly usable way, providing a more natural experience that increases productivity. It also supplies a dash of coolness.

If there's one task that even beginner computer users know how to do, it's to drag an item to the trash. The metaphor is very satisfying—if you don't want it, throw it away! On the other hand, the standard web approach—click the checkbox and press delete—is also well known, but far less satisfying. Our client doesn't want to click checkboxes; he wants to drag stuff to their doom, and have them literally disappear in a puff of smoke to show that it's truly been destroyed.

Figure 7.8 shows an image thumbnail in mid-destruction. The user has selected a photo and dragged it out of the grid and into the trash. The grid of photos is nothing more than a set of `img` tags. You can choose any type of element to be draggable, just as long as you can make it look pretty and work well for your users. A nice touch is to set `cursor: move` on the draggable elements—that way users will see the "grabby hand" icon and know they can drag it.

Figure 7.8. Drag and destroy

As always, we'll start with the markup:

```
chapter_07/14_drag_drop/index.html (excerpt)

<div class="trash">
  <img src="trash.png" alt="trash"/>
  <span id="trash-title">Drag images here to delete</span>
</div>
<div id="photo-grid">
  <img src="../../images/fader_100.jpg" />
  <img src="../../images/beau_100.jpg" />
</div>
```

 Progressive Enhancement

For the sake of illustration, we're including the `.trash div` in the markup here. However, this poses a problem for users with JavaScript disabled: they'll see a trash area, but will be unable to do anything with it! In a real-world app, you'd want to start with a fully functional, HTML form-based interface for deleting images (or whatever it is you intend to use drag and drop for). Then, you'd use all the methods we've seen throughout the book to remove all those interface elements from the page, and replace them with the above drag and drop markup.

Drag and drop can be a real pain to make work across browsers. Instead of reinventing the wheel, we'll look to our trusted jQuery companion, jQuery UI. It provides a couple of very handy interaction helpers—`draggable` and `droppable`—to handle smooth cross-browser drag and drop.

No Theme Required!

You'll need to include the jQuery UI library in your page as we've covered before, but this time no CSS theme file is required; `draggable` and `droppable` are behaviors, with no preset styling necessary. They do, however, give you some quite handy `class` names to apply your own styles to, which we'll be looking at very shortly.

Let's sketch out the basic structure of our interaction code:

```
                                        chapter_07/14_drag_drop/script.js (excerpt)
$(document).ready(function() {
  $('#photo-grid > div').draggable({
    revert: 'invalid'
  });
  $('.trash').droppable({
    activeClass: 'highlight',
    hoverClass: 'highlight-accept',
    drop: function(event, ui) {
      puffRemove($(ui.draggable));
    }
  });
});

function puffRemove(which) {
  // Implement the "puff-of-smoke" effect
}
```

This is the skeleton of our interaction. There's still a lot we need to do to achieve a nice "puff" animation—but, incredibly, that's everything we need for drag and drop! Let's take a closer look at what jQuery UI has given us.

draggable

The `draggable` interaction helper makes whatever you select draggable with the mouse. Try this out for size: `$('p').draggable()`. It can make every <p> tag on the page draggable! Test it out—it's a lot of fun. Naturally, there are stacks of options and events to customize the behavior. Here are some of the more helpful ones:

```
$('p').draggable({axis: 'y', containment: 'parent'});
```

The `axis` option restricts the object to be draggable along either the X or Y axis only, and the `containment` option confines the object to a bounding box; acceptable values are `'parent'`, `'document'`, and `'window'` (to stay within the respective DOM elements), or an array of values to specify pixel boundaries in the form `[x1, y1, x2, y2]`. You can also use the `grid` option to confine dragging to a grid, by specifying a two element array (for example, `grid:[20,20]`).

Let's look at another example:

```
$('#dragIt').draggable({
  handle: 'p:first',
  opacity: 0.5,
  helper: 'clone'
});
```

For this next bunch of options, we're operating on a `div` called `dragIt`, which contains at least one `<p>` tag. We use the `handle` option to designate the first p element as the "handle" users can use to drag the draggable element around. We also specify the `helper` option, which allows you to specify an element to represent the node being dragged around. In this case we've set this option to `clone`. This causes the element to be duplicated, so that the original element will stay in place until you've finished dragging. The `opacity` applies to the helper element.

The other option worth noting is `revert`. If you set this to `invalid` (as we did in our photo dragging example), the element you drag will spring back to its original position if you drop it outside of a droppable target area.

There are also three events you can catch—`start`, `stop`, and `drag`—that fire when you start dragging, stop dragging, and are in mid-drag respectively. In our example we only need to react to drop, but you can easily conceive of situations where the other two events could be put to good use.

droppable

The Bonnie to `draggable`'s Clyde is the `droppable` behavior. Droppable elements are targets for draggable items. A droppable element has far fewer options than a draggable element; we've used the most important, `activeClass` and `hoverClass`, above. The `activeClass` is added to the droppable element when a draggable item is being dragged. Similarly, the `hoverClass` is added when a draggable item is hovering over the droppable element.

You can also specify a selector for the `accept` option, which restricts the draggables that can be dropped. This lets you have multiple drop points, where only certain draggable items can go. This can be great for list manipulation.

The events for a droppable element are similar to draggables. Instead of `start`, `stop`, and `drag` we have `over`, `out`, and `drop`. In our photo grid example, we've used the `drop` event to know when to destroy the draggable item.

Both the `draggable` and `droppable` behaviors are complex beasts. Once you're over the thrill of how easy they are to implement, you should have a further read through the advanced options in the documentation.

The "Puff" Effect

With dragging and dropping all taken care of, you can walk away knowing you've created a powerful yet cool control with just a few lines of code. But with all that time we saved by using the existing drag and drop functionality, rather than writing it ourselves, we might as well make this a little more impressive—and add the "puff of smoke" as the image is removed.

Instead of using jQuery's `animate` function, we'll need to roll our own animation solution. This is because we need to cycle through image frames—like creating cartoons. To do this we'll use a PNG image that has five same-sized frames of animation all stacked on top of each other, and then offset the image to show the correct frame. This means we'll need to change the position of the image in discrete chunks. If we were to use `animate` instead, it would change the background position gradually, resulting in chopped-off images halfway between frames:

chapter_07/14_drag_drop/script.js (excerpt)

```
// Implement the "puff-of-smoke" effect
var $this = $(which);
var image_width = 128;
var frame_count = 5;
```

To start off, we'll store our selection and set up a couple of constants. The `image_width` is the width in pixels of the animation image. The `frame_count` is the total number of frames in the animation (the total height of the image, therefore, should be `image_width * frame_count`). Of course, these will always be the same in our example, but this way, if you ever want to use a different animation image, you can find the numbers you need to change right at the top of the script, instead of hunting through it to change them in multiple places.

We then set up a container to house the image. The container will be exactly the same size, and in exactly the same place as the element we're deleting:

chapter_07/14_drag_drop/script.js *(excerpt)*

```
// Create container
var $puff = $('<div class="puff"></div>')
  .css({
    height: $this.outerHeight(),
    left: $this.offset().left,
    top: $this.offset().top,
    width: $this.outerWidth(),
    position: 'absolute',
    overflow: 'hidden'
  })
  .appendTo('body');
```

With the container in place we can now append the animation image to it. Because the container has its `overflow` set to `hidden`, only a single frame of the image will ever be seen. To make the image fit the container (which is the same size as the element we're deleting), we need to scale it to fit. The scale is determined by dividing the width of the container by the width of the image:

chapter_07/14_drag_drop/script.js *(excerpt)*

```
var scale_factor = $this.outerWidth() / image_width;
var $image = $('<img class="puff" src="epuff.png"/>')
  .css({
    width: image_width * scale_factor,
    height: (frame_count * image_width) * scale_factor
  })
  .data('count', frame_count)
  .appendTo($puff);
```

Preloading the Image

If you have a lot of frames in your animation image, it could wind up being a fairly large file and take a while to load. If your user deletes an element before the image has loaded, the animation will be unable to display. A trick for preloading the image is to load it into a jQuery selector in the document-ready function: `$('<img src="puff.png"/>');`. This will load the image without displaying it, so it will be ready for your animation.

We also add a `count` property to the image via the `data` action. This contains the total number of frames left to show. With all of this in place, we can go ahead and delete the original element that was dropped:

chapter_07/14_drag_drop/script.js (excerpt)

```
// Remove the original element
$this.animate({
  opacity: 0
}, 'fast').remove();
```

While that's fading out, we want to initiate the animation. This is going to require a small amount of JavaScript-fu; we're going to set up a self-contained, self-executing loop that plays the animation through once:

chapter_07/14_drag_drop/script.js (excerpt)

```
// Animate the puff of smoke
(function animate() {  ❶

  var count = $image.data('count');  ❷

  if (count) {  ❸
    var top = frame_count - count;
    var height = $image.height() / frame_count;
    $image.css({
      "top": - (top * height),
      'position': 'absolute'
    });
    $puff.css({
      'height': height
    })
    $image.data("count", count - 1);  ❹
```

```
    setTimeout(animate, 75);  ❺
  } else {
    $image.parent().remove();  ❻
  }
})();
```

Inside this function, we're executing the animation. Here are the highlights:

❶ We've wrapped the function in the `(function myFunction(){})()` construct, which is a way to create and execute an anonymous function that can nonetheless refer to itself by name. This is an odd JavaScript construct, and one that you needn't worry about understanding completely; in this case it's handy as it allows us to create a self-contained piece of functionality that can call itself (this will be useful when we use the `setTimeout` method).

❷ We find out which frame we're up to by checking the `count` data.

❸ If there are still frames left to display, we calculate the offset of the image and move the correct frame into view. (We can use `if (count)` in this way because in JavaScript, the number `0` is equivalent to `false`.)

❹ We decrease the frame count so that the next time the loop runs it will display the next frame in the series.

❺ Finally, we call `setTimeout`, specifying our anonymous function as the callback. This way, after 75 milliseconds, the whole process will run again.

❻ When the count reaches zero and the animation concludes, we remove the puff container from the DOM.

Try it out. Drag an item to the trash, and watch it vanish in a cloud of smoke!

jQuery UI `sortable`

Another great feature of jQuery UI is the `sortable` behavior. An element that you declare as `sortable` becomes a droppable target to its children—and the children all become draggable. The result is that you can reorder the children as you see fit. While sortable allows us to order items within a container, it doesn't actually sort anything: the sorting is up to the user.

This makes it perfect for lists of elements where order needs to be managed. Rather than using the fiddly **move up the list** or **move down the list** buttons that we usually see next to lists, we can apply the sortable behavior to them and allow our users to reorder the list in a much more intuitive way.

On the front page of StarTrackr! there are two lists that show the ranking of the week's top celebrities. One is for the A-list celebrities, and the other for the B-list. This is the perfect opportunity to show our client a cool trick: let's make the lists reorderable by the users. They can move the celebs up and down the lists, and even swap them if they challenge their A/B list status. When they're happy with their reordering, they can click the **Accept** button and the changes will be submitted to the server.

Lists are the primary targets for the sortable behaviour. With a little extra work a `div` can also take up the challenge. For this example, we'll use the following markup:

```
chapter_07/15_sortables/index.html (excerpt)

<ul id="a-list" class="connected">
  <li><a href="#">Glendatronix</a></li>
  <li><a href="#">Baron von Jovi</a></li>
  ⋮
</ul>

<ul id="b-list" class="connected">
  <li><a href="#">Mr Speaker</a></li>
  ⋮
</ul>
```

Like `draggable` and `droppable`, establishing an element as sortable is straightforward:

```
$("#a-list, #b-list").sortable();
```

There's a raft of methods, events, and options that are available when an element becomes sortable, and we can combine them to control the interesting moments that occur during the course of the sorting:

chapter_07/15_sortables/script.js (excerpt)

```
$("#a-list, #b-list").sortable({
  connectWith: '.connected',
  placeholder: 'ui-state-highlight',
  receive: function(event, ui) { adopt(this) },
  remove: function(event, ui) { orphan(this) }
}).disableSelection();
```

We've specified two options and two methods to our sortables, and we'll build on those methods to make our actions a little more user-friendly. A nice touch we can exploit is that accessing `this` inside the callbacks (as we've done above) gives us a reference to the sortable element.

 disableSelection

Chained on the end of our `sortable` instantiation is a nifty action: `disableSelection`. `disableSelection`, and its reverse, `enableSelection`, are two really powerful methods in jQueryUI. Calling `disableSelection` makes it impossible for users to select text inside the target elements. It can be used to stop text from being selected when users are dragging—or sorting—the element, and prevents users from accidentally highlighting text when they just want to drag an item.

Let's look at the two methods we've assigned as event handlers:

chapter_07/15_sortables/script.js (excerpt)

```
function adopt(which) {
  if ($(which).hasClass('empty')) {
    $(which).removeClass('empty').find('.empty').remove();
  }
}

function orphan(which) {
  console.log(which);
  if ($(which).children().length == 0) {
    $(which)
      .append($('<li class="empty">empty</li>'))
      .addClass('empty');
  }
}
```

These methods allow us to add the text "empty" to a list when its last item is removed, and remove the text as soon as a new item is added. The `receive` event is fired when a sortable list receives an item from a connected list. We use it to call our custom `adopt` method, wherein we remove the "empty" text if it's found.

Removing a child from a sortable fires the `remove` event, which we use to call our `orphan` function. This method checks to see if the parent sortable has no children. Should it be empty, we give it a child `<li>` and assign it the `empty` class.

Progress Bar

Our client wants to implement a new feature he calls StarChirp, which will enable his users to communicate via short status messages (presumably about celebrities). We have no idea where he could have come up with this idea, but we're happy to have a go at it. He specifies that he wants to differentiate his product from other status update sites by displaying the remaining character count in the form of a progress bar. This makes sense: it'll display the percentage of how much room is left to type, so users can easily see if they're approaching their word limit.

A progress bar is one of the most recognizable messages a user can see. Thanks to countless bad movies, even the layperson understands that the progress bar is the ultimate technological ticking clock. A progress bar effectively shows how far through a long-running process or set of processes we are—and more importantly, how far we have to go.

The simplest way to simulate a progress bar is to include a block-level element inside another block-level element. The outside element's width is set to the length of the progress bar, and the inside element's width is set to the correct ratio in relation to the outer element. Give the inside element a bit of color and that's it!

As we've been using the jQuery UI library for our recent tasks, we might as well explore the whole gamut and see what the jQuery UI progress bar widget has to offer.

We've coded up a small form to hold the relevant elements, but for the progress bar all that's required is an empty `div`:

```
chapter_07/16_progress_bar/index.html (excerpt)
```

```html
<form>
  <fieldset>
    <legend>StarChirp</legend>
    <textarea id="chirper" rows=""></textarea>
    <div id="console">
      <div id="bar"></div>
      <div id="count">0</div>
    </div>
    <input type="submit" value="Chirp!" />
  </fieldset>
</form>
```

Now we simply need to tell jQuery UI which element we'd like to transform:

```
chapter_07/16_progress_bar/script.js (excerpt)
```

```javascript
$('#bar').progressbar();
```

That's it. The progress bar is ready! There's not much tweaking you can do. If you want the bar to default at a value other than 0%, you can specify it like this: `$('#bar').progressbar({value: 50})`.

For our StarChirp box, we'll monitor the user's key presses in much the same manner as we did for the maximum length indicator earlier in this chapter. This time, however, we need to update the progress bar as the user types:

```
                              chapter_07/16_progress_bar/script.js (excerpt)

$('#chirper')
  .val('')
  .keyup(function(e) {
    var characters = 140;
    var chirp = $('#chirper').val();
    var count = chirp.length;

    if (count <= characters) {
      $('#bar').progressbar('value', (count / characters) * 100);
      $('#count').text(count);
    } else {
      $('#chirper').val(chirp.substring(0,characters));
    }
  });
```

The important point to remember about the jQuery UI progress bar is that its range is from 0 to 100. It's a percentage, so you'll need to figure out the percentage to pass in. We'll divide the current number of characters by the total allowed, and multiply the result by 100. Now we have a valid value to pass to the progress bar via the value option.

If there are already more characters in the box than what's allowed, we'll use the JavaScript substring function to chop off the excess.

The effect is that every character we add will move the progress bar to the right, and every character we remove will move the progress bar to the left.

Dialogs and Notifications

In the olden days, there was little requirement for user messages on our brochure sites; perhaps just a "thanks for submitting the form," or a JavaScript popup dialog telling us we forgot to fill out an email field.

These days, as our Ajax-enabled web applications become more complex, the breadth of information that needs to be conveyed is growing: validation messages, status updates, error handling messages, and so on. Doing it in a way that avoids overwhelming or annoying the user can be quite an art form.

Simple Modal Dialog

Modal dialogs are notifications that pop up in the user's face and must be acted on if the user want to continue. It's quite an intrusion—people tend to dislike popups, so they should only be used if the interaction is essential. Our client informs us it's essential that users agree to an End User License Agreement (EULA) to use the StarTrackr! application. Not all modal dialogs are as disagreeable as our StarTrackr! EULA, however, so they're a useful control to learn to build.

What you might notice from the figure is that a modal dialog looks strikingly like a lightbox. It's a lightbox with some buttons! To supply the contents of a dialog, we'll embed the HTML in a hidden `div`. When we want to show it, we'll copy the contents into the dialog structure and fade it in. That way we can have multiple dialogs that use the same lightbox elements:

chapter_07/17_simple_modal_dialog/index.html (excerpt)

```
<div id="overlay">
  <div id="blanket"></div>
</div>
<!-- the dialog contents -->
<div id="eula" class="dialog">
  <h4>End User License Agreement</h4>
    ⋮
  <div class="buttons">
    <a href="#" class="ok">Agree</a>
    <a href="#" class="cancel">Disagree</a>
  </div>
</div>
```

You'll see that we've included a couple of button links in the bottom of the dialog. These are where we can hook in our events to process the user interaction. It's a fairly simple HTML base so, as you can imagine, CSS plays a big part in how effective the dialogs look. We want to stretch our structure and lightbox "blanket" over the entire screen. The modal dialog will appear to sit on top of it:

```css
#overlay {
  display:none;
  top: 0;
  right: 0;
  bottom: 0;
  left: 0;
  margin-right: auto;
  margin-left: auto;
  position: fixed;
  width: 100%;
  z-index: 100;
}

#blanket {
  background-color: #000000;
  top: 0;
  bottom: 0;
  left: 0;
  display: block;
  opacity: 0.8;
  position: absolute;
  width: 100%;
}

.dialog {
  display: none;
  margin: 100px auto;
  position: relative;
  width: 500px;
  padding: 40px;
  background: white;
  -moz-border-radius: 10px;
}
```

Now to bring the dialog onscreen. We'll create an `openDialog` function that will be responsible for taking the dialog HTML, transporting it to the overlay structure and displaying it. The "transporting" part is achieved via the `clone` action, which creates a copy of the current jQuery selection, leaving the original in place. When we close the dialog we're going to remove the contents, so unless we cloned it each time, we'd only be able to open it once:

```
                         chapter_07/17_simple_modal_dialog/script.js (excerpt)

function openDialog(selector) {
  $(selector)
    .clone()
    .show()
    .appendTo('#overlay')
    .parent()
    .fadeIn('fast');
}
```

Because we've added the behavior to a function, we can call it whenever we need to open a dialog, and pass it the selector of the element we want to show:

```
                         chapter_07/17_simple_modal_dialog/script.js (excerpt)

$("#eulaOpen").click(function() {
  openDialog("#eula");
});
```

The second part is returning everything back to its initial state when the dialog is closed. This is achieved by finding the overlay, fading it out, and then removing the cloned dialog contents:

```
                         chapter_07/17_simple_modal_dialog/script.js (excerpt)

function closeDialog(selector) {
  $(selector)
    .parents("#overlay")
    .fadeOut('fast', function() {
      $(this)
        .find(".dialog")
        .remove();
    });
}
```

We need to call the `closeDialog` function from within the current dialog. But as well as closing it, the buttons in a dialog should have other effects. By adding extra buttons in the dialog's HTML, and hooking on to them in the document-ready part of your code, you can run any arbitrary number of event handlers and process them as you need:

```
                              chapter_07/17_simple_modal_dialog/script.js (excerpt)
$('#eula')
  .find('.ok, .cancel')
  .live('click', function() {
    closeDialog(this);
  })
  .end()
  .find('.ok')
  .live('click', function() {
    // Clicked Agree!
  })
  .end()
  .find('.cancel')
  .live('click', function() {
    // Clicked disagree!
});
```

The important part of this code is that we're using the live action. When we use clone to duplicate a DOM node, its event handlers get lost in the process—but live keeps everything in place no matter how often we clone and delete nodes!

This is a simple, but fairly crude way to handle the button events. In Chapter 9, we'll look at how we can set up a custom event handling system. The advantage of the method used here is that it's extremely lightweight and targeted to our particular needs. But manually creating buttons and handling the related events would become tiring fairly quickly if you have many complicated dialogs to look after, so you'll probably be interested in the jQuery UI Dialog widget.

jQuery UI Dialog

As you'd expect by now, the jQuery UI Dialog component is the complete bells and whistles version of a dialog box. Out of the box it is draggable and resizable, can be modal or non-modal, allows for various transition effects, and lets you specify the dialog buttons programmatically. A sample dialog, styled with the UI lightness theme, is shown in Figure 7.9.

Figure 7.9. A jQuery UI dialog

Just like with our custom dialog box, the main contents are specified in the HTML itself, then hidden and displayed as necessary by the library. This way you can put whatever you like inside the dialog—including images, links, or forms:

chapter_07/18_jquery_ui_dialog/index.html (excerpt)

```
<div id="dialog" title="Are you sure?">
  <p>You've assigned the current celebrity a rating of 0…</p>
  <p>Perhaps you are just judging them on the terrible …</p>
</div>
```

We're using the UI lightness theme for CSS, as it matches up well with the StarTrackr! site—but the dialogs are fully skinnable, and as always you can make a custom theme with the ThemeRoller tool (more on this in the section called "Theme Rolling" in Chapter 9). As you can see from the HTML snippet, the `title` attribute specifies the text to be displayed in the title bar of the dialog. Other than that, there's little going on in our HTML … so where do those buttons come from? Let's have a look at the script:

```
                                    chapter_07/18_jquery_ui_dialog/script.js (excerpt)

$('#dialog').dialog({
  autoOpen: false,
  height: 280,
  modal: true,
  resizable: false,
  buttons: {
    Continue: function() {
      $(this).dialog('close');
      // Submit Rating
    },
    'Change Rating': function() {
      $(this).dialog('close');
      // Update Rating
    }
  }
});
```

Aha, interesting! The buttons, including their text, are specified via the options passed to the `dialog` function.

The buttons are grouped together in an object and assigned to the `buttons` property of the dialog. To define a button, you need to create a named function inside the `buttons` object. The function code will execute whenever the user clicks the button—and the name of the function is the text that will be displayed on the button. If you want your button text to contain a space, you'll need to wrap the function name in quotes. The buttons are added to the dialog from right to left, so make sure you add them in the order you want them displayed. This is quite a neat way to package together the button functions with the dialog—unlike our custom dialog where the functionality was specified independently of the dialog code.

 Quotes

In the above example, the second button's name is in quotes, while the first one isn't. This is simply to illustrate the necessity of enclosing multiple-word buttons in quotes; in your code it might be preferable to put quotes around everything for consistency and simplicity.

By default, the dialog will pop up as soon as you define it. This makes it easy to create small and simple dialogs as you need them. For our example, though, we want to set up the dialog first, and only have it pop up on a certain trigger (when the user gives the poor celebrity a zero rating). To prevent the dialog popping up immediately, we set the `autoOpen` property to `false`. Now, when the page is loaded, the dialog sits and waits for further instructions.

When the user clicks the `rating-0` link, we tell the dialog to display itself by passing the string `'open'` to the `dialog` method. This is a good way to communicate with the dialog after the initialization phase:

```
chapter_07/18_jquery_ui_dialog/script.js (excerpt)

$('#rating-0').click(function() {
  $('#dialog').dialog('open');
});
```

That's a nice looking dialog we have there! We can now execute any required code inside the dialog button functions. As part of the code we'll also have to tell the dialog when we want it to close. If you look back at the button definitions above, you can see we have the line `$(this).dialog('close')`. As you might suspect, the `close` command is the opposite of the `open` command. You can open and close the dialogs as many times as you need.

What else can the plugin do? Well, we've specified the option `modal` to be `true`; that's why we have the nice stripey background—but by default, `modal` will be `false`, which allows the user to continue working with the rest of the page while the dialog is open. Also, we've set `resizable` to `false` (and left the `draggable` option on default—which is `true`). These options make use of the jQuery UI `resizable` and `draggable` behaviors to add some desktop flavor to the dialog.

We specified the dialog's title text in HTML, but you can also do it in jQuery via the `title` property, just as you can set its width and height. One less obvious, but extremely useful alternative is the bgiframe option. If this option is set to `true`, the bgiframe plugin will be used to nfix an issue in Internet Explorer 6 where select boxes show on top of other elements.

In terms of events, you can utilize the dialog's `open`, `close`, and `focus` events if you need to do some processing unrelated to buttons. But there's also an extremely useful `beforeClose` event that occurs when a dialog is asked to close—before it actually does! This is a great place to handle any processes you'd have to do regardless of which button was clicked. It's also useful if you need to stop the dialog from closing unless certain conditions are satisfied.

By now, you're starting to appreciate the depth of the jQuery UI library. All of the controls are well thought out and feature-rich. As always, you need to weight the leaner custom option against the more bandwidth-intensive (but quick to implement and more fully featured) jQuery UI alternative. Which one you choose should depend on your project requirements.

Growl-style Notifications

Our client is worried that StarTrackr! is lagging behind competitors in the real-time web space. He wants to be able to communicate with users and keep them abreast of up-to-the-second information: new Twitter posts, news from the RSS feed … anything to show that StarTrackr! is buzzing with life.

The data is no problem—the back-end team can handle it … but how can we notify the user in a way that's both cool and helpful? Once again we'll look to the desktop for inspiration, and implement Growl-style notification bubbles (Growl is a popular notification system for the Mac OS X desktop).

When we have a message to share with the users, we'll add a bubble to the page. The bubble will be located at the bottom right-hand side of the screen. If we have more messages to share, they'll appear underneath the previous ones, in a kind of upside-down stack. Each bubble will have a close button, enabling users to close them after they've been read. The overall effect is shown in Figure 7.10.

Figure 7.10. Growl-style notifications

The real trick to the bubbles is CSS. It takes care of all the tough stuff involved in positioning the dialogs and making them look really cool. In terms of HTML, all we need is a simple container:

chapter_07/19_growl_style_notifications/index.html *(excerpt)*

```html
<div id="growl"></div>
```

It needs to be able to be positioned in the bottom corner to achieve the effect we're attempting. Placing it in the footer or outside of your page's main container element is common. Let's apply some basic CSS to handle the positioning:

chapter_07/19_growl_style_notifications/style.css *(excerpt)*

```css
#growl {
    position: absolute;
    bottom: 0;
    right: 0;
    width: 320px;
    z-index: 10;
}
```

Now that the container is in place, we can start adding our message bubbles to it. We'll create a simple function that takes a message, wraps it in some structure, and appends it to our positioned bubble holder:

chapter_07/19_growl_style_notifications/script.js *(excerpt)*

```javascript
function addNotice(notice) {
  $('<div class="notice"></div>')
    .append('<div class="skin"></div>')
    .append('<a href="#" class="close">close</a>')
    .append($('<div class="content"></div>').html($(notice)))
    .hide()
    .appendTo('#growl')
    .fadeIn(1000);
}
```

The structure we've added consists of a containing element with an extra div available for styling (we're using it to lay the visible message over a semi-opaque background), a close button, and a container for the message contents.

One other point to note about this function is that any HTML we pass to it is wrapped in the jQuery dollar selector. This means we can pass in either plain text, HTML, or jQuery objects, and they'll be displayed in the box. Again, you can style it all however suits your site—though you'll need to give the bubble container `position: relative`:

chapter_07/19_growl_style_notifications/style.css *(excerpt)*

```css
.notice {
  position: relative;
}

.skin {
  position: absolute;
  background-color: #000000;
  bottom: 0;
  left: 0;
  opacity: 0.6;
  right: 0;
  top: 0;
  z-index: -1;
  -moz-border-radius: 5px; -webkit-border-radius: 5px;
}

.close {
  background: transparent url('button-close.png') 0 0 no-repeat;
}
```

This will position our bubbles correctly and give them some basic styles. Inside the document-ready function, just call the `addNotice` function with a message, and it will fade in at the bottom of the screen:

chapter_07/19_growl_style_notifications/script.js *(excerpt)*

```js
addNotice("<p>Welcome to StarTrackr!</p>");
addNotice("<p>Stay awhile!</p><p>Stay FOREVER!</p>");
```

You can also pass in images, or indeed any HTML you like. Of course, most of the time you'll want to display the result of a user interaction, or an Ajax call—you just need to call `addNotice` whenever you want to display a message to the user. The only problem is … once the bubbles are there, they're unable to be removed—they just keep stacking up! Let's fix this:

```
                              chapter_07/19_growl_style_notifications/script.js (excerpt)

$('#growl')
  .find('.close')
  .live('click', function() {
    // Remove the bubble
  });
```

Instead of adding the `click` handler directly to the close button, we're using the `live` function to keep an eye on any new `.close` elements that are added. This helps us separate out the closing code and keep everything nice and readable. All that's left to do now is handle the actual removing:

```
                              chapter_07/19_growl_style_notifications/script.js (excerpt)

// Remove the bubble
$(this)
  .closest('.notice')
  .animate({
    border: 'none',
    height: 0,
    marginBottom: 0,
    marginTop: '-6px',
    opacity: 0,
    paddingBottom: 0,
    paddingTop: 0,
    queue: false
  }, 1000, function() {
    $(this).remove();
  });
```

The removal code goes looking for the nearest parent container via the `closest` action, and animates it to invisibility in an appealing way. Once it's invisible, the container is no longer needed, so we remove it from the DOM. The `closest` method is another one of jQuery's DOM traversing actions, and has the cool ability to locate the closest parent element that matches the selector you give it—including itself.

1-up Notification

It's Friday afternoon again, and the boss is out of the office. There's nothing left to do in this week's blitz, and there's still an hour left until office drinks. This seems like the perfect time to sneak a cool little feature onto the site. Throughout the book we've concentrated on enlivening tried-and-true controls and recreating desktop effects, but jQuery's best asset is that it lets you try out new effects extremely quickly. We'll embrace the creative spirit and make a notification mechanism that comes straight out of 8-bit video gaming history: the 1-up notification.

The brainchild of web developer Jeremy Keith, 1-up notifications provide a non-modal feedback mechanism to show your user that an action happened. A small message (generally a single word) will appear at the point the action has taken place, then fade upwards and quickly away—exactly like the point scoring notifications in classic platform video games! Perhaps you'd think that this effect is only useful for novelty value—but it turns out to be a very satisfying and surprisingly subtle way to message your users.

As this is jQuery, there are many ways to put this together. Our approach will be to insert a new element that's initially hidden, positioned such that it sits directly centered and slightly above the element that triggers the action. For our triggers, we have some simple anchor tags that act as "Add to wishlist" links. When they're clicked, a notice saying "Adding" will appear above the link and rapidly fade out while moving upwards. Once the animation finishes, the button will change to "Added" and the interaction is complete:

chapter_07/20_1_up_notifications/index.html (excerpt)

```
<a class="wishlist" href="#">Add to wishlist</a>
```

The message elements we'll insert will have the class adding—so let's make sure that when we append them, they'll be invisible and properly located:

chapter_07/20_1_up_notifications/style.css (excerpt)

```
.adding{
  position:relative;
  left:-35px;
  top:-4px;
  display:none;
}
```

When the document is ready, we can then find all our targets and add the new message element to each of them. When a target (an element that has the wishlist class) is clicked, we call a custom function that sets our notification in motion.

The custom function takes a reference to the current object and a callback function to run when the interaction is complete. This function will move the selection to the link (via the `prev` action) and set its text to "Added":

```
chapter_07/20_1_up_notifications/script.js (excerpt)

$('<span>Adding</span>')
  .addClass('adding')
  .insertAfter('.wishlist');

$('.wishlist')
  .click(function(e) {
    doOneUp(this, function() {
      $(this).prev().text('Added');
    });
    e.preventDefault();
  })
```

Our custom function features nothing new to us at this point: it simply moves to the hidden `span` element and displays it. Now the message is visible to the end user. We then kick off an animation that adjusts the span's `top` and `opacity` properties—to move it upwards and fade it out simultaneously:

```
chapter_07/20_1_up_notifications/script.js (excerpt)

function doOneUp(which, callback) {
  $(which)
    .next()
    .show()
    .animate({
      top:"-=50px",
      opacity:"toggle"
    },
    1000,
    function() {
      $(this)
        .css({top: ""})
        .hide(callback)
        .remove();
    });
}
```

Passing Callbacks

Notice the `callback` variable that's being passed around in the example? We supply a function as a parameter to our `doOneUp` code, but we don't do anything with it ourselves; we just pass it along as the callback to jQuery's `hide` action. When `hide` completes, it will run whatever code we gave it. In this case, it's the code to change the link text from "Add to wishlist" to "Added."

This effect is impressive, but it would be more useful if it were customizable, especially with respect to the positioning of the text message; at the moment it's hard-coded into the CSS. It would be good to make this an option in the code, and also provide options to select the distance the message travels and its speed. In short, this effect would be perfect as a plugin! You'll have to wait until (or skip over to) Chapter 9 to learn how to do that.

We're in Good Form

Building usable, accessible, and impressive forms and interface controls is hard work, and to tackle the task we have to use all of the tools we have at our disposal: HTML, CSS, JavaScript, and jQuery. It's a team effort, and as developers, we need to be aware which tool is the right one for the job. Once we've figured this out though, it's all bets off. Forms and controls are the core of application development on the Web—so it's an exciting area to be experimenting in. Striking a balance between impressive, novel, and usable interactions can be tricky, but if you get it right, you can have a significant impact on the way people use and perceive your site.

8

Lists, Trees, and Tables

The popularity of StarTrackr! has just skyrocketed, after exposing an ill-conceived publicity stunt where a celebrity claimed to be trapped inside a large balloon that had been accidentally set loose. Thankfully, the celebrity happened to be "B-grader of the week" on StarTrackr!, with several users alerting the media that his tracking device indicated that he was, in fact, in a local exclusive day spa.

The droves of new users and intrigued old-school media types flocking to the site have created a tidal wave of data, which the site's administration section is struggling to keep up with. Our client is worried that important information might be overlooked, as it's becoming nearly impossible to glean any meaning from the unstructured lists and tables of data currently in there.

The admin area of a site is traditionally the most neglected; it's out of sight of the general public, so we can cut corners and put less thought into usability and the user experience. Out the window go best practices such as progressive enhancement and concerns about accessibility (usually due to extremely tight deadlines, mind you!).

But the rise of the Rich Internet Application is changing that. Clients expect our web-based systems to rival their desktop applications for usability and design. Thankfully with jQuery by our side, that's no problem!

Lists

Lists are the real unsung heroes of the post table-based layout period of the Web. As designers were freed from the constraints of the tyrannical table cell, they started to look for other (semantically correct) ways to recreate common user interface elements such as menus, navigation panels, tag clouds, and so on. And time after time, as the redundant layout cruft was stripped from the underlying data, all that was left behind was—a list!

The StarTrackr! site is already home to an extensive array of lists: they form the basis of our tabs, accordions, menus, image galleries, and more—but there's far more we can do to augment and enhance the humble list.

jQuery UI Selectables

The ocean of user-generated content is proving a handful for our client. Thousands of tags are pouring in from the site's users—but now the legal department is saying that as the manager, he has to approve every single one manually, to avoid a repeat of a recent nasty litigation.

Because the site employs an unconstrained tag system, there are stacks of duplicate tags in the lists—and with the current system that means stacks of extra administration. What the client really wants is a way to easily see tags, select them (and any duplicates), and click a button to approve or reject them.

Our plan of attack is to add jQuery UI's `selectable` behavior to our list. Making an element selectable gives the user the ability to lasso any of the element's children to select them: if you click on one element, then drag over subsequent elements, they become highlighted. You can than process the selection however you see fit. Perfect for administrating boring lists! The behavior we're aiming to create is illustrated in Figure 8.1.

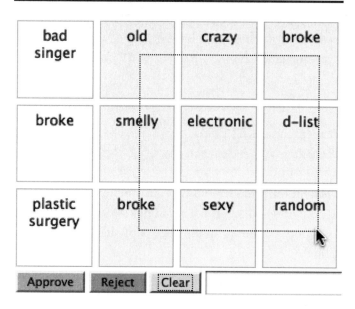

Figure 8.1. Selectable list items

In addition to lassoing, the selectable behavior also lets you add nonsequential items to the list using the **Ctrl** key (as you can do in most desktop applications)—and even navigate the selections with the keyboard.

Keep Your Users in the Loop

Although being able to click and drag selections on a list is very cool and very useful, it's only cool and useful if your users know about it! Making selections in this manner is a nonstandard form of interaction on the Web, so you'll need to provide instructions to your users to teach them how to use your new functionality.

Let's have a look at the markup. The server spits out a long list of tags, which is a fine base for our selector grid. We'll also throw in a few buttons to allow users to approve or reject the tags in their selection, as well as a button to reset the selection:

chapter_08/01_jquery_ui_selectable/index.html (excerpt)

```html
<ul id="tags">
  <li>bad singer</li>
  <li>old</li>
  <li>plastic surgery</li>
  <li>broke</li>
    ⋮
</ul>
<button id="approve">Approve</button>
<button id="reject">Reject</button>
<button id="clear">Clear</button>
```

A big long list is a bit intimidating, so we'll use some basic CSS to make the list into a grid, and convert each tag into a small box. With our grid ready to go, we have to add the jQuery UI library to the page. Now it's time to tell the tag list to become selectable:

chapter_08/01_jquery_ui_selectable/script.js (excerpt)

```javascript
$("#tags").selectable();
```

Fire up your browser and check it out. Hrrm … has anything actually happened? Well yes, it has, but it's invisible! The `selectable` method works by adding `class` attributes to selected items, unless we assign styles to those `class`es, we'll be unable to see anything happening. If you inspect the list items with Firebug as you select them, you'll see the changes occurring. Let's have a stab at styling selected elements:

chapter_08/01_jquery_ui_selectable/style.css (excerpt)

```css
#tags .ui-selecting {
  background: #FEFF9F;
}

#tags .ui-selected {
  background-color:#eEeF8F;
}
```

The `ui-selecting` class is applied as the user is in the process of selecting elements, and the `ui-selected` class is added as soon they stop. If you try it now, you'll see you can lasso some squares. It's quite a natural interaction—which is exactly what you want from your page components. You can also click while holding down the **Ctrl** key to select individual items.

The next task we want to do is help with the duplicate tags. In a tagging system the number of tags for each term is important—so rather than just deleting duplicates, we'll write some code to select any tags that match the user's selection. For instance, if they click on "A-lister," all the "A-lister" tags will be highlighted.

We need to know which events we can hook into from the jQuery UI component. Consulting the documentation,[1] we find that we can capture the `start`, `stop`, `selecting`, `unselecting`, `selected`, and `unselected` events. We could capture the `selecting` event—and remove duplicates as the user moves the mouse—but it might be a bit confusing. We'll stick with the `stop` event, which fires as soon as the user completes the selection:

chapter_08/01_jquery_ui_selectable/script.js (excerpt)

```
$('#tags').selectable({
  stop: function() {
    // The user stopped selecting!
  }
});
```

Now we can begin our quest to find the duplicate tags. Our general approach will be to make a list of all the tags the user has selected, then search for any duplicates of those tags that appear in the greater tag list:

---

[1] http://docs.jquery.com/UI/Selectable

---

chapter_08/01_jquery_ui_selectable/script.js *(excerpt)*

```javascript
var names = $.map($('.ui-selected, this'), function(element, i) {
  return $(element).text();
});

$('li', this)
  .filter(function() {
    if ($.inArray($(this).text(), names) != -1) {
      return true;
    } else {
      return false;
    };
  })
  .addClass('ui-selected');
```

To find the duplicates, we've called on the service of an assortment of new jQuery features, so hold on to your hats!

The first of these is the oddest: `$('.ui-selected', this)`. This looks like a regular jQuery selector, but there's a second parameter. It turns out that the complete definition for the jQuery selector is actually `$(expression, context)`—we've just been omitting the second parameter. The `context` defines where jQuery should look for your selector; by default it looks everywhere on the page—but by specifying our unordered list as the context, the expression will be limited to elements inside the list.

$.map and $.inArray

Next we use a couple of jQuery utility methods: `$.map` and `$.inArray` to juggle the list items. The utility methods jQuery provides are mostly for working on JavaScript arrays—and that's what we're doing here. First we create an array called `names`, which we populate using the `$.map` method.

The `$.map` method allows you to take each element in the array, process it in some way, and return the results as a new array. You use it when you want to transform every element in the same way. We want to transform our jQuery selection into a simple list of tag text—so we pass in the selection, and define an anonymous function to return each element's text. Hey presto: an array of tag text!

We next use the context trick as before to retrieve all the list item elements, and filter them based on whether or not they're duplicates. Our `filter` function uses the `$.inArray` utility method, which searches an array (but only plain JavaScript arrays—not jQuery selections, unfortunately) for a specified value. Given an array and a search term, like `$.inArray(value, array)`, it will return the value's index in the array. Helpfully, it will return `-1` if the value is *not* found in the array. Remember that `filter` expects us to return either `true` or `false`—so we just check to see if `$.inArray` returns `-1`, and return `true` or `false` as appropriate. Using `filter` in this way allows us to search our array of tag texts for each list item's text—if it's in there, it's a duplicate, so we return it to the filter to be selected.

Accessing the Data

Now that we can make selections, how can we use them? The jQuery UI Selectable component works with class names, so we will too. To acquire the list of selected values, we simply search for any items that have the `ui-selected class` on them:

```
                                    chapter_08/01_jquery_ui_selectable/script.js (excerpt)
$('#approve').click(function() {
  $('#tags')
    .find('.ui-selected')
    .addClass('approve')
    .removeClass('ui-selected reject');
});

$('#reject').click(function() {
  $('#tags')
    .find('.ui-selected')
    .addClass('reject')
    .removeClass('ui-selected approve');
});

$('#clear').click(function() {
  $('#tags')
    .find('li')
    .removeClass('ui-selected approve reject');
  $('#approved').val('');
});
```

We're just adding an `approve` or `reject class` when the user clicks on our buttons—also being sure to remove the `ui-selected class`, since we want to style approved tags differently from selected ones.

But what if we wanted to, say, send this information to the server? Perhaps it would be good to store the list of approved tags in a hidden form field, so that the server can access it for processing. Let's update the `#approve` click handler to iterate over the approved items, and append each item's index to a hidden field in a simple pipe-delimited format:

chapter_08/01_jquery_ui_selectable/script.js *(excerpt)*

```
$('#approve').click(function() {
  var approvedItems = "";
  $('#tags')
    .find('.ui-selected')
    .addClass('approve')
    .removeClass('ui-selected reject')
    .each(function() {
      approvedItems += $(this).index() + "|";
    });
  $('#approved').val(approvedItems);
});
```

We'll also add a line to our `#clear` button click handler to clear that input's value:

chapter_08/01_jquery_ui_selectable/script.js *(excerpt)*

```
$('#approved').val('');
```

Thanks to the `index` method, we now know which items in the list have been approved. `index` will tell you an item's position inside its parent element. Our control is impressive in how easy it is to use. The jQuery UI `selectable` behavior is doing a lot of work behind the scenes to allow lists to be selectable—but the end result is a natural-feeling component, and that's exactly what we want.

Sorting Lists

With the tag system under control, it's time to turn to some of the other lists that are scattered throughout the admin section. Many of these lists are populated by the server in the order they were entered into the system. This is good for seeing what's new, but bad for finding particular items. Our client has asked us to build some sorting capabilities into all of the lists in the admin section, so he can click a button and have the lists sorted in ascending or descending alphabetical order.

The markup we'll be dealing with is a simple unordered list made up of links:

```
                                    chapter_08/02_sorting_lists/index.html (excerpt)

<ul class="sortable">
  <li><a href="#">Beau Dandy</a></li>
  <li><a href="#">Glendatronix</a></li>
  <li><a href="#">BMX Spandex Corporation</a></li>
  <li><a href="#">Maxwell Zilog</a></li>
  <li><a href="#">Computadors</a>
</ul>
```

jQuery objects lack any built-in sorting functionality. This makes sense, after all; a selection could include different kinds of elements located in different parts of the page, so sorting them in a consistent manner would be impossible. To sort our jQuery selections, therefore, we need to fall back on some JavaScript array methods. jQuery selections aren't actually arrays, but they're "array-like," and they allow us to use the JavaScript sort function on them.

We'll try to build a reusable list-sorting widget. We'll call it SORTER, and we'd call SORTER.sort(list) to sort a list in ascending order, and SORTER.sort(list, 'desc') to sort in descending order. We'll assume that the selector passed in will match ordered or unordered lists, but let's see if we can make that happen:

```
                                    chapter_08/02_sorting_lists/script.js (excerpt)

var SORTER = {};
SORTER.sort = function(which, dir) {
  SORTER.dir = (dir == "desc") ? -1 : 1;
  $(which).each(function() {
    // Find the list items and sort them
    var sorted = $(this).find("> li").sort(function(a, b) {
      return $(a).text().toLowerCase() > $(b).text().toLowerCase() ?
        SORTER.dir : -SORTER.dir;
    });
    $(this).append(sorted);
  });
};
```

That code is deceptively short, because it happens to be doing a lot! First up, we check to see if `desc` was passed in as the `dir` parameter, and set the `SORTER.dir` variable accordingly. All we need to do is grab all of the first-level children list elements and give them a sort. We only want the first-level items; if we grabbed further levels, they'd be sorted and dragged up to the parent level. Because calling `sort` reverts our selections to raw JavaScript, we need to rewrap them in the `$()` to be able to call the jQuery `text` method and compare their values. We also convert the values to lowercase—which makes the sorting case-insensitive.

 The sort Function

The `sort` function is plain old JavaScript: it sorts an array based on the results of the function you pass to it. `sort` will go over the contents of the array and pass them to your function in pairs. If your function returns `1`, `sort` will swap the items and place the second one first. If your function returns `-1`, JavaScript will put the first item first. Finally, if your function returns `0`, `sort` will consider that both items are equal and no sorting will take place.

We're doing a little magic to let us use the same function for sorting in ascending and descending order: we've set our `SORTER.dir` variable to `-1` or `1`, depending on the direction. Then in the `sort` comparison function, we do a further calculation: if `a` is less than `b`, we return `-SORTER.dir`. If the direction comes in as `-1`, we process it as `-(-1)`, which is `1`—so if we're trying to sort descending, the return values are swapped.

Once we've sorted the items, we can reinsert them into the list in the correct order. Remember, the `append` function removes the element first—so it removes the item and appends it in the correct position.

To test it out, we'll add some buttons to our HTML and call `SORTER.sort` from their `click` event handlers:

chapter_08/02_sorting_lists/script.js *(excerpt)*

```
$('#ascending').click(function() {
  SORTER.sort('.sortable');
});
$('#descending').click(function() {
  SORTER.sort('.sortable', 'desc');
});
```

Manipulating Select Box Lists

Although we covered forms in the previous chapter, there's still time to have a look at certain form elements in the context of lists. Here we're going to examine `select` elements, especially those with `multiple="multiple"` (that is, select boxes which appear as selectable lists of items).

Swapping List Elements

The StarTrackr! client has asked us to improve the admin functionality for assigning celebrities to the A-list. The current functionality consists of two select elements: one contains the A-list celebrities, and the other contains every other celebrity in the system. But the world of popularity is extremely fickle—and an A-lister today can be a nobody tomorrow. So the client wants to be able to easily swap the celebrities between each list. We'll add a few controls to the interface to let him do just that, as shown in Figure 8.2.

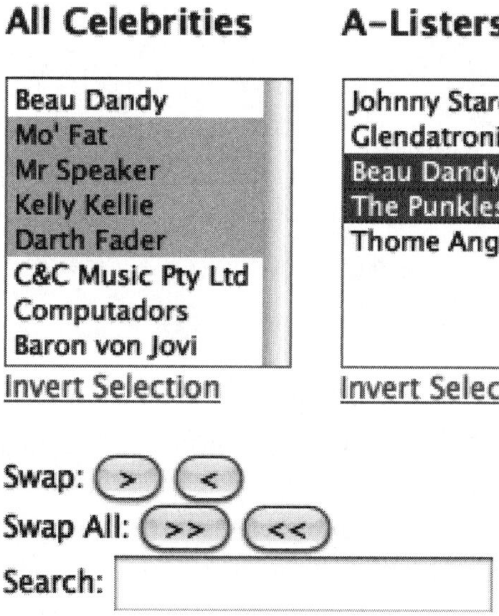

All Celebrities   **A-Listers**

Beau Dandy
Mo' Fat
Mr Speaker
Kelly Kellie
Darth Fader
C&C Music Pty Ltd
Computadors
Baron von Jovi

Johnny Stardust
Glendatronix
Beau Dandy
The Punkless Brewster
Thome Angeles

Invert Selection   Invert Selection

Swap: (>) (<)
Swap All: (>>) (<<)
Search: [   ]

Figure 8.2. List boxes with controls

This is the HTML we're dealing with, consisting of the two `select` elements, and a few buttons for performing various operations:

```
                              chapter_08/03_select_lists/index.html (excerpt)

<select id="candidates" multiple="multiple" size="8">
  <option value="142">Beau Dandy</option>
  ⋮
</select>
<select id="a-listers" multiple="multiple" size="8">
  <option value="232">Johnny Stardust</option>
  ⋮
</select>
<div id="controls">
  <input type="button" id="swapLeft" value="&gt;" />
  <input type="button" id="swapRight" value="&lt;" />
  ⋮
</div>
```

As stated, the client wants the ability to swap selected items from one list to another. We'll make a SWAPLIST object that will contain all the functionality we'll build. This can then be reused anytime we need to play with select elements:

```
                                chapter_08/03_select_lists/script.js (excerpt)

var SWAPLIST = {};
SWAPLIST.swap = function(from, to) {
  $(from)
    .find(':selected')
    .appendTo(to);
}
```

We've defined a swap function that accepts selector strings targeting two lists: a source list and a destination list. The first task we want to do is to grab any items that are currently selected. We can do this using the find action with the :selected form filter. This filter will return any form elements that have the attribute selected set. Then we can move the selection over to the destination list with appendTo. Easy! And once we've defined this functionality, we can apply it to any two lists by calling our swap method from appropriate click handlers:

```
                                chapter_08/03_select_lists/script.js (excerpt)

$('#swapLeft').click(function() {
  SWAPLIST.swap('#candidates', '#a-listers');
});
```

```
$('#swapRight').click(function() {
  SWAPLIST.swap('#a-listers', '#candidates');
});
```

Now selected items can be swapped back and forth at will! Let's add some more functionality to our SWAPLIST object. How about swapping *all* elements? That's even easier:

chapter_08/03_select_lists/script.js (excerpt)

```
SWAPLIST.swapAll = function(from,to) {
  $(from)
    .children()
    .appendTo(to);
}
```

We just take all the child elements (instead of only the selected elements) and append them to the bottom of the destination—the whole list jumps from source list to destination list.

Inverting a Selection

The next client request is to add a button that inverts the current selection, to make it easier for his staff when dealing with large selections. When this link is clicked, all currently selected items in the target list become deselected, and vice versa. Let's make a function inside the SWAPLIST object that does this:

chapter_08/03_select_lists/script.js (excerpt)

```
SWAPLIST.invert = function(list) {
  $(list)
    .children()
    .attr('selected', function(i, selected) {
      return !selected;
    });
}
```

All we have to do is retrieve every list item and swap its selected attribute. We use the attr function to set our list items to !$(this).attr('selected'). The JavaScript NOT (!) operator (the exclamation mark) inverts the Boolean value, so if the value was true it becomes false, and if it was false it becomes true!

Calling `attr` with a Function Parameter

This is a great trick: we've used the `attr` action—but it's not the version we're used to. Previously we used the `attr(key, value)` action to set attributes to a static value, but `attr` also lets us pass in a function to determine the value. The function will be passed two parameters: the index of the element and its current value. The return value of the function becomes the attribute's new value. For our `invert` method, we return the opposite of the element's current selection value—so each element is toggled. We can do this kind of dynamic processing with stacks of commands: `text`, `html`, `val`, `addClass`, `wrap` ... and many more!

Searching through Lists

After having to listen to the client whine on and on about how hard it is to find the celebrities he's trying to select, you decide to throw in a little freebie: a quick search feature that lets him type some characters and automatically select any matching elements:

chapter_08/03_select_lists/script.js (excerpt)

```
SWAPLIST.search = function(list, search) {
  $(list)
    .children()
    .attr('selected', '')
    .filter(function() {
      if (search == '') {
        return false;
      }
      return $(this)
        .text()
        .toLowerCase()
        .indexOf(search) > - 1
    })
    .attr('selected', 'selected');
}
```

What's going on here? First, we're grabbing all list items and then clearing any previous selections (by setting `selected` to an empty string). Next, we're using the `filter` action to find any elements we're searching for.

The `filter` action accepts a function as a parameter, and runs that function against every jQuery object in the selection. If the function returns `true`, the element stays in the selection. But if the function returns `false`—it's gone ... out of the selection, and unaffected by further processing.

To find elements we care about, we check to see if the text they contain has the text we're looking for in it. To do this we use the `text` action that gives us a string. We convert it to lower case (so the search will be case-insensitive), and check to see if our source text is located in the element string. The JavaScript `indexOf` method will find the position of a string inside another string; for example, `"hello".index-Of('ll');` will return 2 (the index starts at 0, as usual). If the substring is not found, `indexOf` will return `-1`, which is what we're checking for here.

Whichever elements remain in the jQuery selection after the `filter` function runs must contain the keyword we're looking for—so once again we use the `attr` method to select them.

To use the search method we created, we could attach it to a `click` handler—so the user types a word and then clicks a search button. Even better is to attach a `keyup` handler to the `input` itself, so it selects as you type:

chapter_08/03_select_lists/script.js *(excerpt)*

```
$('#search').keyup(function() {
  SWAPLIST.search("#a-listers, #candidates", $(this).val());
});
```

Trees

"This is another mess. We have several subcategories of celebrities ... you know, A-listers who are in bands, or who are famous because their parents are rich; B-listers who came in second on some reality TV contest, stuff like that. Right now they're all in one big list. I need to see how the categories fit inside each other! Can you build something to help me?"

The client's talking about a tree. Trees are few and far between on the Web for two reasons: they're hard to do well, and there are few situations where they make sense. However, a nested set of categories *is* a valid use of a tree structure (a more common one is representing a directory structure), so let's dive in!

Expandable Tree

Here's the secret about trees: they're really just nested lists! The key to dealing with trees in jQuery is to make sure your HTML is consistent—so we can figure out where we are, and open and close the correct branches. The control we'll build will look like the one in Figure 8.3. We've kept the styling deliberately sparse, but as always the potential for improving the appearance is limited only by your CSS skills!

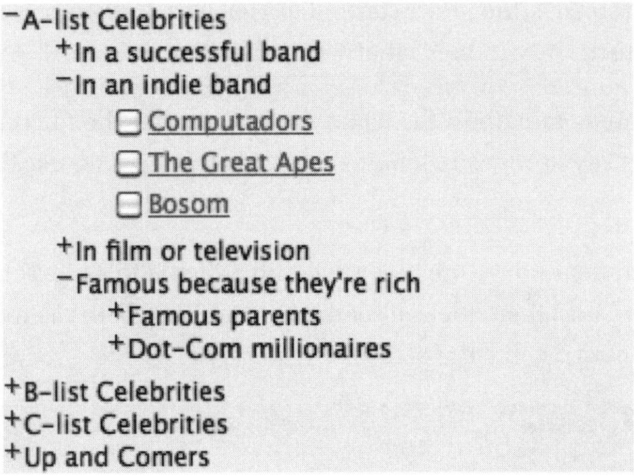

```
⁻A-list Celebrities
    ⁺In a successful band
    ⁻In an indie band
            ☐ Computadors
            ☐ The Great Apes
            ☐ Bosom

    ⁺In film or television
    ⁻Famous because they're rich
        ⁺Famous parents
        ⁺Dot-Com millionaires
⁺B-list Celebrities
⁺C-list Celebrities
⁺Up and Comers
```

Figure 8.3. Tree

The important part of our markup is the span that contains each category (or directory) name. We'll use this span as a base for inserting a small plus/minus graphic—to act as the branch toggle. Here's a subset of the markup we'll be working with:

chapter_08/04_expandable_tree/index.html *(excerpt)*

```html
<ul id="celebTree">
  <li><span>A-list Celebrities</span>
    <ul>
      <li><span>In a successful band</span>
        <ul>
          <li>Johnny Stardust</li>
          <li>Glendatronix</li>
        </ul>
      </li>
      ⋮
      <li><span>Famous because they're rich</span>
        <ul>
```

```
<li><span>Dot-Com millionaires</span>
  <ul>
    <li>Joel Mynor</li>
    ⋮
```

The tree can nest as far as is needed—just repeat the structure inside the appropriate child list item. Because it's nice and consistent, you can easily generate the HTML on the server.

With the list on the page, the next step is to pretty it up with some CSS. That's in your court, but our code will add a few extra classes you can use to customize the display. The handle class will be assigned to the element we'll insert to act as the toggle handle. When a branch of the tree is opened, it'll receive the opened class; otherwise it'll have the closed class. We've used these classes below to add a CSS sprite, which will change between a plus sign and a minus sign:

chapter_08/04_expandable_tree/script.js *(excerpt)*

```css
.handle {
  background: transparent url(tree-handle.png) no-repeat left top;
  display:block;
  float:left;
  width:10px;
  height:10px;
  cursor:pointer;
}
.closed { background-position: left top; }
.opened { background-position: left -10px; }
```

The code for the tree is remarkably simple, thanks to the recursive nature of a tree: we just have to do one small piece of code, and attach it to each subcategory. Our plan of attack for creating the expanding/collapsing tree effect is to first hide all of the nested ul categories. Then we'll add in a new element before the category title that contains a click event handler—this will open and close its branch:

```
chapter_08/04_expandable_tree/script.js (excerpt)

$('#celebTree ul')
  .hide()
  .prev('span')
  .before('<span></span>')
  .prev()
  .addClass('handle closed')
  .click(function() {
    // plus/minus handle click
  });
```

Six chained actions. Bet you're feeling some of that jQuery power coursing through your veins right about now! Here we see where consistent markup helps us out: in each subcategory list we look for the previous span element—that's the subcategory title. Then we insert a new span element right before the title.

Because our handle was added before the title, we need to move back to it with the prev action. We add the handle and closed (it's closed by default because of the hide action) classes to it, and an event handler for when it's clicked.

At this stage the tree will be fully collapsed, with our brand-new handle prepended to the titles. All that's left to do is toggle the branches when we click on it:

```
chapter_08/04_expandable_tree/script.js (excerpt)

// plus/minus handle click
$(this)
  .toggleClass('closed opened')
  .nextAll('ul')
  .toggle();
```

When the handle is clicked, we toggle the closed and opened classes with toggleClass. If you specify multiple class names with toggleClass, any specified class that exists on the element is removed, and any that are absent from the element are added.

Advanced `toggleClass`

Another neat trick of `toggleClass` is that it accepts a second parameter: a Boolean value that specifies whether the `class` should be added or removed. This might sound strange, but it's a nice shortcut. Consider this code:

```
if (x == 1) {
  $(this).addClass('opened');
} else {
  $(this).removeClass('opened');
}
```

With the `toggleClass(class, switch)` syntax, we can replace the `if` statement with the following concise syntax:

```
$(this).toggleClass('opened', x == 1);
```

Finding the subcategory that we need to open and close is easy, thanks to the `nextAll` action. jQuery will check the next sibling, see that it's a `span` element (the category title), filter it out based on our expression, and move to the next sibling … which is a `ul` item. Bingo! We just toggle this and the tree swings open and closed.

Event Delegation

Event delegation is a topic that's applicable everywhere, but is particularly important if you're dealing with large trees. The idea is that instead of applying individual event handlers to every node in your tree, you apply a single event handler to intercept the click—and then figure out who the click was aimed at and run the appropriate action.

If you've been following along closely this might sound a bit familiar to you. We covered the `live` method in the section called "Prepare for the Future: `live` and `die`" in Chapter 6. `live` handles event delegation for you—that's the magic that makes it possible—but it comes with a potential gotcha that you need to be aware of.

To acquire a better understanding of how event delegation works and why it is important, let's use it for real. We'll start with the following HTML that displays our products in a categorized list:

```
                              chapter_08/05_event_delegation/index.html (excerpt)
<span>Selection:</span>
<span id="current">--Choose a celebrity--</span>
<ul id="picker">
  <li class="category">
      <span class="title">A-List</span>
      <ul>
        <li>Beau Dandy</li>
        <li>Glendatronix</li>
      </ul>
  </li>
  <li class="category">
      <span class="title">B-List</span>
      <ul>
        <li>Mo' Fat</li>
        <li>DJ Darth Fader</li>
      </ul>
  </li>
</ul>
```

When users clicks on a celebrity, their selection should appear above the list in the format "category > celebrity" as in Figure 8.4. So what's the best way to capture this information?

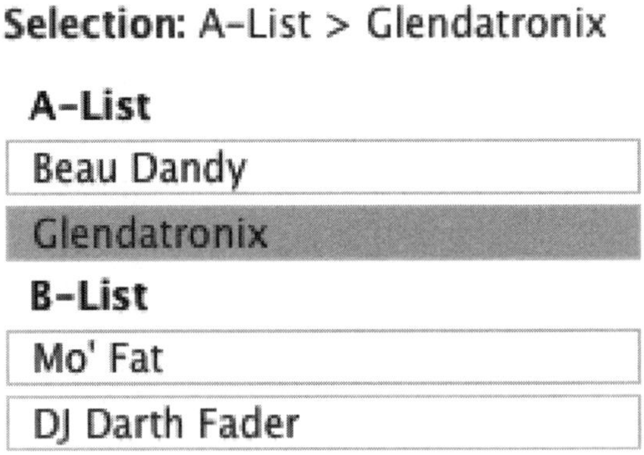

Selection: A–List > Glendatronix

A-List

Beau Dandy

Glendatronix

B-List

Mo' Fat

DJ Darth Fader

Figure 8.4. Delegating events

If we added a click event handler to every single list item—$('#picker li').click(…)—we could end up with hundreds of handlers. This would severely impact performance, as the browser would need to keep track of them all and check them all whenever a click occurred on the page. With event delegation, we add our lone event handler to the parent of the list, and then access the target of the event to determine the element that was actually clicked on. The `target` property of an event is the actual DOM element—so it needs to be wrapped in the jQuery selector to obtain a jQuery object:

```
$('#picker').click(function(e) {
  $('#current').text($(e.target).text());
});
```

Our list acts as if each item has its own handler! Nice, but what was the gotcha mentioned earlier? Event delegation works because of event bubbling (which we looked at in the section called "Event Propagation" in Chapter 5)—the events will bubble up until our parent handler catches them. The problem occurs if a handler catches the event before the parent and stops the event from propagating (with `e.stopPropagation`, or `"return false"`). If the event is stopped on its way up, event delegation will fail! That's why it's important that you know how events are being handled under the hood—it'll save you a lot of headaches when dealing with otherwise incomprehensible bugs.

We've handled any clicks with a single handler, but we now need to find out a bit more about where the element is located. Specifically, how can we find out which category the element is in? How about this:

```
                                                              (excerpt)

$('#picker').click(function(e) {
  var celebrity = $(e.target).text();
  var category = $(e.target)
    .closest('.category')
    .find('.title')
    .text();
  $('#current').text(category + " > " + celebrity);
});
```

We've asked the `closest` method to find the closest element with the `category` class. If the element itself doesn't have that `class`, `closest` will check its parent … and so on until it finds a matching element. This saves us having long strings of `parent().parent().parent()`, and also lets us be more flexible in how we structure our HTML.

Tables

If HTML lists are the unsung heroes of the new Web, tables are that bad kid who ends up turning out good. The tables themselves were never to blame—we misused and abused them for years as a hack to lay out our web designs in a reasonable cross-browser manner. But that's what CSS is for, not poor old tables. And now that CSS has come of age, we can finally return to using tables solely for their original purpose: displaying tabular data.

StarTrackr! has stacks of data to display. So much so that it's growing out of hand: the tables are becoming overly large and unreadable, the information has no paging or sorting mechanisms, and there's no way to edit the information easily. We saw how easy it was to add zebra striping and row highlighting to tables in Chapter 2; this will give us a few quick wins, but to address the more serious table issues, we're going to need some extra help from jQuery.

Fixed Table Headers

The header row of a table is of paramount importance: without it, you'd be stuck with rows of meaningless data. But if you're dealing with a large number of rows, you'll find that the headers become less and less helpful, as they scroll out of sight and out of mind. Paging the data generally takes care of the problem—but if you need to have all the data on one page at the same time, you'll have to think of another option.

Keeping the header row fixed at the top of the table is an effective way to keep track of what our columns are about, and it also looks really cool! As the user scrolls the table to reveal new data, the header follows along. You can see this in action in Figure 8.5.

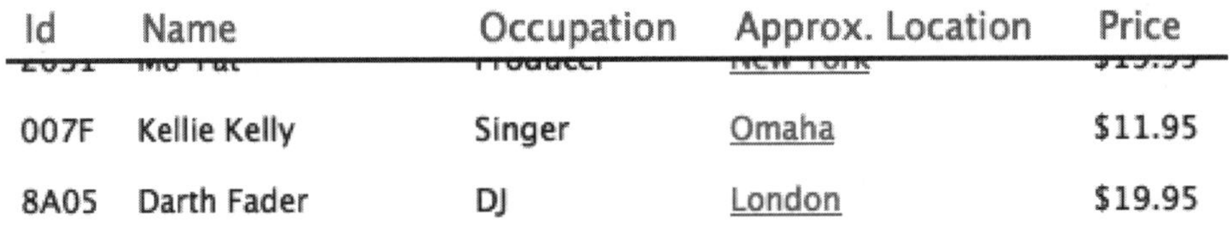

Id	Name	Occupation	Approx. Location	Price
~~2031~~	~~Mo Fat~~	~~Producer~~	~~New York~~	~~$19.95~~
007F	Kellie Kelly	Singer	Omaha	$11.95
8A05	Darth Fader	DJ	London	$19.95

Figure 8.5. Fixed header row

If your table is the only element on the page, `position: fixed` can be used to affix the `thead` element in place. However, `position: fixed` can only position an element relative to the viewport, rather than its containing element. This means that for tables contained inside other elements (which will almost always be the case), we need to turn to jQuery.

Let's have a look at how we can achieve this effect. Our markup is the same Celebrities table we added zebra-striping to back in Chapter 2:

chapter_08/06_fixed_table_headers/index.html (excerpt)

```
<table id="celebs">
  <thead>
    <tr>
      <th>Id</th>
      <th>Name</th>
      <th>Occupation</th>
      <th>Approx. Location</th>
      <th>Price</th>
    </tr>
  </thead>
  <tbody>
    ⋮
  </tbody>
</table>
```

Moving the `thead` around is tricky. Some browsers let you move it with impunity, while in others it's surprisingly resistant to styling. So we'll employ a trick: we'll duplicate the contents of the `thead` in the form of an unordered list, styled to look exactly like the `thead`. Then we'll give that `position: absolute;`, and move it around the screen as the user scrolls.

We start by creating a `TABLE` widget to hold our code, with a `fixHeader` method that we'll use for our fixed headers effect. The method will expect to receive a selector string pointing at a table on the page. We start by storing a few selections inside variables and in `data`, to speed up our subsequent code:

```
var TABLE = {};

TABLE.fixHeader = function(table) {
  $(table).each(function() {
    var $table = $(this);
    var $thead = $table.find('thead');
    var $ths = $thead.find('th');
    $table.data('top', $thead.offset().top);
    $table.data('left', $thead.offset().left);
    $table.data('bottom', $table.data('top') + $table.height() -
➥$thead.height());
    ⋮
```

We first declare a closure to hold on to our widget's context. Then we select any tables that match the selector passed in to our method. We loop over them with `each`, and store a reference to the `table` itself (`$table`), the `thead` (`$thead`), and the collection of `th` elements it contains (`$ths`). Finally, we store the left and top offsets of the `$thead`, as well as the location of the bottom of the table (to avoid the header moving past the bottom!).

 Use each When Writing Selector-based Functions

When writing this sort of utility function, you should always anticipate the possibility of your selector returning more than one element. In this case, our page only has one table on it, so the method would work fine if we omitted the `each` loop. But in the interests of preparing for the future, and making our code reusable, we've included the loop anyway; even if the `table` selector returns multiple tables, our function will handle them all with grace.

Next, we create our *faux* header—a `ul`—and copy over the contents of the table header:

```
                              chapter_08/06_fixed_table_headers/script.js (excerpt)

var $list = $('<ul class="faux-head"></ul>');
$ths.each(function(i) {
  _th = $(this);
  $list.append($("<li></li>")
    .addClass(_th.attr("class"))
    .html(_th.html())
    .width(_th.width())
    .click(function() {
      _th.click()
    })
  ).hide().css({left: _table.left});
});
$('body').append($list);
```

With the real `th` elements collected in `$ths`, we use an `each` action to go through each one and craft our mimics. We copy the original elements' `class`, HTML contents, width, and `click` event handlers. Some of this is unnecessary in our simple example, but it's good to be prepared! After the list is fully populated, we hide it and position it directly over our real `thead` before slipping it into the page.

 Append as Infrequently as Possible

You may wonder why we wait until the list is fully constructed before appending it to the page. While appending the list to the page first, and subsequently appending each item to it would have the same desired effect, the method we've chosen to adopt executes much more quickly in the browser.

Every time you insert a new element into the DOM, the browser needs to recalculate the position of every element on the page. If you do this a lot (especially if you do it in a loop!), your script can become very slow. The method we've used above—storing the new elements in a variable, processing them as necessary, and then appending them all in one fell swoop—ensures optimal performance.

With our `thead` mimic now nicely in place, we need to react to the scroll event and position it appropriately:

```
                                chapter_08/06_fixed_table_headers/script.js (excerpt)

$(window).scroll(function() {
  setTimeout(function() {
    if ($table.data('top') < $(document).scrollTop() &&
➥$(document).scrollTop() < $table.data('bottom')) {
      $list
        .show()
        .stop()
        .animate({
          top: $(document).scrollTop(),
          opacity: 1
        });
    } else {
      $list.fadeOut(function() {
        $(this).css({top: $table.data('top')});
      });
    }
  }, 100);
});
```

We set the timeout for 100 milliseconds after the `scroll` event fires; it's a very short time, but enough to ensure that we avoid constantly animating as the user scrolls. We check to see if we've scrolled the `thead` out of the viewport, but not past the bottom of the table; if we have, we reveal our mimic and animate it to the correct position. If we've scrolled back high enough so that the original `thead` is visible, or down past the bottom of the table, we fade out the impostor list (and position it back at the top, so that it animates from the correct position when it reappears).

And there you have it! We can call our `TABLE.fixHeader("#celebs")` and scroll the page, and the new "`thead`" follows along to keep the identifying labels visible at all times.

Repeating Header

Another approach to the disappearing header row problem is to simply repeat the header at regular intervals. This is particularly handy if the intention is for the data to be printed out—as cool as it looks, our animated table header is unhelpful if you need to sort through a dozen pages of printed tables! The goal would be to take the first row of the table, and copy it every, say, ten rows.

The result is shown in Figure 8.6.

Id	Name	Occupation	Approx. Location	Price
203A	Johny Stardust (bio)	Front-man	Los Angeles	$39.95
6636	Glendatronix	Keytarist	London	$39.95
141B	Beau Dandy (pic)	Singer	New York	$39.95
2031	Mo' Fat	Producer	New York	$19.95
007F	Kellie Kelly	Singer	Omaha	$11.95
8A05	Darth Fader	DJ	London	$19.95
203A	Johny Stardust (bio)	Front-man	Los Angeles	$39.95
6636	Glendatronix	Keytarist	London	$39.95
141B	Beau Dandy (pic)	Singer	New York	$39.95
2031	Mo' Fat	Producer	New York	$19.95
Id	Name	Occupation	Approx. Location	Price
007F	Kellie Kelly	Singer	Omaha	$11.95
8A05	Darth Fader	DJ	London	$19.95

Figure 8.6. Repeating the table header

Copying the header row and putting it elsewhere should be old hat for you by now. But how exactly do we add the header every ten rows? Do we loop over every row and check its index? Well, we could … but yet again jQuery comes to the rescue with a powerful built-in filter:

```
chapter_08/07_repeating_table_header/script.js (excerpt)
$('#celebs')
  .find('tr:first')
  .clone()
  .insertAfter('#celebs tr:nth-child(10n)');
```

This solution starts out simply enough—grabbing the first table row, then cloning it with the clone method. Then comes the clever bit: the **nth-child** selector is perfect for adding the rows right where we want them. You might be a little baffled by the way we've used it, though, as its syntax differs a bit from the other filters we've seen. At its most basic, if you give it a simple integer, it will select that index. For example, if you selected :nth-child(2), you'd receive the third child element.

But the `:nth-child` selector also accepts other values, which cause it to select multiple rows as the same time. If you pass in the text values even or odd, you'll select all of the even or odd child elements. Coolest of all, you can pass it an equation to figure out which children to select!

You can use the letter "n" to indicate repetition; for example, `:nth-child(10n)` will select every tenth row. You can then augment this with a plus or minus to offset which rows are selected. For example, if you want to select the third row, and then every tenth row after that, you could use `:nth-child(10n+3)`. Finally, if you like to think backwards, you could achieve the same result with `:nth-child(10n-7)`.

That all works okay, but it does have a bug: if the last row of the table matches our equation, the header row will be repeated as the final row—which looks a bit weird. Also, we want to apply the repeating header to a couple of tables, and want to avoid having to copy/paste code. Next chapter, we'll look at making our code reusable via plugins—but for now, we'll keep it simple and stick with a trusty widget object:

chapter_08/07_repeating_table_header/script.js (excerpt)

```
var TABLE = {};

TABLE.repeatHeader = function(table, every) {
  $(table).each(function() {
    var $this = $(this);
    var rowsLen = $this.find('tr:not(:first)').length;

    $(this).find('tr:first')
      .clone()
      .insertAfter($this.find('tr:nth-child(' + every + 'n)'));

    if ((rowsLen) % every === 0) {
      $this.find('tr:last').remove();
    }
  });
}
```

We've created a function that accepts the selector string for our table, and a number representing how many rows to leave between each repeat of the header. We then cycle through each element our selector finds (so our function can be applied to more than one table on the same page). For each item, we set up a shortcut to the `$(this)` element and grab the number of rows in the table. It's important to store the number of rows in advance, because when we repeat our table headers, the number of rows is going to change!

Next comes the workhorse: we copy out the first row (as we did before) and insert it every "nth" row. This needed to be slightly rewritten with a `find` action, so it could be run on any of a number of tables matched by the selector—but otherwise it's exactly the same as our first effort. The final part of the code does a small bit of math to determine whether we've added a header as the final row of the table; if the total number of rows divides evenly by our repeater number, we need to remove the last row.

Data Grids

"These changes to the admin section are just great," says our client in a *here comes a big request* kind of way, "but it would be great if we could replace the old desktop application that the marketing manager uses. It hooks into the same database, but it lets her sort and move around the data, and edit different cells—all on the one page! But I suppose that's impossible, right?"

Sure, he's gone and laid the old reverse psychology on us, but it works every time. "Of course it's possible!" you laugh, looking at the crusty Windows application he's demonstrating. "In fact, I could do it even better—it's just a matter of taking …"

"Great!" says the client, slapping you on the back. "Let me know when we can have a look at it." And out he walks—off to another one of his "business meetings." Looking back at the application, you realize that, yes, indeed you can do it better. What you need to do is transform our simple table into a data grid.

There's no set definition for what constitutes a data grid, but some common features are sorting, filtering, searching, paging, column resizing, and row editing. Let's have a go at some paging and inline editing.

Pagination

A huge long table can be quite scary to encounter on a web site—especially as screen real estate is so valuable. Adding paging to a table lets us display a small subset of the data at any one time, while allowing the user to move through it easily with navigation buttons.

Pagination is often handled by the server. The user can request a specific page of data and the server will return it. This makes a lot of sense for massive amounts of data: if you loaded 10,000 table rows into your browser it might become a little sluggish. But for smaller sets, it can make sense to load everything onto the page at once; all data is stored locally, and there are no refreshes every time the user wants to move through the data. Our jQuery pagination widget is shown in Figure 8.7.

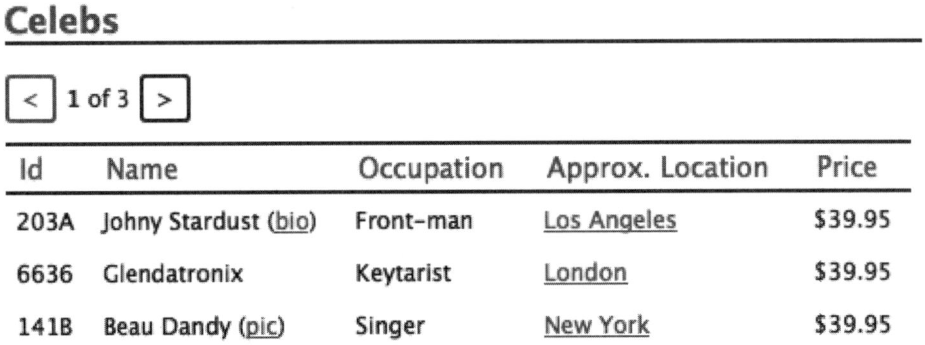

Celebs

| < | 1 of 3 | > |

Id	Name	Occupation	Approx. Location	Price
203A	Johny Stardust (bio)	Front-man	Los Angeles	$39.95
6636	Glendatronix	Keytarist	London	$39.95
141B	Beau Dandy (pic)	Singer	New York	$39.95

Figure 8.7. Paging tables

The table paging widget that we'll create will have clickable **Next** and **Previous** buttons, as well as a display of the current page and total number of pages. The structure of the HTML is quite important, as jQuery will need to traverse from the paginated table to the navigation items:

chapter_08/08_pagination/index.html *(excerpt)*

```
<div class="table-wrapper">
  <div class="wrapper-paging">
    <ul>
      <li><a class="paging-back">&lt;</a></li>
      <li><a class="paging-this"><b>0</b> of <span>x</span></a></li>
      <li><a class="paging-next">&gt;</a></li>
    </ul>
  </div>
  <div class="wrapper-panel">
    <table id="celebs">
    ⋮
    </table>
  </div>
</div>
```

Adding the Controls Dynamically

Another option would be to build the navigation controls completely in jQuery. This means you could easily apply it to any table, and the controls would be added automatically. Such an approach is often favored by plugin authors.

You can style the controls however you see fit—but it's a good idea to hide the controls container in CSS, then show it with jQuery when the page loads. This is so anyone without JavaScript enabled can avoid seeing the redundant controls.

Our widget skeleton looks like this:

chapter_08/08_pagination/index.html *(excerpt)*

```
var TABLE = {};
TABLE.paginate = function(table, pageLength) {
  // 1. Set up paging information
  // 2. Set up the navigation controls
  // 3. Show initial rows
  pagination = function (direction) {
    reveal = function (current) {
      // 5. Reveal the correct rows
    };
    // 4. Move previous and next
  }
};
```

It looks as if there's a lot to cover—but be assured, it's stuff you already know. To start off, we grab the table and rows we want to paginate, and do some calculations to figure out how many pages there'll be:

chapter_08/08_pagination/script.js *(excerpt)*

```
// 1. Set up paging information
var $table = $(table);
var $rows = $table.find('tbody > tr');
var numPages = Math.ceil($rows.length / pageLength) - 1;
var current = 0;
```

Now we have to configure the navigation controls. This is where our structure is important, as we find the controls by climbing up the DOM from our table selection to the wrapper `div`, then back down to the navigation section. This approach lets you apply the same code to any tables that have been structured appropriately:

chapter_08/08_pagination/script.js *(excerpt)*

```
// 2. Set up the navigation controls
var $nav = $table
  .parents('.table-wrapper')
  .find('.wrapper-paging ul');
var $back = $nav.find('li:first-child a');
var $next = $nav.find('li:last-child a');
```

We then set the text in the display boxes for the current page and the total length (adding one, because our counters are zero-based). Next, we attach the event handlers for the **Previous/Next** buttons. When these buttons are clicked, we call our `pagination` function with the direction we want to move:

chapter_08/08_pagination/script.js *(excerpt)*

```
$nav.find('a.paging-this b').text(current + 1);
$nav.find('a.paging-this span').text(numPages + 1);
$back
  .addClass('paging-disabled')
  .click(function() {
    pagination('<');
  });
$next.click(function() {
  pagination('>');
});
```

The last part of the setup is to limit how many rows the user sees to begin with. The easiest way to do this is to hide all the table rows, and show only the rows within the range we're interested in. But how can we select a range of elements with jQuery? We could use the `:lt()` and `:gt()` filters—but when it comes time to show, say, rows 10 to 20, the selectors will get a bit messy. Luckily for us there's the `slice` action, which takes a start index and an end index as parameters, and returns only the objects within that range:

chapter_08/08_pagination/script.js *(excerpt)*

```
// 3. Show initial rows
$rows
  .hide()
  .slice(0, pageLength)
  .show();
```

Everything looks in order now: our navigation controls are showing the correct page and total, and the first page of data is displaying correctly. But our paging buttons have no function yet. We'll add some logic to move the current page, and work out whether we should disable buttons (if we're at either end of the table):

chapter_08/08_pagination/script.js *(excerpt)*

```
// 4. Move previous and next
if (direction == "<") { // previous
  if (current > 1) {
    reveal(current -= 1);
  }
  else if (current == 1) {
    reveal(current -= 1);
    $back.addClass("paging-disabled");
  }
} else { // next
  if (current < numPages - 1) {
    reveal(current += 1);
  }
  else if (current == numPages - 1) {
    reveal(current += 1);
    $next.addClass("paging-disabled");
  }
}
```

We update the `current` variable—but not the table itself. To do so, we create an internal function called `reveal`:

```
// 5. Reveal the correct rows
var reveal = function (current) {
  $back.removeClass("paging-disabled");
  $next.removeClass("paging-disabled");

  $rows
    .hide()
    .slice(current * pageLength, current * pageLength + pageLength)
    .show();

  $nav.find("a.paging-this b").text(current + 1);
}
```

reveal starts by clearing the disabled classes, so that our buttons avoid becoming stranded in a disabled state. We then use the slice method again to select the correct rows to display.

Nested Functions

The structure we've used here is a little odd—but when you think about it, it's straightforward: we've nested a function declaration inside another function. All this does is restrict the scope of the function (see the section called "Scope" in Chapter 6), so it can only be called from within its parent function. Why is this a good idea? In this case our function has no purpose outside its parent, and placing it in a wider scope would only put it at greater risk of conflicting with other function or variable names.

Editing a Row

We've already handled inline editing on a single element, but what if you want to make an entire table editable? We'll add editing functionality to the data grid by inserting an Edit button at the end of each row, turning that entire row of cells into input elements, as shown in Figure 8.8.

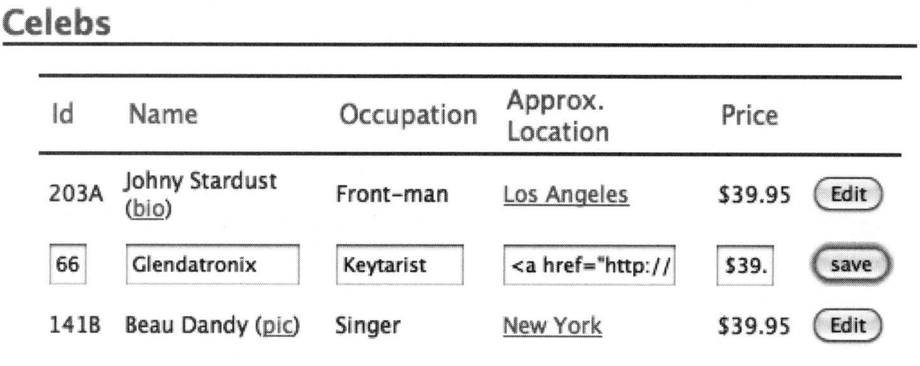

Celebs

Id	Name	Occupation	Approx. Location	Price	
203A	Johny Stardust (bio)	Front-man	Los Angeles	$39.95	(Edit)
66	Glendatronix	Keytarist	<a href="http://	$39.	(save)
141B	Beau Dandy (pic)	Singer	New York	$39.95	(Edit)

Figure 8.8. Editable rows in action

The cells that contain your tabular data provide an excellent opportunity to store information as we manipulate the markup; this is actually a trick we used in our form controls. What we've yet to experience, though, is a row element to group our work area. Let's see how to use it:

```
                          chapter_08/09_editable_table_cells/index.html (excerpt)
<form action="null" method="post">
  <table id="celebs">
    <thead>
      <tr>
        <th>ID</th>
        <th>Name</th>
        <th>Occupation</th>
        <th>Approx. Location</th>
        <th>Price</th>
      </tr>
    </thead>
    <tbody>
      <tr>
        <td>203A</td>
        <td>Johny Stardust</td>
        <td>Front-man</td>
        <td>Los Angeles</td>
        <td>$39.95</td>
      </tr>
      ⋮
```

Looks quite normal, right? And so it should, as all the editable features will be added progressively—the better to keep your visitors happy and coming back for more!

And there's another payoff: by not including any of the editing controls in the table's HTML, we can easily add any number of rows to it, relying on jQuery to do our heavy lifting.

We'll start with a setup method, to initialize our table and add the required buttons:

```
chapter_08/09_editable_table_cells/script.js (excerpt)

TABLE.formwork = function(table) {
  var $tables = $(table);

  $tables.each(function () {
    var _table = $(this);
    _table
      .find('thead tr')
      .append($('<th class="edit"> </th>'));
    _table
      .find('tbody tr')
      .append($('<td class="edit"><input type="button"
value="Edit"/></td>'))
  });

  $tables.find('.edit :button').live('click', function(e) {
    TABLE.editable(this);
    e.preventDefault();
  });
}
```

Our `TABLE.formwork` method looks for the selector we pass in, and then the rows in the `thead` and `tbody`, adding an extra `edit` cell to each. The `thead` cell is empty, but it's there to retain the table's column structure, and the `tbody` addition holds the button that switches the row into edit mode. Even though we know that the buttons exist prior to attaching our `click` event, event delegation through `live` is the way of the future. This is why we're using it to ensure that no matter how we move our buttons around, remove them, or reinstate them, the `click` handlers will stay in place.

The other point to remember here is that we're applying the `live` method outside the `each` loop. By applying it to `$tables` outside the loop, rather than `_table` inside, we ensure that the event listener is only added once. We achieve the full effect, but our code runs faster. And ninjas love fast code!

Now comes the good part. We want our buttons to work in two states—an edit mode and a save mode—and we want all the cells other than our button-containing cells to become editable. Here's how we're going to do it:

```
TABLE.editable = function (button) {
  var $button = $(button);
  var $row = $button.parents('tbody tr');
  var $cells = $row.children('td').not('.edit');

  if ($row.data('flag')) { // in edit mode, move back to table
    // cell methods

    $row.data('flag', false);
    $button.text('Edit');
  }
  else { // in table mode, move to edit mode
    // cell methods

    $row.data('flag', true);
    $button.text('Save');
  }
};
```

The live `click` event from `TABLE.formwork` passes in the button for the row we want to edit, so we'll use that to cache references to the parent row and the other cells it contains. We use `parents` on the `$button` object to find the row, and `children` on the `$row`—excluding the edit cell with `not`—to find all the other cells.

In the `if` statement, we set a `data` flag to let us know that the row is in edit mode, and change the button text to reflect that. All that remains is to switch out the cell contents.

We'll look at the code in reverse order, to present the simpler code first. The easiest part of what we need to do is *exit* edit mode:

```
$cells.each(function () {
  var _cell = $(this);
  _cell.html(_cell.find('input').val());
});
```

To move out of edit mode, we take the `val` of the `input` in the `_cell`, and add it as the `_cell`'s `html`. Since we need to refer to the cell more than once (even if it's only twice!), we save it in a variable first to speed up performance.

Now for the code required to change *into* edit mode:

chapter_08/09_editable_table_cells/script.js *(excerpt)*

```
$cells.each(function () {
  var _cell = $(this);
  _cell.data('text',_cell.html())
    .html('');

  var $input = $('<input type="text" />')
    .val(_cell.data('text'))
    .width(_cell.width() - 16);

  _cell.append($input);
});
```

To make the cells editable is only slightly trickier. We'll need to empty out the current cell contents before we can add in the `inputs`, or we'll break the layout. Before we empty each cell, though, we store the current contents in `data` so we can use them later.

We're going to `append` an `input` we create, and as we have seen, it's important to manipulate anything we create *before* we add it to the DOM. The `input`'s width is set smaller than the width of the cell to avoid any layout breakage, and we grab the data we just saved to serve as the input element's default value.

Try it out, and you'll be impressed by how smoothly it works. Bet you're starting to feel like a ninja now!

DataTables Plugin

We've started down the path of creating a reusable data grid. There are infinite number of ways to go from here; the table could do with being sortable by column, or searchable—we could pack it with every crazy feature imaginable. But if you're pressed for time, and need a lot of features fast, you'll want to research the plugin options that are out there, such as the DataTables plugin.[2]

---

[2] http://www.datatables.net/index

DataTables is a truly impressive plugin for turning your HTML tables into fully functional data grids, complete with pagination, column sorting, searching, ThemeRoller support, Ajax loading, and more. As always, the decision to use a plugin or build custom functionality comes down to how much time you have, how many features you need, and how big a file you're willing to serve to your visitors. Oh, and also how much fun you think you'd have developing the functionality yourself!

For the moment we've been able to add all the features required for our client's table-based needs on our own, and we've learned a lot about jQuery in doing it. Before we move on to the next (and final) chapter, let's revisit our check-all checkboxes in the context of tables.

Selecting Rows with Checkboxes

Another feature that the public are becoming increasingly used to having is the ability to select rows of a table (or any kind of list) by checking a checkbox associated with the row. As well as selections being able to be made on an individual basis, there are often shortcuts for selecting all items, selecting none, or inverting the current selection of checkboxes. None of this is new to us: we've already built check-all checkboxes and selection-inverting buttons.

But, dissatisfied with this, some users also want to be able to select continuous rows by using the **Shift** key—just like in their desktop applications.

Selecting a Column of Checkboxes

Dealing with columns of data is much trickier than dealing with rows of data. They may appear closely tied when viewed together onscreen, but when it comes to the DOM they're merely distant relatives. There are no handy `next` or `previous` functions we can hook into.

Naturally, jQuery can help us out. Thanks to its sophisticated selector engine, we can do whatever we want—it might just require a bit of thinking. To start with, we know we need to grab the table; in our case, it's good old `#celebs`.

Next, we want to retrieve the table rows: `#celebs tr`, and then the first columns of each row `#celebs tr td:nth-child(1)`. Finally, we make sure we're only selecting checkboxes: `#celebs tr td:nth-child(1) :checkbox`. That's quite the selector! How far we've come from our simple `$('tr:odd')`.

We place another checkbox (with an id of `checker`) in the `thead` of our table. Because it's in a `th` rather than a `td`, our selector will ignore it. We can attach a `click` handler to this to turn all the checkboxes on and off:

```
                        chapter_08/10_select_column_checkboxes/script.js (excerpt)
var chkSelector = 'tr td:nth-child(1) :checkbox';

$('#checker').click(function() {
  $('#celebs ' + chkSelector)
    .attr('checked', $(this).attr('checked'));
});
```

Shift-selecting Checkboxes

All on or all off is one thing … but our client now has high expectations of us. He demands that he be able to **Shift**+Click on checkboxes to select a bunch at a time within a range of rows. Just like in his webmail client.

Shift-selecting presents some fun problems. For starters, how do we know if the user is pressing **Shift**? Luckily for us, jQuery events tell us! We can find out from an event the state of the **Shift** key by checking the Boolean property `e.shiftKey`. That was easy! How about finding out which row was clicked on? We can just jump up the DOM and find the parent row of the checkbox, and fetch its index using `index`. Another easy one.

Next, we have to know where the user *last* clicked, so we can have a start and end point for checking boxes. The easiest way for us to do this is to store each click in the table using the `data` method. That's a lot of information we have, so let's put it into practice:

```
                chapter_08/10_select_column_checkboxes/script.js (excerpt)

$('#celebs ' + chkSelector).click(function(e) {
  var $table = $(this).parents('table');
  var lastRow = $table.data('lastRow');
  var thisRow = $(this).parents('tr').index();

  if (lastRow !== undefined && e.shiftKey) {
    var numChecked = 0;
    var start = lastRow < thisRow ? lastRow : thisRow;
    var end = lastRow > thisRow ? lastRow : thisRow;
    $table
      .find(chkSelector)
      .slice(start, end)
      .attr('checked', true);
  }
  $table.data('lastRow', thisRow);
});
```

We spring into action only when there's a lastRow value (it will be undefined the first time through, before we've stored a click value on the table), and the user is also holding down **Shift**.

With the source and destination rows in hand, we need to figure out which is further down the table, so we can make sure that the starting point is before the end point. Then we slice up our checkbox selection with jQuery's slice method. With our freshly sliced jQuery selection in hand, we can finish it off by checking all the remaining checkboxes in the selection. Now you can easily select ranges of rows in a highly intuitive manner!

We've Made the A-list!

We've transformed the admin section of StarTrackr! from a horrible mess of poorly formatted data into a usable desktop-style application—and in the process transformed raw data into useful information. The ease with which jQuery lets us mold standard HTML elements into powerful application-like controls means that the holy grail of responsive, impressive, and accessible Rich Internet Applications is well within our grasp.

What's truly awesome to note at this stage, is that in terms of the core jQuery library, almost all the functions we find ourselves using we've seen before at some earlier stage. Surely this means we're gaining a strong understanding of this powerful tool! Now you just need to start trying out your own ideas—the time of automatically reaching for the plugin should be well behind you. Try implementing a quick proof of concept yourself, and you'll be surprised how easy it is to reach the results you're looking for. Before long, you'll find your code is as good as (if not better than!) what you find in the plugin repository.

Speaking of the plugin repository—that's one of the last legs in our jQuery journey. In the next chapter, you'll learn how to take all this fantastic functionality you're building and make it available to the whole world, in plugin form. We'll also cover a few other advanced topics to round out your jQuery ninja training nicely!

9

Plugins, Themes, and Advanced Topics

jQuery, like the game of chess, or any version of Tetris, is simple to learn but difficult to master. Thanks to its seamless integration with the Document Object Model, jQuery feels natural and easy to use. But jQuery is a quiet achiever: it doesn't like to brag about it, but under the hood lies an extensible architecture, a powerful event handling system, and a robust plugin framework.

Plugins

"Hey, now that everything's in place—can you just go back and put that menu from phase three into the admin section? And can you add the cool lists you made in the last phase to those lists on the front end—and add the scroller effect you did … you can just copy and paste the code, right?"

Ah, copy/paste: our good friend and worst enemy. Sure, it may seem like a quick way to get a piece of functionality up and running—but we all know that this kind of code reuse can so easily degenerate into our worst JavaScript nightmares. And we can't let that happen to our beautiful jQuery creations.

You've seen throughout the book how extremely useful the jQuery plugin architecture is. We've made use of all manner of third-party creations—from styleable scrollbars, to shuffling image galleries, to autocompleting form fields. The good news is that it's extremely easy to package your code as a plugin for reuse in your other projects—and, if your code is really special, in other developers' projects as well!

Creating a Plugin

It will only be a short time into your jQuery-writing life before you have the urge to turn some of your code into a plugin. There's nothing better than seeing a bit of your own code being called from the middle of a jQuery chain! The best part is that it's a very simple process to convert your existing jQuery into a plugin, and you can make it as customizable as you like.

Setting Up

Before we start, we need an idea for our plugin. Some time ago the client mentioned that he'd like to highlight all the text paragraphs on the page, so that when users moved their mouse over the paragraphs, text would become unhighlighted to indicate it had been read. While you'll agree it's far from being the best user interface idea, it's sufficiently simple to demonstrate how to make a plugin, without having to concentrate on the effect's code itself.

All we have to do to make a plugin callable like regular jQuery actions is attach a function to the jQuery **prototype**. In JavaScript, the `prototype` property of any object or built-in data type can be used to extend it with new methods or properties. For our plugin, we'll be using the `prototype` property of the core `jQuery` object itself to add our new methods to it.

The safest (only!) way to do this is to create a private scope for the `jQuery` function. This JavaScript trick ensures that your plugin will work nicely, even on pages where a person is using the $ function for non-jQuery purposes:

```
(function($) {
  // Shell for your plugin code
})(jQuery);
```

This code can go anywhere in your script, but standard practice is to put it in a separate JavaScript file named **jquery.pluginname.js**, and include it as you'd include any plugin. Now that you have a stand-alone file, you can easily use it in future projects or share it with the world!

Inside this protective shell we can use the `$` alias with impunity. That's all there is in the way of preliminaries—so it's time to start to writing a plugin. First we need to give it a name, `highlightOnce`, and attach it to the jQuery plugin hook, `$.fn`:

chapter_09/01_plugins/jquery.highlightonce.js (excerpt)

```
(function($) {
  // Shell for your plugin code
  $.fn.highlightOnce = function() {
    // Plugin code
  }
})(jQuery);
```

Internally `$.fn` is a shortcut to the `jQuery.prototype` JavaScript property—and it's the perfect place to put our plugins. This is where jQuery puts its actions, so now that we've added our custom action we can call it as if it was built into jQuery.

At this point our code *looks* like a jQuery plugin, but it won't act like one—there's still one more task left to do. If we were to perform some operations inside our plugin code now, we would actually be working on the *entire selection at once*; for example, if we ran `$('p').highlightOnce()`, we'd be operating on every paragraph element as a single selection. What we need to do is work on each element, one at a time, and return the element so the jQuery chain can continue. Here's a fairly standard construct for plugins:

chapter_09/01_plugins/jquery.highlightonce.js (excerpt)

```
// Plugin code
return this.each(function() {
  // Do something to each item
});
```

So you now have a nice skeleton for creating simple plugins. Save this outline so you can quickly create new plugins on a whim!

Adding the Plugin's Functionality

Our highlightOnce plugin is ready to roll, so let's give it a job to do. All the structure we've added so far is just the scaffolding—now it's time to create a building! The type of code we can run in the guts of our plugin is exactly the same as the code we're used to writing; we can access the current object with the $(this) construct and execute any jQuery or JavaScript code we need to.

The first function our plugin needs to accomplish is to highlight every selected element, so we'll just set the background to a bright yellow color. Next, we need to handle when the user mouses over the element so we can remove the highlight. We only want this to happen once, as soon as the element is faded back to the original color (don't forget, we need the jQuery UI Effects component to do that):

```
                    chapter_09/01_plugins/jquery.highlightonce.js (excerpt)

// Do something to each item
$(this)
   .data('original-color', $(this).css('background-color'))
   .css('background-color', '#fff47f')
   .one('mouseenter', function() {
     $(this).animate({
       'background-color': $(this).data('original-color')
     }, 'fast');
   });
```

There just happens to be a jQuery action that fits our needs exactly: the one action. Functionally, the one action is identical to the bind action we saw earlier, in that it lets us attach an event handler to our element. The distinction with one is that the event will only ever run *once*, after which the event will automatically unbind itself.

For our code, we save the current background color in the element's data store, then bind the mouseover event to the DOM elements that are selected. When the user mouses over the element, our code runs and the background color is animated back to the original. And with that, our plugin is ready to be used:

chapter_09/01_plugins/script.js *(excerpt)*

```
$('p')
  .hide()
  .highlightOnce()
  .slideDown();
```

It's quite exciting: our functionality is captured in a chainable, reusable plugin that we've nestled in between the `hide` and `slideDown` actions. Seeing how 11 lines of code was all that was required (and six of those are stock-standard plugin scaffolding!), you can see it's worth turning any functionality you intend on reusing into a plugin!

Adding Options

jQuery plugins are an excellent way to produce reusable code, but to be truly useful, our plugins need to be applicable outside the context for which we created them: they need to be *customizable*. We can add user-specified options to our plugins, which can then be used to modify the plugin's behavior when it's put to use.

We're familiar with how options work from a plugin user's perspective, as we've passed in options to just about every plugin we've used throughout the book. Options let us modify the plugin's functionality in both subtle and more obvious ways, so that it can be used in as wide a range of situations as we can imagine.

There are two types of plugin options: simple values and object literals. Let's start with the simpler one to see how this works. For our highlightOnce plugin, it seems quite limiting to have the color hard-coded. We'd like to give developers the choice to highlight their elements in any color they'd like. Let's make that an option:

chapter_09/02_plugin_options/jquery.highlightonce.js *(excerpt)*

```
$.fn.highlightOnce = function(color) {
  ⋮
  $(this).css('background-color', color  ||  '#fff47f')
  ⋮
};
```

The plugin can be called with a color, but can also be called without parameters—in which case a default value will be used (thanks to the JavaScript || operator). Let's highlight our paragraphs in green:

```
$('p')
  .hide()
  .highlightOnce('green')
  .slideDown();
```

If you have one or two simple options that are always required, this approach is fine. But when your plugins start to become more complicated, you'll end up with numerous settings, and your users will want to override some and keep the default values for others. This is where we turn to the more complex object literal notation.

It's not scary—you already know how to define this type of settings object. We've used them for `animate`, `css`, and most jQuery UI components. The key/value object has the benefit of only one parameter needing to be defined, in which users will be able to specify multiple settings. Our first step is to set up default values for each option:

```
$.fn.highlightOnce.defaults = {
  color : '#fff47f',
  duration : 'fast'
};
```

We now have the defaults as an object, so we need to make use of the jQuery `$.extend` function. This handy function has several uses, but for our purposes, we'll use it to extend an object by adding all of the properties from another object. This way, we can extend the options the user passes in with our default settings: the plugin will have values specified for every option already, and if the user specifies one of them, the default will be overridden. Perfect! Let's look at the code:

```
$.fn.highlightOnce = function(options) {
  options = $.extend($.fn.highlightOnce.defaults, options);

  return this.each( … );
};
```

Our `options` variable contains the correct settings inside it—whether they've been defined by the user, or by the default object. Now we can use the settings in our code:

```
chapter_09/03_plugin_options_with_defaults/jquery.highlightonce.js (excerpt)

$(this)
  .data('original-color', $(this).css('background-color'))
  .css('background-color', options.color)
  .one('mouseenter', function() {
    $(this).animate({
      'background-color': $(this).data('original-color')
    }, options.duration);
  });
```

As the plugin user, we can specify the color or duration of the highlight—or accept the defaults. In the following example we'll accept the default color, but override the duration to be 2,000 milliseconds rather than "fast":

```
chapter_09/03_plugin_options_with_defaults/script.js (excerpt)

$('p')
  .hide()
  .highlightOnce({color: '#COFFEE', duration: 2000})
  .slideDown();
```

Adding Callbacks

You have seen how callback functions and events can be very useful. Many of the effects and controls throughout the book have relied on them—and many of the plugins we've used have given us access to callbacks to customize their functionality. Callbacks are a mechanism for giving your plugin's users a place to run their own code, based on events occurring inside your plugin. Generally you'll have a fairly good idea of what events you'd like to expose to your users. For our highlightOnce plugin, for example, we might want to run additional code when the effect is set up, when the effect concludes, and perhaps when the fade-out commences.

To demonstrate, let's try exposing a `setup` event (which will run after the `mouseover` handlers are attached), and a `complete` event (which will run after the final `animate` action concludes):

```
                chapter_09/04_plugin_callbacks/jquery.highlightonce.js (excerpt)
$.fn.highlightOnce.defaults = {
  color : '#fff47f',
  duration : 'fast',
  setup : null,
  complete: null
};
```

The callback functions shouldn't do anything by default, so we'll set them to `null`. When the time comes to run the callbacks, there are a few possible ways of proceeding. If our callback needs to run in the place of a jQuery callback, we can simply provide the function passed in by our users to the jQuery action. Otherwise, we'll need to call the function manually at the appropriate location:

```
                chapter_09/04_plugin_callbacks/jquery.highlightonce.js (excerpt)
$(this)
  .data('original-color', $(this).css('background-color'))
  .css('background-color', options.color)
  .one('mouseenter', function() {
    $(this).animate(
      {'background-color': $(this).data('original-color')},
      options.duration,
      options.complete
    );
  });

// Fire the setUp callback
$.isFunction(options.setup) && options.setup.call(this);
```

Above we can see both types of callbacks. The `complete` callback handler is easy: the effect is completed when the `animate` action is finished, and the `animate` action accepts a callback function itself, so we just pass the function along. No such luck with the `setup` handler, though—we'll have to fire that one ourselves. We turn to jQuery and a dash of advanced JavaScript to execute the code. First, we check to see if the callback is a function with the handy `$.isFunction` jQuery action that returns a Boolean value: `true` if the callback is a function, `false` if it's not. If it's the latter (which is most likely because the user left the defaults as they were, in which case it will still be `null`), there's no point trying to execute it!

More Utility Functions

In addition to $.isFunction, jQuery also provides the following functions: $.isArray (for testing if a variable is an array), $.isPlainObject (for simple JavaScript objects), and $.isEmptyObject (for an object that has no properties). These functions provide you with a number of ways to ascertain the nature and properties of a JavaScript construct.

If the callback *has* been defined, we need to run it. There are several ways to run a JavaScript function, and the easiest is to just call it: options.setup(). This will run fine, but the problem is that it's called in the scope of the default object, instead of in the scope of the event's target element (as we're used to). So the callback function would be unable to determine which DOM element it was dealing with. To remedy this, we use the JavaScript method call. The first parameter you pass to call will override this in the method you're calling. In our example, we pass in this, which is the DOM element we want.

With the scope corrected, we can now use $(this) inside the complete event handler to slide up the element once the effect is done and dusted:

chapter_09/04_plugin_callbacks/script.js *(excerpt)*

```
$('p')
  .hide()
  .highlightOnce({
    color: '#FFA86F',
    complete: function() {
      $(this).slideUp();
    }
  })
  .slideDown();
```

jQuery-style Callback

You might have noticed that the jQuery callbacks seem better integrated than our plugin's named events. For example, in the hide action, you can specify the callback function as either the first (and only) parameter, or you can include the speed parameter and then the callback function. It's unnecessary to include a key/value pair as we did above. What's the secret? It turns out to be a little bit of a JavaScript hack. If you detect that the first parameter is a function, rather than an object, you can assume that only a callback has been specified, so you shift the parameters over.

Here's a (truncated) example from the jQuery core library, part of the Ajax `load` action. The `params` parameter is optional, so if it isn't supplied the second parameter is assumed to be the callback:

```
load: function( url, params, callback ){
  // If the second parameter is a function
  if ( jQuery.isFunction( params ) ){
    // We assume that it's the callback
    callback = params;
    params = null;
```

The `params` parameter is supposed to be an object filled with various settings. But if we detect that it's actually a function, we assign the function to the `callback` variable and clear the `params` variable. It's a cool trick and a good way to make your plugins feel more jQuery-ish.

Let's modify our highlightOnce plugin to use this callback detection trick:

```
                    chapter_09/05_jquery_style_callbacks/jquery.highlightonce.js (excerpt)
$.fn.highlightOnce = function(options, callback) {
  if ($.isFunction(options)) {
    callback = options;
    options = null;
  }
  options = $.extend($.fn.highlightOnce.defaults,options);

  return this.each(function() {
    // Do something to each item
    $(this)
      .data('original-color', $(this).css('background-color'))
      .css('background-color', options.color)
      .one('mouseenter', function() {
        $(this).css('background-color', '');
        $.isFunction(callback) && callback();
      });
  });
};
```

Advanced Topics

Eventually the thrill of creating plugins will wear off a smidgen, and you'll start to wonder if there are any other gems hidden in jQuery's underbelly. And you'd be right to wonder. In addition to the fantastic plugin architecture we've just explored, jQuery provides a mechanism for extending and overwriting its core functionality, and a flexible event system for defining and fine-tuning how your components respond to your users—and to other components.

Extending jQuery

Plugins are not the only jQuery mechanisms for code reuse and extensibility; at your disposal is a system to add plugin-like functionality, as well as customize and override elements of the core jQuery system on the fly. If you have a chunk of code you'd like to execute in a native jQuery fashion, you can extend jQuery with your new functionality without creating a plugin, directly from inside your script. This way you can fine-tune your code to more closely fit the jQuery feel, and fine-tune jQuery to suit your exact requirements.

Adding Methods to jQuery

Sometimes sections of the code you're writing are such a pivotal part of your application that you find yourself using them over and over again. When this happens, you may have found a candidate for extending jQuery. Hidden away in the plugins section of the jQuery core library, the `extend` method is normally the domain of the plugin developer. But don't let that stop you!

`jQuery.fn.extend()`, or `$.fn.extend()`, accepts an object that allows us to provide a new set of methods to *extend* jQuery—adding new actions that can be performed on jQuery selections. This is closely linked to `jQuery.extend()`, which extends the jQuery object itself. The net result is exactly the same as the plugins we wrote earlier. Generally you'll use the `extend` method when you have a group of small related methods you want to add, or when you want to override some existing functionality (we'll look at that shortly).

So let's take a look at some code we've already created and see how it evolves using `extend`. Back in Chapter 8 we looked at sorting lists:

```
var SORTER = {};
SORTER.sort = function(which) {
  // Sort the selected list
}
```

Having to call our widgets like this lacks that jQuery feel. So we'll convert the reverse method to integrate it more closely with jQuery, using extend:

chapter_09/06_extending_jquery/script.js *(excerpt)*

```
$.fn.extend({
  sorter: function() {
    return this.each(function() {
      var sorted = $(this).children('li').sort(function(a,b) {
        // Find the list items and sort them
        return $(a).text().toLowerCase() >
➥$(b).text().toLowerCase() ? 1 : -1;
      });
      $(this).append(sorted);
    });
  }
});
```

Inside the new sorter and reverser methods, we return the results of running the functions from our original example against each member of the selection on which we called the action. This return structure allows us to use the action in a chain:

chapter_09/06_extending_jquery/script.js *(excerpt)*

```
$('#ascending').click(function() {
  $('ul.sortable')
  .hide()
  .sorter()
  .slideDown();
});
```

The biggest change from our original SORTER widget is that once the extend is in place, we no longer call the functions and pass in parameters; instead, we treat it like a normal jQuery action, much as we would had we packaged it into a plugin. Of course, you could take this same code and make it into a plugin! Doing it on the fly like this is just another option available to you.

$. Prefixed Functions

At the beginning of the book we praised jQuery for being a very consistent library: each time we call upon it we have a selector, an action, and perhaps a few parameters. Once you learned that basic pattern, it would be essentially all you had to remember. Then, only a few paragraphs later, we snuck in some code that didn't use a selector at all! Since then, we've seen several of these kinds of actions: `$.ajax`, `$.map`, `$.slice`, `$.trim`, and more.

The `$.` prefixed functions don't work on a selection; rather, they're general utility commands that can have a place outside a jQuery command chain. For example, `$.map` can be used to map any arbitrary array—but it can also be used to modify a jQuery selection.

The client liked the Ajax Twitter-search component we developed in Chapter 6, but wanted a more human-readable time displayed for the tweets: for example, rather than "56 seconds ago," he'd like it to say "about a minute ago." This sounds like a good candidate for adding to the jQuery object, since it's the sort of functionality you'd like to be able to use outside of a selection. Any time we need a friendly looking time period, we'd like to be able to call `$.lapsed(time)` and obtain a nice string.

To get underway, we'll omit the actual logic for a second while we look at the function's structure. The skeleton looks very similar to the plugins we created —passing the jQuery object to the wrapped function—so our code will work even if the $ alias has been redefined:

chapter_09/07_$_prefixed_functions/script.js *(excerpt)*

```
(function($) {
  $.lapsed = function(time) {
    var then = new Date(Date.parse(time));
    var now = new Date();
    var minutes = Math.round((now-then) / 60000);
    var lapsed;

    // Determine pretty time
    :
  };
})(jQuery);
```

Now we just need to attach our function to the jQuery object itself. Because we're extending jQuery, you'll have to be careful to avoid unintentionally overwriting any of the built-in function names. The code we'll use to determine the "pretty" time is nothing more than a series of `if`/`else` structures. To keep the example simple, our helper will only go as far as "more than a minute ago"—but you'll want to extend this to account for larger time spans:

chapter_09/07_$_prefixed_functions/script.js *(excerpt)*

```javascript
// Determine pretty time
if (minutes == 0) {
  var seconds = Math.round((now - then) / 1000);
  if (seconds < 10) {
    lapsed = "less than 10 seconds ago";
  }
  else if (seconds < 20) {
    lapsed = "less than 20 seconds ago";
  }
  else {
    lapsed = "half a minute ago";
  }
}
else if (minutes == 1) {
  var seconds = Math.round((now-then) / 1000);
  if (seconds == 30) {
    lapsed = "half a minute ago";
  } else if (seconds < 60) {
    lapsed = "less than a minute ago";
  } else {
    lapsed = "1 minute ago";
  }
} else {
  lapsed = "more than a minute ago";
}
return lapsed;
```

To use this extension in our jQuery code, we pass a timestamp to the new `lapsed` function, and append the result wherever we need it. Our functionality is neatly encapsulated, and ready for use on any number of future projects:

```
chapter_09/07_$_prefixed_functions/script.js (excerpt)
.append('<span class="time">' + $.lapsed(this.created_at) +
➥'</span>')
```

Overwriting Existing Functionality

One of the main differences between adding plugins via $.fn.myPlugin rather than
$.extend({ myPlugin : … }), is that the extend mechanism *augments* the element
you're extending, rather than replacing it entirely. This is what makes it possible
to extend jQuery itself (or existing plugins) with additional functionality. As well
as adding new methods to jQuery, as we did above, we can also extend the functionality of existing methods!

As a simple example, we're going to extend the functionality of the $.trim method.
$.trim takes a string and removes any leading or trailing spaces. We'll add an extra
parameter to the method that, if set to true, will remove *all* spaces from the given
string:

```
chapter_09/08_overwriting_existing_function/script.js (excerpt)
(function($) {
  var _trim = $.trim;
  $.extend({
    trim:function(text, clear) {
      if (clear) {
        return text.replace(/\s+/g,'');
      }
      return _trim.call(this, text);
    }
  });
})(jQuery);
```

First, as always, we're playing nice for people who don't want to use the $ for jQuery
(see the section called "Plugins"). Next, we're storing the original trim function in
a variable so we can access it later on. Finally, we reach the important bit: extending
the trim function. Our version of trim is going to accept an extra Boolean parameter.
If it's set we run our custom regular expression to remove *all* whitespace, and if it's
not set, we call the original jQuery trim function.

Extending code in this way is particularly useful when dealing with more complex objects; for example, if you need to modify the $.ajax method to do some additional processing on every request. In that situation you'd only want to modify the particular aspects of the code that you needed to, and leave everything else alone. By storing the original function, and referring to it as necessary, this becomes a simple task.

Create Your Own Selectors

Ten basic filters, four content filters, two visibility filters, six or so attribute filters, four child filters, and 14 form-focused filters. This is more than just the makings of a wicked Christmas carol: jQuery's built-in filters allow you to easily select just about anything on the page! But what do we do when we want all the advertisement units in a page, or all the links that were clicked to leave a page, or all the break-out items that are below the fold?

 The Fold

"Above the fold" in web design terms refers to the area of a page visible on pageload, without scrolling. Hence, "below the fold" refers to the total area beneath that, which is invisible without scrolling.

The term originates from newspapers, which are generally folded in half for display. It was therefore considered advantageous to have a headline or advertisement appear above the fold, visible to anyone passing by. In particular, important stories would be positioned here in order to attract attention and entice people to buy the paper.

These are admittedly odd requests, but let's use the opportunity to examine custom filters in detail; besides, in certain situations they can definitely work in your favor.

Rather than finding elements *below* the fold, let's turn to a more useful purpose, and detect when an element is visible, or *above the fold*, on pageload. If the element is above the fold, we can load its content via Ajax straight away. If not, we can delay the Ajax request until later, saving both bandwidth and pageload time:

chapter_09/09_custom_selectors/script.js *(excerpt)*

```
$.extend($.expr[':'], {
  abovethefold: function(el) {
    return $(el).offset().top < $(window).scrollTop() +
➥$(window).height();
  }
});
```

We've already looked at `$.extend` a few times, so accessing the selector engine should be quite familiar. The `$.expr[:]` object is what we need to extend in order to add our custom filters. We pass in a key/value pair, where the key is the name of our filter, and the value is a function that takes a reference to an element. The function should return `true` or `false`. If it returns `true`, the element tested (`el`) will be added to the selection. Otherwise, it will be filtered out:

chapter_09/09_custom_selectors/script.js *(excerpt)*

```
$('p:abovethefold').css('color', 'red');
```

If we test our new `:abovethefold` filter once the page has loaded, we'll see that only paragraphs visible without scrolling will be turned red.

The extensibility of the selector engine is a little-known feature of jQuery, and one that distinguishes the novices from the ninjas!

Events

The event system in jQuery is very powerful. Its primary purpose is to normalize all browser events to match the W3C standards, thus allowing us to perform cross-browser event handling with relative ease—but that's just the tip of the iceberg. A lot of thought has gone into the internal event system in the core library, and this functionality has also been exposed to those developers who are looking to do more than just react to simple events.

Event Properties

With a standardized event in your hands, you can rely on the features that the standards set out. So what exactly does that mean? The jQuery event wrapper gives you a lot of properties and events to play with, though there's too many to list here (the full list is in the section called "Events" in Appendix A). You've already seen many of the commonly used features throughout the book—the `pageX` and `pageY` properties, and the `stopPropagation` and `preventDefault` methods. But where do those events you assign actually exist? How does a lowly paragraph tag know to react when it's clicked? jQuery gives you a way to see what a particular element is set up to do by storing the events, using the `data` action under the key `'events'`.

To see this in action, we've set up a paragraph tag and attached three events to it: two separate `click` events, and one `mouseover` event. We've given the functions names so that we can easily identify them inside our debugger:

chapter_09/10_event_properties/script.js (excerpt)

```
$('p:first').click(function firstClick() {
  // first click handler
})
.click(function secondClick() {
  // second click handler
})
.mouseover(function firstMouse() {
  // first mouseover click handler
});
```

Should you want to access the details of those event handlers at a later point in your code, you need only call `.data('events')` on your paragraph:

chapter_09/10_event_properties/script.js (excerpt)

```
var events = $('p:first').data('events');
console.log(events);
```

The `data('events')` call gives us back an object containing references to all of the events attached to that paragraph. You can see an output of the event data in the Firebug console (see the section called "Troubleshooting with `console.log`" in Chapter 4) in Figure 9.1.

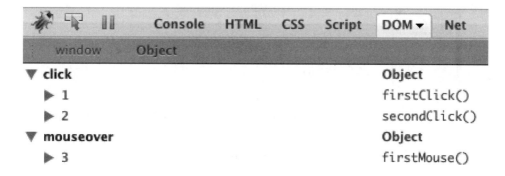

Figure 9.1. data('events') inspected in Firebug

The event data contains both the event type and the event handlers themselves, nested inside the object.

Custom Events

We saw earlier that `bind` and `trigger` do all the real work for the events that we fire; they're behind the scenes of `click`, `mouseover`, `toggle` … every one of them! The shorthand actions make for shorter, more readable code, and the expanded `bind` and `trigger` syntax provides exactly the same functionality. Why use `bind` and `trigger` then? It turns out that they're far more versatile and powerful than we've witnessed thus far. For starters, we can break away from browser-specified events and start creating some of our own!

Creating your own events helps to make your code clearer; for instance, a function buried in a `click` handler needs to be analyzed to determine its purpose, whereas an event with a specific name might be easier to comprehend at a glance. Let's have a look at creating a custom `do-toggle` event. To do so, we'll go all the way back to the disclaimer message example we saw in Chapter 2:

chapter_09/11_custom_events/index.html *(excerpt)*

```html
<p id="disclaimer">
  Disclaimer! This service is not intended …
</p>
<input type="button" id="toggleButton" value="toggle" />
```

This time, instead of the button being responsible for toggling the disclaimer, the disclaimer will be responsible for toggling itself:

```
chapter_09/11_custom_events/script.js (excerpt)

$('#disclaimer').bind('do-toggle', function() {
  $(this).toggle('slow');
});
```

We have bound our custom `do-toggle` event to the disclaimer element. When the `do-toggle` event fires, the function will run and the disclaimer will hide or show itself. But how do we fire the `do-toggle` event? By using the `trigger` method:

```
chapter_09/11_custom_events/script.js (excerpt)

$('#toggleButton').click(function() {
  $('#disclaimer').trigger('do-toggle');
})
```

When the button is clicked, the disclaimer is toggled. It might seem like the long way round compared to just hiding and showing with the toggle button, but now we've done two very important tasks: we've moved the code responsibility to the element itself, and given ourselves the ability to fire the event from any other location. Whether we want to toggle the disclaimer via our toggle button, or via a small icon at the top of the screen, there's no need to replicate the code—we just fire the do-toggle event from wherever we like.

But wait, there's more! The `bind`/`trigger` system also lets you append parameters when you fire events. Each triggering element can pass different data, so the event handler can customize its response. This makes custom events very powerful; you can now create widgets that can elegantly be controlled by multiple other elements on the page, so you can cleanly separate and isolate page behavior and make your code far more reusable.

As an example, we're going to put an alternate trigger mechanism on the page for our animated content panes from the section called "Bouncy Content Panes" in Chapter 3. In this example, we made cool-looking content panes showing celebrity biographies that bounced open and closed when their headings were clicked. For clarity here, we'll omit the bouncing effect, so when the user clicks on the biography headings the panes will toggle instantly.

However, there'll also be a `select` box above the panes. When a celebrity is chosen from the list, the biography will toggle in the same manner; the same event handler will fire, except this time we'll have a nice sliding effect.

Our `select` box trigger contains a list of the available biographies that the user can view. Later, we'll attach a `change` event handler to it to trigger the sliding effect:

chapter_09/12_custom_events_with_params/index.html (excerpt)

```html
<select id="chooser">
  <option>Beau Dandy</option>
  <option>Johny Startdust</option>
  <option>Glendatronix</option>
</select>
```

Here is the important part. We are binding our custom `reveal` event to all of the biography headings. The code will accept an extra parameter, which we'll use to determine how to display the biographies. If the `effect` parameter is set to `ease`, we'll `slideToggle`, otherwise the user will see the standard nonsliding toggle:

chapter_09/12_custom_events_with_params/script.js (excerpt)

```javascript
$('#bio h3').bind('reveal', function(e, effect) {
  if (effect == 'ease') {
    $(this).next().slideToggle();
  } else {
    $(this).next().toggle();
  }
})
.click(function() {
  // Trigger 1 : plain toggle
  $(this).trigger('reveal');
});
```

Because our first trigger has no need to add any effect, we won't add any parameters to the `trigger` call. When the `bind` code runs, it finds no `effect` parameter, so it does the regular toggle:

```
chapter_09/12_custom_events_with_params/script.js (excerpt)

$('#chooser')
  .change(function() {
    // Trigger 2: slidey toggle
    $('#bio h3:contains(' + $(this).val() + ')')
      .trigger('reveal', 'ease');
  });
```

When the user changes the current selection in the `select` list, we find the correct content pane and trigger the `reveal` event again. But this time we add the `'ease'` parameter, so the user experiences the fancy sliding version.

Adding data to custom events is a fantastic way to encapsulate your widget's code, and expose an interface that other d evelopers can use to customize your functionality. To pass multiple items to the `bind` function, you need to wrap the `trigger`'s parameters in an array:

```
chapter_09/12_custom_events_with_params/script.js (excerpt)

$('#bio h3:contains(' + $(this).val() + ')')
  .trigger('reveal', ['ease',2000]);
```

Unbinding and Namespacing

jQuery can create some amazing effects with just a handful of actions: the majority of our controls used no more than a few actions, and very little JavaScript code. As you start to expand your controls and effects—converting them to plugins and using multiple controls together to make bigger, cooler controls—you'll find that your events start to become a bit unwieldy. Handlers are attached and never removed, even after your effect has finished, and this can clash with any new behavior that you attempt to add later on. We're not always able to rely on the set-it-and-forget-it approach we've been using so far.

The jQuery library provides us with two mechanisms for dealing with this problem: **event unbinding** and **event namespacing**. Event unbinding lets us remove event handlers from objects, and event namespacing provides a way for us to break our event handlers into logical groups that can be unbound without affecting other events. This is especially useful when we're developing plugins.

Event unbinding is simple: we use the `bind` action to add events to an object, so we use the `unbind` action to remove them! There are three ways we can use `unbind`: to remove *all* events from objects in a selection, to remove all events *of a particular type* from our selection, or to remove *one specific* event handler. Here's the first form:

```
$('p').unbind();
```

This will remove all event handlers associated with all paragraphs on the page. It's a little extreme—more commonly, we'll just want to remove events of a certain type. For example, to remove of all the `mouseover` events, we pass the event type into the `unbind` action:

```
$('p').unbind('mouseover');
```

And finally, to unbind a single event handler, we pass the function we want to unbind. This is a little more complicated, because we need to have named the function when we bound it. For our example, we `bind` two functions to the `click` event. We then `unbind` one of the events:

chapter_09/13_event_unbinding/script.js (excerpt)

```
var doToggle = function() { $(this).toggle(); };
var doSlide = function() { $(this).slideToggle(); };

$('p')
  .click(doToggle)
  .click(doSlide);

$('p').unbind('click', doToggle);
```

Thanks to our unbind call, any subsequent clicking on the paragraph tags would still trigger the `doSlide` method, but no longer trigger the `doToggle` method.

Shorthand Unbinding?

You can also use the shorthand `click` and `mouseover` methods to bind events, so are there `unclick` and `unmouseover` shorthand methods too? Nope. Those methods *used to* exist in jQuery, a long time ago, but they were removed because they made the core API a lot bigger, and were very seldom necessary.

As extensive as all those unbinding options seem, they're unable to cater for all situations. When you're doing lots of binding and unbinding, it's easy to lose track of what's going on—so jQuery provides a way to group related events together via event namespacing. Namespaced events can be triggered independently of other events of the same type, and all events in the same namespace can be unbound with a single command.

To define a namespace, you append a period (.) and your namespace name to the event you want to attach a handler to. Without doing anything further, the event will work just like a regular non-namespaced event; but you now have a handle that you can use to be more specific about which events are fired, without needing to maintain a reference to each event's function (as we did above):

```
                               chapter_09/14_event_namespacing/script.js (excerpt)
$('p').bind('mouseover.colorize', function() {
  $(this).css('background-color', 'lemonchiffon')
})
.bind('mouseout.colorize', function() {
  $(this).css('background-color', '');
})
.click(function() {
  $(this)
    .trigger('mouseout.colorize')
    .unbind('.colorize');
});
```

In this example, we've bound regular `mouseover` and `mouseout` event handlers to every paragraph on the page. This creates a simple and convincing highlight effect as the user moves a mouse over the elements. But there's an extra trick to this highlight: when the user clicks on an element, the highlight will be removed.

When the `click` occurs, the user will be hovering over the element; if we remove the handlers, the `mouseout` code will never run and the element will remain highlighted. To combat this, we trigger the `mouseout` manually. Because we've namespaced the event, we can specify that only the `mouseout` code relating to our effect should run. Any other `mouseout` handlers will remain dormant.

With our element unhighlighted, we can remove all of the event handlers in our effect's namespace with a single unbind command. We target the namespace by passing only '.colorize' as a parameter.

Namespacing your events is particularly useful when you're creating plugins. You now have an easy way to control all the events that your plugin adds to the DOM without worrying about what the user (or other plugins) might have also attached. When it comes time to tear everything down, you can clean up with a simple unbind.

If you want to trigger only non-namespaced events, you can add an exclamation mark (!) to the end of your trigger parameter. If we wanted to run the mouseover events that were outside of our (or any other) namespace, we would execute: $('p').trigger('mouseout!').

 Multiple Namespaces

You're not limited to playing with a single namespace: if you need to target multiple namespaces in one statement, simply concatenate them with periods.

Binding the iPhone: Non-standard Events

As if the jQuery event system hasn't proven itself to be a little winner already, it has yet another trick up its sleeve: it can respond to events it should have no knowledge of! This ability is going to become more and more important as we start to move away from the PC as our primary tool for accessing the Web. The number and type of devices on which people will be viewing your pages in the future is going to explode: iPhones, other mobile phones, PSPs, Chumbys, "the next big thing," and so on. While most of them are going to have to respect the DOM, they will all try to add something of their own to improve human-computer interaction.

And that will mean new hardware-triggered events for us to handle. The iPhone's touch interface is a great example of this. Although the iPhone can react to mousedown and mouseup events, there are other preferred events to use. There's a collection of specific events that handle interaction with the touchscreen which don't make sense on most other devices. Although jQuery doesn't provide direct access to these events (it would soon be a huge library if it had to support every device's events!), the bind method is generic enough to catch any events that are fired:

```
$(document).bind('touchstart', function(e) {
  var original = e.originalEvent;

  var x = original.changedTouches[0].pageX;
  var y = original.changedTouches[0].pageY;

  $('#block').css({top: y, left: x});
});
```

The touch events are defined by a third party, but as long as we have access to the documentation about the events (or can collect our own data with Firebug, or another debugging tool), we can easily capture and respond. In our example, we're catching the `touchstart` event that's fired whenever the user touches the screen.

Because jQuery has no knowledge of `touchstart`, we need to access the `originalEvent` from the jQuery event object that's passed to our callback function. `originalEvent` gives us access to the unwrapped JavaScript event, free of any of jQuery's additions. We can now make use of the event exactly as it's documented. We're grabbing the X and Y position of the screen touch, and updating an absolutely positioned block element at the touch location.

 Disable mousedown and mouseup

If you're writing handlers for the iPhone, you might need to disable the default actions for `mousedown` and `mouseup`. You can do this by capturing them on the `$(document)`, and using the `event.preventDefault` action. Otherwise, you run the risk of running the same code twice, because you'll be triggering both touch and mouse events.

The `special` Event

Creating your own custom events is undoubtedly quite advanced—but jQuery's `special` event construct is downright ninja-like. If you're feeling a bit restricted by the regular old DOM events, this is for you! Using `special` is a way to create native-seeming events of your own, or overwrite and augment existing events. You can do some custom code handling every time a handler is bound, as well as when the event is removed (which occurs during the `beforeUnload` phase). A `special` event is a first-class jQuery citizen.

`click` events fire when the user clicks something, `load` events fire when an element has loaded … Now we're going to create an event that fires when the user hovers multiple times over an element. By default, when an element receives three mouseovers, the bound event handler runs, but we'll see how this can be customized on an element-by-element basis. As with regular events, it's up to you to specify the code that executes in the event handler.

To create a special event you attach a JavaScript object to the `$.event.special` namespace. The event system provides four hooks for you to define how the event works. The `setup` function runs when the event is first bound, the `add` function runs *every time* it's bound, the `remove` function runs when it's unbound, and the `teardown` function runs when the *last* event is unbound (that is, when no more events of this type remain bound to handlers).

Let's have a look at the skeleton of our `multihover` event:

chapter_09/15_special_event/script.js *(excerpt)*

```
jQuery.event.special.multihover = {
  setup: function(data, namespaces) {
    // Do when the first event is bound
  },
  add: function(handler, data, namespaces) {
    // Do every time you bind another event
  },
  remove: function(namespaces) {
    // Do when an event is unbound
  },
  teardown: function(namespaces) {
    // Do when the last event is unbound
  },
  handler: function(e) {
    // Do your logic
  }
}
```

Once you've created your event, you can bind it as you would any event. Obviously there's no shortcut method to bind your custom events, so you have to use the `bind` method to attach it to page elements:

```
$('p').bind('multihover', {times: 4}, function() {
  $(this).css('background-color', 'lemonchiffon');
});
```

We've bound our new `multihover` event to all the paragraphs on the page, and then specified how many times we want to hover over an element before the event fires. We saw in the the section called "Custom Events" that you can pass data to an event with the `trigger` method, but now we learn that you can also specify data to pass to an event when you bind it as well!

Our `special` event isn't going to use the `add` or `remove` hooks, because we only want to allow one `multihover` event to be attached to each element. In the `setup` hook, we'll store the required number of hovers on the element itself using the `data` action. We'll default to 3 in the absence of a user-specified value. Next up, we bind our custom event handler (which we call `jQuery.event.special.handler`) to the `mouseover` event, since we'll need to perform our logic there to determine when the third hover has taken place:

```
setup: function(data, namespaces) {
  $(this)
    .data('times', data && data.times || 3)
    .bind('mouseover', jQuery.event.special.multihover.handler);
},
⋮
teardown: function(namespaces) {
  $(this)
    .removeData('times')
    .unbind('mouseover', jQuery.event.special.multihover.handler);
```

 The `data` Parameter

The `data` parameter on the `bind` method is not specific to the `special` event. It'll work exactly the same on any of your events, so take advantage of it!

We also undo all this setup in the corresponding `teardown` handler. Here we remove the `data` item we added, and unbind the `mouseover` binding. This tidies everything up. Now we have a new event that calls our custom handler every time a `mouseover` event occurs, so let's implement our `multihover` logic:

```
chapter_09/15_special_event/script.js (excerpt)

handler: function(e) {
  // Do your logic
  var times = $(this).data('times') || 0;
  times--;
  $(this).data('times', times);

  if (times <= 0) {
    e.type = 'multihover';
    jQuery.event.handle.apply(this,arguments);

    $(this).unbind('multihover');
  }
}
```

This is the meat of the functionality. We've separated it into its own function only to keep it clear—we could have just as easily handled it with an anonymous function.

The `multihover` logic first subtracts 1 from the `times` data item. When it reaches 0 (which is to say that all the hovers are done), we modify the event property `type` and set it to `multihover`, then call the internal `handle` function. This will cause any bound callbacks that the user has specified to be executed, just like a native event.

The `special` event is a beautiful way to wrap up custom events to be reused throughout your projects. As well as creating new functionality, like our `multihover` event, you can also redefine existing events; for example, you could overwrite the internal `click` event by providing the appropriate hooks to `$.event.special.click`. Creating `special` events is a relatively rare requirement—but when you do need them, you'll see that they're a killer advanced feature of jQuery.

A jQuery Ninja's Miscellany

Even once we've explored the full-blown systems and frameworks on offer within jQuery, there are still countless treasures planted throughout the library for you to take advantage of. Some of these are well-documented functions, though perhaps quite specific; others are more obscure advanced topics.

Avoiding Conflicts

As we mentioned, the $ and jQuery objects and methods we use when writing our code are namespaces, just like those we've been creating ourselves. jQuery, as a namespace, scores well on the uniqueness and clarity fronts, and is also fairly short.

And while the dollar sign certainly scores points for shortness, it misses the mark widely on uniqueness. This lack of uniqueness can be cause for concern if another developer overwrites what we assume to be $. Prototype.js, for example, uses $() as shorthand for the JavaScript getElementById method, and if we're careless, such namespacing conflicts can be catastrophic. To prepare for this occurrence, jQuery gives us access to noConflict:

```
jQuery.noConflict();
```

At its most basic, this means that jQuery will relinquish any rights to the $ namespace, but still respond to the jQuery namespace:

```
jQuery.noConflict();
// Do something with jQuery
jQuery("div p").hide();
// Do something with another library's $()
$("content").style.display = 'none';
```

This would mean that you'd have to remove any references to the $ in your code, replacing them with jQuery, and frankly that might be unfeasible. But there's a way to ease that workload:

```
jQuery.noConflict();
(function($) {
  $(function() {
    // more code using $ as alias to jQuery
  });
})(jQuery);
// other code using $ as an alias to the other library
```

By wrapping all our jQuery commands in an anonymous function and passing in references to `jQuery` and `$`, we create a shell that protects the jQuery methods and properties inside. And there's yet another option available to us: a further trick we can employ is to assign `noConflict`'s return value to a variable, and use that instead of `jQuery` or `$`. In this case, we've chosen to use `trkr` as the jQuery alias:

```
var trkr = jQuery.noConflict();
// Do something with jQuery
trkr ("div p").hide();
// Do something with another library's $()
$("content").style.display = 'none';
```

There's one further process we can use, and that's to assign the `noConflict` to a new namespace:

```
var trkr = {};
trkr.$ = jQuery.noConflict(true);
```

Among all these options you're bound to find a solution that will suit your needs!

Queuing and Dequeuing Animations

Despite the multitude of animation options you have at your disposal, sometimes they fall short of what you need; you might want an animation to pause, or perhaps have an element outside the animation react when the animation reaches a certain point. There are plenty of interesting moments in an animation sequence, and it would be nice to be able to harness them. And you can, with `queue`!

Generally speaking, actions we chain together on a selection are asynchronous, happening more or less at the same time:

chapter_09/16_queue_dequeue_animations/script.js *(excerpt)*

```
$('#button1').click(function() {
  $(this).animate({
    height: 200,
    width: 200
  }, 'slow').text("rollin'");
});
```

When you click that button, it will slowly grow to a size of 200x200 pixels, but the text will update almost immediately. When we use the `animate` action, it adds an `fx` stack to the element, and any animations we add will go on that stack. The `text` action, though, ignores the `fx` stack, being animation-focused, while `queue` honors the stack:

chapter_09/16_queue_dequeue_animations/script.js *(excerpt)*

```
$('#button2').click(function() {
  $(this).animate({
    height: 200,
    width: 200
  }, 'slow').queue(function() {
    $(this).text('rolled!');
  }).text("rollin'");
});
```

Now the `animate` and `text` actions happen together, but the `queue` also changes the text once the animation has concluded. And it doesn't stop there ... or more accurately, it does! If we add another `animate` action to the chain, the `queue` will hold the `fx` stack and will stop the chained action from proceeding:

chapter_09/16_queue_dequeue_animations/script.js *(excerpt)*

```
$('#button3').click(function() {
  $(this).animate({
    height: 200,
    width: 200
  }, 'slow').queue(function() {
    $(this).text('rolled!');
  }).text("rollin'").animate({ // This animate won't fire
    height: 100,
    width: 100
  }, 'slow');
});
```

The queue action now needs some help to release the stack once more. Just as live has die, and animate has stop, queue also has its opposite: dequeue.

The dequeue method is just a little peculiar; rather than being linked into the jQuery chain, the dequeue action is called from within queue's callback:

chapter_09/16_queue_dequeue_animations/script.js *(excerpt)*

```
$('#button4').click(function() {
  $(this).animate({
    height: 200,
    width: 200
  }, 'slow').queue(function() {
    $(this).text('rolled!');
    $(this).dequeue();
  }).text("rollin'").animate({ // This animate won't fire
    height: 100,
    width: 100
  }, 'slow');
});
```

When we click the button now, its text will change to "rollin'," it will grow to 200x200; then its text will change to "rolled," and finally it will shrink to 100x100. Not an animation that will change your world, perhaps, but queue will likely change the way you look at animations.

Treating JavaScript Objects as jQuery Objects

jQuery works by selecting DOM elements and then acting on them. But a little-known secret is that jQuery can act on more than just the DOM; it can be applied to regular JavaScript objects as well. This is less a deliberate feature than a consequence of the library's internal design. Although at first glance it might appear a little bizarre (why would you want to slideUp a JavaScript object?), it does have some potentially interesting ramifications.

First off, though: of course it's impossible to slideUp a JavaScript object—after all, it lacks a height property, or any visible properties for that matter. But you can nonetheless select it just as if it were a DOM element:

```
$(myobj);
```

There are a number of jQuery actions unrelated to visual properties, but which we could imagine employing on a generic object. For example, the amazingly useful data action is used to store arbitrary data against the selected element. We can use this to add metadata to any object in our code. For example, we could establish a bidirectional link between two JavaScript objects. In the example below, we want to store additional information on a map. The map holds locator pins for the locations of celebrities, and we want to attach additional information to the locator that can be retrieved when the pin is clicked:

```
// Our map pin location's meta data
var locationData = {
  name : "Bourgeois Burger Cafe",
  celebCount : 3,
  lat : latitude,
  lon : longitude,
}
// Get a pin locator from our fictional mapping service
var locator = Map.getLocator(latitude, longitude);
```

We have two objects: the third party locator pin object, and our locationData object that contains data relating to the pin. If we select the locator with jQuery, we can apply the data action and attach the locationData object. Internally jQuery will store the relationship in the data store—so neither object is actually modified:

```
// Attach our data object to the JavaScript pin object
$(locator).data('pin_data', locationData);
```

Now at a future point when the user clicks on the map and the locator's click handler fires, we'll have access to the `locationData` object:

```
// Later, when a location is clicked...
var currentData = $(clickedLocation).data('pin_data');

// We can retrieve the metadata stored on the object!
alert("You selected the location: " + currentData.name);
});
```

Although in many cases we'd probably want to store the element reference in the object itself, when the objects are coming from third-party code, you have to be very careful with adding or removing properties. As well, since any changes the third party makes in the future could affect your code, it's best to play it safe. The `data` action lets us augment the object without changing it.

Theme Rolling

Throughout the preceding pages we've traversed and conquered much of the jQuery UI API. One of the most attractive features of jQuery UI is ... its attractiveness! Out of the box the UI components look great—and (as much as we might hate to admit it) looking great is incredibly important. Sometimes it can be even more important than the functionality itself! There's nothing worse than showing a colleague or boss a technically brilliant proof of concept for a control you've created, only to be met with criticism about its design. Worse still, sometimes your lack of initial thought regarding skinning and theming results in a product that's inherently difficult to style.

This is not a problem for jQuery UI components; there's a gallery of themes available—and picking or customizing a new funky design is simple, thanks to the ThemeRoller web application.[1] ThemeRoller lets you tweak, design, and download jQuery UI themes. Additionally, if you follow some simple conventions when creating your own controls, you can easily take advantage of existing and customized themes to ensure everything you create looks as awesome as it works.

---

[1] http://jqueryui.com/themeroller/

Using Gallery Themes

We've mentioned themes on a few occasions on our jQuery UI expedition—it's one of the options we had to specify when we downloaded the library. By default you receive the UI lightness theme, but we've also made use of the Sunny theme, and perhaps you've had a look at a couple more as you went along. To see what default themes you can use, head over to the ThemeRoller site.

Now click the **Gallery** tab in the left sidebar. Here you can view various predesigned themes and find one that fits your needs. Then if you hit the download button, you'll be taken to the familiar jQuery UI build screen. If you need the whole library, customize the components you want. The theme you choose will be preselected in the theme drop-down box.

If, on the other hand, you just wanted the theme, don't worry about which components are selected and just download the library. The bundled files will include your theme, so just copy the **css** folder out of the download and into your project. Then update the theme name in the style sheet link inside your page, so that your components will look for the correct CSS file. That's all there is to it.

Rolling Your Own

Chances are the default themes may prove unsuitable for your site. Thankfully the ThemeRoller tool is here to make customizing the available themes a breeze. ThemeRoller is a web application that provides a simple interface to modify every aspect of a jQuery UI theme. As you update properties in the sidebar, the changes are instantly reflected in the preview area, as illustrated in Figure 9.2.

Figure 9.2. The jQuery UI ThemeRoller

Once you've tweaked your theme to perfection, you can download it by hitting the **Download theme** button. The changes are passed over to the jQuery UI download builder, just like a regular gallery theme—except that the theme drop-down box will now say "Custom Theme." If you were to download the bundle now your theme would be called custom-theme (so your CSS files would be stored in the **custom-theme** folder). If you feel your creation demands a more fitting title, drop down the **Advanced Theme Settings** panel and update the **Theme Folder Name** input box.

Limited IE6 Support

Although ThemeRoller themes are incredibly nice-looking and easy to use, there's a catch. The jQuery UI team is less obsessed with supporting Internet Explorer 6 than its jQuery core counterparts, and as a result, the themes use some CSS3 styles and semitransparent PNGs that will look quite ugly in IE6. It recommends that you use a PNG support library to have nice icons—and you'll have to find a non-CSS solution to your round-corner woes!

Making Your Components Themeable

ThemeRoller may have a groovy-sounding name, and the results you gain from it may be fairly impressive—but all it's really doing is generating a block of CSS classes that can be used to style any set of DOM elements. If you build your own custom

UI components in a way that follows the jQuery UI's markup and naming conventions, they'll be also be skinnable.

In Figure 9.3 we've applied the appropriate CSS classes to the bouncy content panes from Chapter 3, so now we have a very jQuery UI-like component. The default themes (or our custom ThemeRoller themes) can be included at the top of our page, and our chameleon widget will instantly have a new look and feel (the figure shows the UI lightness, Dot Luv, and Eggplant predesigned themes in action).

Figure 9.3. ThemeRolled content panes

If you're accustomed to building semantically correct structures, you'll probably only need to add a `class` here and there to access all of the ThemeRoller goodness. The themes assume your widget will have at least a containing element that it can use as the base for styling. Our original HTML for the biography panes looked like this:

```
<div id="bio">
  <h3>Beau Dandy</h3>
  <div>
    <img class="pic" src="glendatronix.png" />
    <span>Glendatronix is the queen of … </span>
  </div>
  <h3>Mr Speaker</h3>
  <div>
    <img class="pic" src="mrspeaker.png" />
    <span>After smashing into the limelight … </span>
  </div>
  ⋮
</div>
```

To start off, we'll designate the #bio div as the container by applying the ui-widget class. Then we'll reset any styles we may have already applied that might mess up the widget styling, by adding ui-helper-reset:

chapter_09/17_themable_components/index.html *(excerpt)*

```
<div id="bio" class="ui-widget ui-helper-reset">
```

This already gives us a lot: the fonts and colors of the current theme. Next, we can start to work additional classes into our component to style the heading and content areas:

chapter_09/17_themable_components/index.html *(excerpt)*

```
<h3 class="ui-widget-header ui-corner-all">Johnny Stardust</h3>
<div class="ui-widget-content">
  <img src="johnnystartdust.png" />
  <span>After smashing into the limelight … </span>
</div>
```

The ui-widget-header gives us the shiny toolbar look, and the ui-corner-all will make the widget nice and round (where supported, of course). You can specify ui-corner-all or the more specific classes that style individual edges—such as the ui-corner-tl for the top-left edge or ui-corner-bottom for both bottom edges, to achieve rounded corners on most elements.

We've also added the dramatic "SOLD OUT!" message to our panes using some additional classes that display as warnings and icons:

chapter_09/17_themable_components/index.html *(excerpt)*

```
<div class="ui-state-error">
  <span class="ui-icon ui-icon-alert"></span>SOLD OUT!
</div>
```

The ui-state-error class gives the strong error-looking messages, and the ui-icon-alert adds a small icon to the span.

As you'd expect from witnessing the jQuery UI library in full flight, there are a lot more options available for controlling how your code is styled by the ThemeRoller themes. There are classes for defining interaction states of buttons, disabled form elements, component shadows, and some great helper classes for z-index fixes (for Internet Explorer 6), as well as shortcut links for accessibility. The documentation[2] is quite detailed and will give you a good grounding for most of your widgets.

The best way to get your head around everything that's available is to read over the documentation, see what elements are affected in the ThemeRoller tool, and inspect the classes applied to elements in the jQuery UI library. Also, remember that when you're making plugins that have a strong UI focus, you can easily add the Theme-Roller classes via jQuery in your plugin code; this will give your users fully skinnable components with very little effort!

StarTrackr!: Epilogue

"We stand here today as creators of the most notorious celebrity hunting web site on the planet!" booms the client to a room full of employees and shareholders. The final phase of the project is live, and your work is coming to an end. It sure has been a long journey since our client asked us to spruce up his site's disclaimer message—a journey that has taken us through fading and sliding, easing and scrolling, enhancing and Ajaxifying. A journey that has taken us, in other words, from novice to ninja.

"But there was one person who made all of this possible," the client continues. "One person we owe all of this to …" and he turns to face you, but the space you'd previously occupied is empty. You've performed one last $("#ninja").hide()—and mysteriously vanished without a trace.

You have no need for the thanks and praises of your clients and co-workers; your reward is that good web development practices have been instilled into yet another project. That, and the significant payments you received. A bit of both, really.

---

[2] http://jqueryui.com/docs/Theming/API

Appendix A: Reference Material

jQuery is all about being flexible, and applicable to as many situations as possible. Both the core library and the plugin architecture encourage this philosophy. The most common usage scenarios are usually catered for straight out of the box, so jQuery's flexibility rests in the ability to override those defaults. This results in a lot of options! There's no need to memorize them all, though—just have a good reference on hand, and always check jQuery's online documentation.[1] And don't be afraid to dive into the jQuery or plugin source code to look for anything the documentation may have missed.

$.ajax Options

The powerful array of Ajax functions in jQuery is underpinned by a single method: $.ajax. This method accepts a plethora of options, giving it the flexibility to be used in countless situations. We examined some of the options throughout the book, but as always with jQuery, there's more!

Flags

The "flaggable" options accept a Boolean value—true or false—to enable or disable the given functionality. Most of the time the defaults will be satisfactory, but it's easy to override them to customize your request.

async

The async option is true by default, but if you need to do a synchronous request (which you should try to minimize—it locks the browser while it's working!), you can set this to false.

cache

Caching data can be an issue when performing Ajax requests; if a user's browser stores old requests, it might not fetch the latest data. To disable caching, you can set the cache option to false. Script and JSONP requests are uncached by default.

---

[1] http://api.jquery.com/

global

We saw that we could handle events from any Ajax request using global event handlers. You also have the option of stopping global event handlers from handling a particular event by specifying `false` for the `global` parameter.

ifModified

By setting the `ifModified` flag, you can force a request to be "successful" (that is, to fire the `success` handler) *only* if the document was modified since the last request. This can be useful if you only want to do some processing when there's new data to display.

processData

When you have data to send along with your request, jQuery will process it and convert it to an appropriate query string value. If this is undesirable (for example, if you need to pass a DOM document, or some other sort of structure) you can set the `processData` flag to `false`.

Settings

Many of the Ajax options allow you to specify more than just a simple on/off value; they generally accept strings or objects to customize and define your Ajax request.

contentType

The `contentType` setting allows you to set the content type for the request. By default it's `application/x-www-form-urlencoded`, which is fine for most cases.

context

When Ajax callbacks execute, their context is the `window` object, which is generally not very useful. You set the `context` option so that the `this` property in a callback refers to something handy, like a custom JavaScript object or a jQuery element.

data

To pass data to the server, you specify a string, JavaScript array, or object for the `data` setting. If you pass in an array or object (and you haven't disabled the `processData` flag), the data will be serialized with the `jQuery.params` utility function. This takes the input and coverts it into a query-string format (very handy)! If it's a `GET` request, the string will be appended to the URL.

dataType

Where `contentType` set the content type of the data you were sending to the server, the `dataType` parameter sets the type of data you're expecting to *receive* from the server. The default type is "everything" (`*/*`), but you could specify `xml`, `html`, `script`, `json`, or `text`—in which case jQuery will use the appropriate content type string.

jsonp

When you make JSONP calls (which allow cross-domain requests) it's expected that the callback function name will be `callback`. If the service you're using requires a different name, you can define it with the `jsonp` setting.

password

Authentication requests require your username and password. You can specify the latter in the `password` setting.

scriptCharset

The `scriptCharset` property allows you to specify the character set of `script` tags injected by `script` or `jsonp` Ajax calls.

timeout

The `timeout` parameter has the honor of being the only `ajax` setting that accepts a number: it defines how many milliseconds need to elapse before aborting an Ajax request.

type

One of the most important settings for an Ajax request, the `type` property defines the HTTP request type: `GET`, `POST`, `PUT`, or `DELETE`.

url

The other most important setting along with `type`, the `url` string defines the address of the location you want to call.

username

Last but not least, the `username` option specifies the username to send with any authentication requests.

Callbacks and Functions

Finally, there are a bunch of callbacks and functions you can define to tweak your request and handle events that occur during the request's life cycle.

The event handlers have already been covered in Chapter 6. The `complete` handler will fire whenever an `$.ajax` call completes—regardless of success or failure—so it's a good place to clean up any loose ends. The `error` handler is called whenever the call fails, and the `success` handler fires whenever it completes correctly.

As well as the event callbacks, there are also a handful of functions existing as hooks; these let you modify various parts of a request on a call-by-call basis. The `beforeSend` function fires before the send message is executed, and gives you a place to modify the request if you require. Your handler is given the request object and the current jQuery object. This is a common place to modify the request headers when it's required. Also, it's your last chance to stop anything from happening: if you return `false` from this function, the request will be aborted.

At the lowest level, the magic of Ajax comes from the browser's implementation of the `XMLHTTPRequest` (or XHR for short) object. This is the fellow that lets us communicate with the server from the client. By default, jQuery looks for the appropriate XHR object and uses this for any Ajax calls. You can modify this if you want to augment or replace it by specifying your own `xhr` function. The function needs to return the object that should be used.

The last hook that's available is the `dataFilter` function. This is called after a request successfully returns, and is a place for you to make sure the response data is okay. If you need to do any data sanitizing, this is the spot. The `dataFilter` function is passed the raw response data and the type; you should return the data once you've processed it so the request cycle can continue.

$.support Options

In the old days, we'd use browser sniffing to determine which version of which browser was being used, and adjust our code to work around known bugs. Today, this method is frowned upon—it's just too flaky. Where possible we should use feature detection to check whether the browser supports a particular piece of functionality, and supply a workaround or fallback if needed.

If you use pure jQuery, most of these issues are taken care of internally, but if you're dirtying your hands with some raw JavaScript, there's a nifty mechanism for feature detection available via the `support` action. We looked at this in Chapter 6, but only briefly spoke of the options available. There are many. They all return a `true` or `false` value to indicate if they're supported, which can then be used in an `if/then/else` block to provide support for both cases. For example:

```
var domObject = document.getElementById('content');
if ($.support.cssFloat) {
  domObject.style.cssFloat = "left";
} else {
  domObject.style.styleFloat = "left";
}
```

Here are the available properties:

boxModel

The `boxModel` property (which is initially set to `null`, and changed to `true` or `false` after the document has loaded) will be `true` if the browser renders in accordance with the W3C box model.

changeBubbles

Detecting browser features as they pertain to events can be a tricky business—it used to be a very common reason to do browser sniffing. Thankfully some clever people figured it all out, so now if you want to know if you can (reliably) react to the `change` event, you can check the `changeBubbles` property.

cssFloat

We saw the `cssFloat` in action in the example above. It detects whether the browser uses the `cssFloat` label to address the float style in JavaScript. (It's impossible to simply `float`, because that's a JavaScript keyword referring to floating-point numbers). Internet Explorer uses `styleFloat` instead of `cssFloat`.

hrefNormalized

Some browsers fiddle around with links that they've determined have been constructed incorrectly—which is a problem if it's unexpected! The `hrefNormalized` property will return `true` if the browser modifies the links.

htmlSerialize

If you need to make sure that link elements (such as `link` and `script` tags) are serialized correctly when using `innerHTML`, you can use the `htmlSerialize` property. Internet Explorer has problems with this—and you'll need to wrap the offending tags in your own wrapper elements if you want it to play nice.

leadingWhitespace

The `leadingWhitespace` option lets you know if the browser leaves the first node in a DOM child as whitespace or not. When `innerHTML` is used, Internet Explorer strips out the first child if it's a whitespace text node; this can mess up your jQuery code if you're relying on a set number of children.

noCloneEvent

When you clone a DOM node, some browsers will also clone the event handlers that are attached to it, while others won't. If events aren't cloned the `noCloneEvent` property will be `true`.

opacity

We're all big fans of opacity: it makes sites look futuristic. Unfortunately some browsers are unable to play with opacity via JavaScript (of course, if you use jQuery you're safe). The `opacity` property tests to see if the rendering engine understands opacity—otherwise you'll need to resort to using the browser's filters.

scriptEval

Browsers also behave differently with regard to executing scripts with injected `script` tags. The `scriptEval` property will let you know if it's safe to inject via `appendChild`, or if you should use the `script.text` property.

style

To find the style currently applied to an element, you can use the `getAttribute` method and ask for `style`—in some browsers. To test whether or not `getAttribute("style")` will work on your user's browser, you can check the `style` property.

submitBubbles

Another event you can check for is the `submit` event via the `submitBubbles` property. Internally, this uses the same feature detection tricks as `changeBubbles`.

tbody

And finally, in some browsers a `tbody` element will be automatically inserted into an empty `table`—which can mess up your DOM manipulations. To check whether you need to look out for this, there's the `tbody` property. This will return `true` (confusingly) if you can have a table without a `tbody` element being automatically inserted.

The best part about the `support` action is that it forces you to understand exactly what bugs you're working around. With browser sniffing it's easy to become complacent and start putting more code than is necessary in conditional blocks. By using `support` you only target very specific aspects, ensuring your users enjoy a consistent (or at least acceptable) experience, regardless of how the vendors modify their browser code.

Events

We've spent a lot of time looking at events, and as we've mentioned on a few occasions, jQuery simplifies the cross-browser event handling process by normalizing events to conform to the W3C standard. A normalized event object has a stack of properties and methods that can be useful to us. We've used some of them throughout the book, and now we'll look at the ones that got away! You can find the full list of event properties in the jQuery Events documentation.[2]

Event Properties

We saw this briefly in Chapter 9: the `type` property will give you the name of the event that fired (even for custom events, if you've named them).

When an event handler is called, you can obtain the DOM element that was the source of the event via the `target` property. This can also be wrapped in a jQuery selector to escape the pesky DOM and back into happy jQuery land. Additionally, if the event is a mouse movement, you can find the element that was the previous target (where the mouse previously was) with the `relatedTarget` property. And if the event is moving up through the hierarchy—when you're dealing with bubbling events—the `currentTarget` will inform you of the target for the current bubbling phase.

---

[2] http://docs.jquery.com/Events/jQuery.Event

A final, extremely useful property is the event's `timeStamp`. This gives you the precise time when the event occurred, and it's most commonly employed when implementing time-based effects. For example, if you wanted to create a special triple-click event on your page, you could consult the events' timestamps to see if three clicks had occurred in a given span of time.

Event Methods

We've seen a bunch of the event methods we could use, like `preventDefault` and `stopPropagation`, which let us control how events bubble and are handled by the browser. There are a couple of extra methods though. One more in the same vein is the `stopImmediatePropagation` method, which is a bit more hardcore than `stopPropagation`. While `stopPropagation` prevents parent handlers from running, `stopImmediatePropagation` stops any further event handlers from running—even on the same element.

The rest of the methods simply report whether or not any of the other methods have been called. The `isDefaultPrevented`, `isPropagationStopped`, and `isImmediatePropagationStopped` methods return a Boolean value that would be `false`, unless the respective commands had been issued.

DIY Event Objects

While we're talking about events, there's one final aspect you might like to know about them: you can create your own event objects and pass them directly to handlers. Check out this code:

```
// Regular event binding
$('p').bind('click', function(e) {
  $(this).text(e.pageX);
});
// Home-made event object!
var e = $.Event('click');
e.pageX = 100;
e.pageY = 100;
$('p').trigger(e);
```

We've created an artificial click event and manually set its `pageX` and `pageY` properties. This gives you ultimate control over the details of the event that triggers an event handler.

Appendix B: JavaScript Tidbits

We can't stress this enough: jQuery is just JavaScript—so the best way to improve your jQuery skills is to brush up on your JavaScript knowledge! We'll have a look now at a few aspects of JavaScript we used throughout the book that you might be wondering about.

 Learning More about JavaScript

If you're looking to take your JavaScript to the next level, we highly recommend Douglas Crockford's *JavaScript: The Good Parts* (Sebastopol: O'Reilly, 2008). It's not particularly light reading, but it's a succinct and pragmatic explanation of how and why JavaScript rocks!

Type Coercion

JavaScript is what's known as a loosely typed language. Some languages, such as Java, are strictly typed: this means that the type of a variable must be set when the variable is declared. JavaScript, on the other hand, allows for variables to be **coerced**. That is, their type can change depending on what we require of them:

```
var a = 2;
var b = "two";
var c = "2";
alert(typeof a);// alerts "number"
alert(typeof b);// alerts "string"
alert(typeof c);// alerts "string"
```

No surprises there—the variables are behaving as we expect. Things look different, though, when we ask JavaScript to take its best guess at what type we *want* the variables to be:

```
alert(a * a);// alerts 4
alert(a + b);// alerts 2two
alert(a * c);// alerts 4
alert(typeof (a * a));// alerts "number"
alert(typeof (a + b));// alerts "string"
alert(typeof (a * c));// alerts "number"
```

When we "add" a string and a number using the + operator, JavaScript assumes we're trying to concatenate the two, so it creates a new string. It would appear to change the number's variable type to `string`. When we use the multiplication operator (*) though, JavaScript assumes that we want to treat the two variables as numbers.

The variable itself remains the same throughout, it's just treated differently. We can always explicitly tell JavaScript how we intend to treat a variable, but if we don't, we need to understand just what JavaScript is doing for us. Here's another example:

```
alert(a + c);// alerts 22
alert(a + parseInt(c));// alerts 4
```

Equality Operators

The equal sign (=) and its related operators can also provide a trap for young players. And where it was once just a little odd, it became even more so in JavaScript 1.3. The first trick is that the equal sign has a different meaning than what you remember from your school mathematics classes:

```
var a = 2;
var b = "2";
```

A single equal sign is an **assignment operator**, and is used to assign values to variables. We all knew what it did, but now we know what it's called:

```
var c = (a == b);
```

Two = signs together, ==, is known as the **equality operator**, and establishes a Boolean value. In our example, the variable c will have a value of `true`, as JavaScript compares the values before and after the equality operator, and considers them to be equal. Using the equality operator, JavaScript pays no heed to the variable's type, and attempts to coerce the values to assess them.

Switch out the first equal sign for an exclamation mark, and you have yourself an **inequality operator** (!=). This operator will return `false` if the variables are equal, or `true` if they aren't:

```
var d = (a != b);
```

The variable d will now have a value of `false`, since a and b are equal. It may be a little complex, but at least it's consistent.

In JavaScript 1.3, the situation became less simple still, with the introduction of one further operator: the **strict equality operator**, shown as ===.

```
var e = (a === b);
```

The strict equality operator differs from the equality operator, in that it pays strict attention to *type* as well as value when it assigns its Boolean. In the above case, d is set to `false`: while a and b both have a value of 2, they have different types.

And as you might have guessed, where the inequality operator was paired with the equality operator, the strict equality operator has a corresponding **strict inequality operator**:

```
var f = (a !== b);
```

In this case the variable f will return `true`, as we know the two compared variables are of different types, though similar values.

Suffice it to say that some equal signs are more equal then others!

Truthiness and Falsiness

JavaScript's Boolean type has two possible values—`true` and `false`:

```
var jQueryIsFun = true;
var javaScriptIsJava = false;
```

But we know that JavaScript likes to be trickier than this. In reality, there are a multitude of ways that variables can evaluate to `true` or `false`. These values are referred to as being **truthy** or **falsy**. So when we write if(variable) { … }, variable need not be a Boolean value: the code between the brackets will run if variable contains the number 5, or the string `"Hello World!"`, or even an empty array. Any value that acts as though it were the Boolean value `true` in this type of context is called *truthy*, and any value that acts like `false` is called *falsy*.

JavaScript treats all these values as truthy:

- `true`
- `1` (because it's a non-zero number)
- `"0"` (because it's a non-empty string)
- `"false"` (because it's a non-empty string)
- `function() {}` (any function)
- `{}` (any object)
- `[]` (any array)

And these values are falsy:

- `false`
- `0` (the number zero)
- `""` (an empty string)
- `null`
- `undefined`
- `NaN` (a special number value meaning Not a Number)

These values can be combined with the logical NOT operator to great effect. A single exclamation mark is used:

```
var a = 0;
var b = 1;

if (!b) {
  // do something
}
else if (!a) {
  // do something else
}
```

The logical NOT operator returns `true` if the value of the variable is `false` and, conversely, it will return `false` if the value is `true`. In the example above, b is truthy and so `!b` returns `false`, and a is falsy so `!a` returns `true`—so the code in the `else if` block would execute.

It's important to remember that while a value may be == `true`, it may only be truthy, and not strictly `true`:

```
var a = true;
var b = 1;

alert(a == b);// alerts true
alert(a === b);// alerts false
alert(a != b); // alerts false
alert(a !== b); // alerts true
```

If you have the option, always elect to use the Boolean values of `true` and `false`. If there's one thing that's undoubtedly true, it's that hunting down a truthy or falsy logic error is truly painstaking!

Appendix C: Plugin Helpers

There are a few jQuery properties and actions that, although applying to any jQuery selection, are particularly useful for plugin development. The reason they're hidden away in this appendix is that they're uncommonly used. Despite this, they're quite powerful, and you should familiarize yourself with them if you intend to spend time developing plugins.

Selector and Context

The first ones we'll look at are the `selector` and `context` properties. These work together to show you what jQuery thinks it's working on.

The `selector` property returns a string value of the current jQuery selector string: so the command `$('p:first').selector` will return the string `"p:first"`. This is useful in your plugins if you need to know what the user originally selected.

You might think that the optional second parameter to the jQuery selector, which is called `context`, is what you'd obtain with the `context` property—but it's a bit trickier than that. In fact, if you supply `context` as a string, it's converted internally to a regular jQuery statement, which will actually affect the `selector` property:

```
var selector = $('p:first', '#content').selector
var context = $('p:first', '#content').context
```

In the above example, the `selector` resolves to `"#content p:first"` and the `context` resolves to `Document` (the context that all your selectors will default to). The `context` property is only modified if you supply an actual DOM node to it:

```
var domContext = $('#content')[0]; // Get the DOM element
var selector = $('p:first', domContext).selector;
var context = $('p:first', domContext).context;
```

In this case, the `selector` will be reported as `"p:first"`, and the `context` will be the DOM element itself (for this example, it's the `<div id="content">` element).

Specifying the DOM node provides no guarantee that your queries will run faster; internally jQuery's selector engine will only search inside the context you specify anyway, even though the `context` property will be reported as `Document`.

The jQuery Stack

To make our plugins play nicely with jQuery, we've learned that we should return each jQuery element from our code, so that commands can continue to be chained after our plugin. Generally, we just modify elements in the selection before we pass them back, but sometimes we want to alter the items that are returned—perhaps remove some elements, or add some new ones. The best way to accomplish this is via the `pushStack` action. This is a convenient way to create a jQuery selection for inclusion in the chain.

By way of example, we'll set up a small plugin that retrieves the elements that surround the selected element. The use case might be to highlight the next and previous items in a list of elements. Our plugin will also wrap around if the selected item is the first or last in the list:

```
jQuery.fn.surrounds = function() {
  var prev = this.index() == 0 ?
    this.siblings(':last') :
    this.prev();
  var next = this.index() == this.siblings().length ?
    this.siblings(':first') :
    this.next();

  var newStack = prev.add(next);
  return this.pushStack(newStack, 'surrounds', '');
};
```

The plugin retrieves the previous and next elements, and combines them into one selection with the `add` action. This new collection is returned via `pushStack`, which accepts the collection, a name for it, and a name for the selector string. The two name parameters will be readable by the `selector` property we looked at above. To use this plugin, we might apply it to an unordered list called categories, like so:

```
$('#categories li:first')
  .surrounds()
  .css('color', 'red')
  .end()
  .css('color', 'blue');
```

This will select the two elements that surround the first list item, then color them red. Because we've used `pushStack`, the jQuery chain remains intact; we can then use the `end` command to move back to the original selection (the first list item), and color it blue. You can use `pushStack` anytime you want to manipulate the chain like this.

The last trick we'll look at in regard to the jQuery internal chain is the ability to access other steps in the chain. As you might remember, the `end` action takes you back up one level to the last command that modified the jQuery selection. If you look into the jQuery core, you'll see that `end` is implemented using the `prevObject` property. Inside your plugin you can gain access to the previous jQuery object by using `this.prevObject`. If the previous object has a previous object, you can access this too!

Minification

You know there are two versions of jQuery, jQuery UI, and many jQuery plugins: an uncompressed version and a minified version. Why is this so?

Regardless of which one you choose, when you add them to your page you gain access to all the features of jQuery (or the plugin in question). The difference is, of course, that the file size of the ".min" version is markedly smaller. With jQuery 1.3.2 coming in at around 118KB and the minified version at 55.9KB, you save over half the file size in bandwidth.

And if the file is half as big, it's delivered twice as fast. Faster downloads mean faster pageloads, so you may be wondering how to enjoy the benefit of minified files with your own script files, and—more importantly—your plugins.

There are a number of utilities you can use to compress your files, so we'll go over a few of the more commonly used ones.

Douglas Crockford's JSMin[1] was first released in December of 2003, and currently comes in both the original executable version (along with the C source code), as well as a host of other language options: C#, Java, JavaScript, Perl, PHP, Python, OCaml, and Ruby.

Of a similar pedigree, but slightly more accessible to use, is Dean Edwards' Packer.[2] It's primarily accessed via a web page interface, but it also has .NET, Perl, and PHP applications available for download.

Both solutions work by eliminating whitespace—line breaks and extraneous spaces—and by shortening variable and function names. The code becomes obfuscated by human standards, but the browser's JavaScript engine has no trouble interpreting the code output. So, for example, this human-readable code:

```
$growl.animate({
    border: "none",
    height: 0,
    marginBottom: 0,
    marginTop: "-6px",
    opacity : 0,
    paddingBottom: 0,
    paddingTop: 0,
    queue: false
}
```

… would be shortened to this:

```
$growl.animate({border:"none",height:0,marginBottom:0,marginTop:
➥"-6px",opacity :0,paddingBottom:0,paddingTop:0,queue:false}
```

The second statement has the whitespace removed, and you can already see that it's taking up less space to achieve the same results. You can also see how it's become more difficult to read. Multiply this effect by the 4,377 lines in the jQuery source, and you can imagine how difficult it would be to make any sense of it. And that's without altering any names.

---

[1] http://www.crockford.com/javascript/jsmin.html

[2] http://dean.edwards.name/packer/

Of these two methods, Packer is arguably the more extensive, not only removing whitespace but also converting names to base 62. Its compressed footprint can therefore be smaller, yet this mightn't necessarily result in the fastest solution, as it means the minified code must be "unpacked" when delivered to the browser. Edwards' most recent modifications have seen some astounding increases in unpacking speeds, but this overhead should be considered when adopting a final solution.

Two other popular options for minifying your JavaScript are Yahoo's YUI Compressor[3] and Google's Closure Compiler.[4]

The teams behind all four methods—well, three, as Crockford is fairly much sorted with JSMin—are continually refining their solutions, and are responsive to industry and community feedback.

---

[3] http://developer.yahoo.com/yui/compressor/
[4] http://code.google.com/closure/compiler/

Index

E

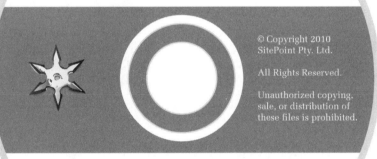

© Copyright 2010
SitePoint Pty. Ltd.

All Rights Reserved.

Unauthorized copying,
sale, or distribution of
these files is prohibited.

JQUERY: NOVICE TO NINJA

CD-ROM

The CD-ROM is not missing.
Download all the code in this book from:
http://www.sitepoint.com/books/jquery1/code.php